COLUMBIA CRITICAL

Emily Brontë

Wuthering Heights

EDITED BY PATSY STONEMAN

Series editor: Richard Beynon

COLUMBIA UNIVERSITY PRESS ◣◢ NEW YORK

31883)

Columbia University Press
Publishers Since 1893
New York
Editor's text copyright © 1998 Patsy Stoneman

First published in the Icon Critical Guides series in 1998 by Icon Books Ltd.

Library of Congress Cataloging-in-Publication Data

Emily Brontë : Wuthering Heights / edited by Patsy Stoneman.
     p.   cm. — (Columbia critical guides)
   Includes bibliographical references and index.
   ISBN 0–231–11920–8 (alk. paper). — ISBN 0–231–11921–6 (pbk. : alk. paper)
   1. Brontë, Emily, 1818–1848. Wuthering Heights.   I. Stoneman, Patsy   II. Series.
   PR4172.W73W88   2000
   823'.8—dc21   99–41367

∞

Casebound editions of Columbia University Press books are printed on permanent and durable acid-free paper.

Printed in the United States of America

c 10 9 8 7 6 5 4 3 2 1
p 10 9 8 7 6 5 4 3 2 1

Contents

Since the Bibliography is very long, this 'brief guide' indicates one or two
essential titles in a number of categories.

A complete list of all the critical works referred to in the book.

A NOTE ON SOURCES AND REFERENCES

Bibliographical References

Because critical books and articles are the subject-matter of this book, almost all such works are identified in the text by author and date and often by title. In these cases, full bibliographic details will be found in the alphabetic Bibliography at the end of the book, and page references will be included in the text. Numbered endnotes will be reserved for explanatory material and for references given within the critical extracts, which may not appear in the Bibliography.

Anthologies

Many of the articles referred to in this book have been reproduced in anthologies, sometimes several times. To allow maximum choice in tracking down references, the following anthologies have been given a key letter which will appear after relevant items in the Bibliography. For nineteenth-century articles which may be difficult to locate, I have given page references to Miriam Allott's *Critical Heritage* collection in addition to the original source. Where my page references are to an anthology rather than an original source, they will appear as follows: (*CH* p. 1).

CH   Allott, Miriam (ed). *The Brontës: The Critical Heritage*. London: Routledge, 1974.

A   Allott, Miriam (ed). *Emily Brontë: Wuthering Heights*. A Casebook. 1970. New ed. Basingstoke: Macmillan, 1992.

B   Bloom, Harold (ed). *Emily Brontë's Wuthering Heights*. Modern Critical Interpretations. New York and Philadelphia: Chelsea Books, 1987.

E   Everitt, Alastair (ed). *Wuthering Heights; An Anthology of Criticism*. London: Frank Cass, 1967.

G   Gregor, Ian (ed). *The Brontës: A Collection of Critical Essays*. Englewood Cliffs, N.J.: Prentice-Hall International, 1970.

L&M Lettis, Richard and William E. Morris (eds). *A Wuthering Heights Handbook*. New York: Odyssey Press, 1961.

O   O'Neill, Judith. *Critics on Charlotte and Emily Brontë*. Readings in Literary Criticism. London: George Allen and Unwin, 1970.

PL   Peterson, Linda H. (ed). *Wuthering Heights*. Case Studies in Contemporary Criticism. Boston: Bedford Books of St Martin's Press, 1992.

PJ   Petit, Jean-Paul (ed). *Emily Brontë*. Penguin Critical Anthology. Harmondsworth: Penguin, 1973.

S&D   Sale, William M. Jr. and Richard J. Dunn (eds). *Wuthering Heights*. A Norton Critical Edition. 1963. 3rd ed. New York and London: Norton, 1990.

SA   Smith, Anne (ed). *The Art of Emily Brontë*. London: Vision Press, 1976.

SP   Stoneman, Patsy (ed). *Wuthering Heights*. A New Casebook. Basingstoke: Macmillan, 1993.

V   Vogler, Thomas A. (ed). *Twentieth-Century Interpretations of 'Wuthering Heights': A Collection of Critical Essays*. Englewood Cliffs, N.J.: Prentice-Hall, 1965.

Texts of *Wuthering Heights*

My own references to *Wuthering Heights* will appear as follows: (*WH* p. 1) and will refer to:

Brontë, Emily. *Wuthering Heights*. 1847. Ed. Ian Jack. Intro. Patsy Stoneman. The World's Classics. Oxford: Oxford University Press, 1995.

Other editions will be identified as follows:

Clarendon: Brontë, Emily. *Wuthering Heights*. 1847. Ed. Hilda Marsden and Ian Jack. Oxford: Clarendon Press, 1976.
Penguin: Brontë, Emily. *Wuthering Heights*. 1847. Ed. David Daiches. Harmondsworth: Penguin, 1965.

INTRODUCTION

WUTHERING HEIGHTS is one of those rare texts which appeals to 'the general reader' while also providing endless material for critical debate. The fascination and the puzzle of the text are increased by the circumstances of its publication. *Wuthering Heights* is Emily Brontë's only novel; it was published in 1847 and in 1848 she died. In 1846, she had joined her sisters, Charlotte and Anne, in publishing a collection of poems, and almost a hundred years later a substantial collection of her poetry was published by C.W. Hatfield (1941).

Apart from the manuscripts of her poems, however, together with a handful of brief, functional letters and three 'diary papers' written at four-year intervals in 1837, 1841 and 1845, we have nothing written in Emily's hand. The prose narratives which once accompanied the poems are lost or destroyed. The 'new novel' on which she is thought to have been working at the time of her death has never been found. The manuscript of *Wuthering Heights* itself has disappeared, and it seems that the proof corrections which Emily made to the first edition of *Wuthering Heights* were never incorporated into the printed text, so that the normal authority of the 'first edition' is undermined. This means that in our encounter with 'the words on the page' we are unusually dependent on editors and commentators to reconstruct an acceptable text. This process of reconstruction began very soon after Emily's death, when Charlotte undertook to edit a second edition of *Wuthering Heights* (1850), altering its bizarre punctuation and moderating the dialect to make it more acceptable to a southern audience. Information about the processes of editing will be found in the Clarendon edition of *Wuthering Heights* – but there are so many 'authoritative texts' now in circulation that quotations by different critics will often be found to include minor variations. A well-documented hypothesis about the construction of the novel has, however, recently been made by Edward Chitham in *The Birth of Wuthering Heights* (1998), where he argues that the novel was written in several phases and, in particular, was substantially rewritten and augmented after its rejection in July 1846. This means that the 'second-generation' story, which has struck most readers as 'second thoughts', may have been just that.

Debate about the meaning and value of *Wuthering Heights* began immediately after its publication. Now, a hundred and fifty years later, there is such a vast quantity of critical commentary that my task in providing a 'critical guide' to this material has been very challenging. Such is the variety and proliferation of the work, with many different kinds of criticism appearing sometimes in the same year, that a simple chronological treatment would have been confusing. I have, therefore, adopted a compromise arrangement. Chapter one deals with the three phases of Emily's Victorian reputation – the first two years, when her identity was not known, the next thirty years or so when the propriety of her work was debated in the context of female authorship, and the final years of the century when she began to be adopted by the aesthetic movement. Chapter two attempts to sketch in the vast sweep of critical movements which has taken place during the twentieth century, from humanist through formalist to deconstructive approaches. Within this general framework, chapter three focuses on psychoanalytic readings, chapter four on source studies and dissemination studies, and chapter five on political readings, divided into Marxist, postcolonial and feminist readings.

I have tried to include substantial extracts from those essays and books which have been most influential; the enormous quantity of interesting material has meant, however, that I have often had to quote briefly or summarise essays which deserve more attention. As well as the 'big names', I have tried to give a sense of critical debate by linking and cross-referencing within and between chapters. My decision to include an essay under 'feminism', say, rather than 'discourse theory' or 'psychoanalysis', has often been determined less by its intrinsic features than by its place in such a dialogue.

Finally, there is the bibliography. Huge as it is (and I think it is probably the most comprehensive currently existing), it is not exhaustive; I have exercised discrimination in excluding work which is not original or has not been taken up in the ongoing debate. It is, nevertheless, overwhelming, and I have therefore added a 'Brief Guide to Further Reading' to help readers new to the subject to know where to begin.

The process of following through, in a largely chronological sequence, the different interpretations of *Wuthering Heights* has been a fascinating one for me and I hope that I have succeeded in providing a 'guide' through the prolific and competing theories provoked by this elusive novel. If the book works in the way I have intended, it provides a history of critical movements in the nineteenth and twentieth centuries, focused on a single, endlessly productive text. Although I have tried to present the different theories in their own terms, the process of preparing this book has confirmed my belief that a novel is not a fixed 'icon' for contemplation, but a 'text in process', revealing new faces to every new age and reader.

CHAPTER ONE

Victorian Responses: Power, Propriety and Poetry

Ellis Bell

NOWADAYS, WHEN 'Emily Brontë's *Wuthering Heights*' seems an indivisible whole, it is difficult to reconstruct the impact made in 1847 by a new novel by an unknown writer called 'Ellis Bell'. The problem then posed to readers by pseudonymous publication was more acute than it would be now. Readers of modernist and postmodernist texts are used to having to piece together meanings for themselves, but mid-nineteenth-century readers expected literature to be a message from the author, so that reading a pseudonymous novel had the disturbing effect of listening to a masked speaker. *Wuthering Heights* itself compounded these problems by not conforming to recognised categories of writing – too down-to-earth to be a gothic fantasy, too brutal to be a novel of manners, and with no recognisable 'moral'. It is not surprising, then, that the first reviewers of *Wuthering Heights* struggle to find an appropriate register to describe powerful writing which flouted normal criteria.

Charlotte Brontë, in her 1850 'Biographical Notice' of her sister, represents the early reviews as unanimous in condemnation, and Elizabeth Gaskell reinforces this impression in her *Life of Charlotte Brontë* (1857). Gaskell quotes from a letter from Charlotte written less than a month before Emily's death:

■ As I sat between them at our quiet but now somewhat melancholy fireside, I studied the two ferocious authors. Ellis the 'man of uncommon talents but dogged, brutal and morose', sat leaning back in his easy chair drawing his impeded breath as he best could . . . I wonder what the Reviewer would have thought of his own sagacity, could he have beheld the pair, as I did . . . [1] □

The quoted phrase is from E. P. Whipple in the *North American Review*

(1848), and does represent a repeated complaint about the 'morbid' (unhealthy), violent and 'coarse' nature of the writing. It was, in fact, the American reviews which were most intemperate in their attack. The American *Graham's Magazine* is apoplectic:

■ How a human being could have attempted such a book as the present without committing suicide . . . is a mystery. It is a compound of vulgar depravity and unnatural horrors, such as we might suppose a person, inspired by a mixture of brandy and gunpowder, might write for the edification of fifth-rate blackguards. □

They were most incensed by the fact that the book seemed to cast a spell over them; the *Literary World* writes:

■ It is 'a dark tale darkly told;' a book that seizes upon us with an iron grasp, and makes us read its story of passions and wrongs whether we will or no. Fascinated by strange magic we read what we dislike, we become interested in characters which are most revolting to our feelings, and are made subject to the immense power, of the book . . . In the whole story not a single trait of character is elicited which can command our admiration . . . and yet, in spite of this, spite of the disgusting coarseness of much of the dialogue, and the improbabilities and incongruities of the plot, we are spell-bound, we cannot choose but read. □

It is, however, E. P. Whipple, the *North American Review* critic quoted by Charlotte Brontë, who is most expansive about 'Acton Bell's' depravity (there was confusion in America, encouraged by Emily and Anne's unscrupulous publisher, Newby, about which 'Bell brother' wrote which novel):

■ Acton . . . appears to think that spiritual wickedness is a combination of animal ferocities, and has accordingly made a compendium of the most striking qualities of tiger, wolf, cur, and wild-cat, in the hope of framing out of such elements a suitable brute-demon to serve as the hero of his novel . . . This epitome of brutality, disavowed by man and devil, Mr Acton Bell attempts in two whole volumes to delineate, and certainly he is to be congratulated on his success. As he is a man of uncommon talents, it is needless to say that it is to his subject and his dogged manner of handling it that we are to refer the burst of dislike with which the novel was received . . . It must be confessed that this coarseness, though the prominent, is not the only characteristic of the writer . . . he aims further to exhibit the action of the sentiment of love on the nature of the being whom his morbid imagination has created. This is by far the ablest and most subtle portion of his labours, and indicates that strong hold upon the elements of character, and that decision of touch in the delineation of the most evanescent qualities of emotion, which distinguish the mind of the whole family. For all practical purposes, however, the power evinced in *Wuthering Heights* is power thrown away. Nightmares and dreams, through which devils dance and wolves howl, make bad novels. □

The British reviewers also objected mainly to the subject-matter of the novel (rather as a modern audience might object to 'sex and violence' on television). Elizabeth Rigby (Lady Eastlake), notorious for her attack on *Jane Eyre*, is even less satisfied with *Wuthering Heights*, finding 'the Jane and Rochester animals in their native state, as Catherine and Heathfield [*sic*], . . . too odiously and abominably pagan to be palatable even to the most vitiated class of English readers' (*CH* p. 111). James Lorimer is more specific. The novel, he says:

■ commences by introducing the reader to a perfect pandemonium of low and brutal creatures, who wrangle with each other in language too disgusting for the eye or the ear to tolerate, and unredeemed, so far as we could see, by one single particle either of wit or humour, or even psychological truth, for the characters are as false as they are loathsome. □

(p. 486; *CH* p. 115)

The British reviewers were, however, on the whole more generous about the power which even Whipple acknowledged.[2] H. F. Chorley, who finds it 'a disagreeable story', also acknowledges 'much power and cleverness' and offers more explanation for the almost universal feeling that although the story might be 'true', it was not appropriate for representation; it deals with 'those physical acts of cruelty which we know to have their warrant in the real annals of crime and suffering, – but the contemplation of which taste rejects' (*CH* p. 218). The *Examiner* also hopes that the author will not again 'drag into light all that he discovers, of coarse and loathsome . . .' (*CH* p. 222).

These comments help to explain why reviewers at this time seem to argue both that the events in *Wuthering Heights* are realistic (because they could happen) and that they are not probable (because they do not normally happen in novels). The *Examiner* complains that the 'realistic' elements do not match his idea of 'romantic love':

■ we entertain great doubts as to the . . . *vraisemblance* of the main character. The hardness, selfishness, and cruelty of Heathcliff are in our opinion inconsistent with the romantic love that he is stated to have felt for Catherine Earnshaw. □

(*CH* p. 221).

The *Atlas*, while agreeing with other reviewers about the painful and shocking nature of the story, disagrees with the *Examiner* about *vraisemblance* (verisimilitude), arguing that despite its improbability on the large scale, *Wuthering Heights* persuades us by the relentless accuracy of its detail. The turn from disapproval to approval here hinges on the word 'natural', which carries the meanings both of 'unformed' and 'true to life':

■ *Wuthering Heights* is a strange, inartistic story. There are evidences in every chapter of a sort of rugged power – an unconscious strength – which the possessor seems never to think of turning to the best advantage. The general effect is inexpressibly painful. We know nothing in the whole range of our fictitious literature which presents such shocking pictures of the worst forms of humanity . . . A more natural story we do not remember to have read. Inconceivable as are the combinations of human degradation which are here to be found moving within the circle of a few miles, the *vraisemblance* is so admirably preserved; there is so much truth in what we may call the *costumery* . . . – the general mounting of the entire piece – that we readily identify the scenes and personages of the fiction; and when we lay aside the book it is some time before we can persuade ourselves that we have held nothing more than imaginary intercourse with the ideal creatures of the brain. The reality of unreality has never been so aptly illustrated as in the scenes of almost savage life which Ellis Bell has brought so vividly before us . . .

Wuthering Heights . . . is only a promise, but it is a colossal one. □

Douglas Jerrold's Weekly Newspaper shares the view of the *Atlas* that the book is a law unto itself:

■ *Wuthering Heights* is a strange sort of book, – baffling all regular criticism; yet, it is impossible to begin and not finish it . . .

In *Wuthering Heights* the reader is shocked, disgusted, almost sickened by details of cruelty, inhumanity, and the most diabolical hate and vengeance, and anon come passages of powerful testimony to the supreme power of love . . . The women in the book are of a strange fiendish-angelic nature, tantalizing, and terrible, and the men are indescribable out of the book itself . . .

It is very puzzling and very interesting . . . we must leave it to our readers to decide what sort of book it is. □

(p. 77; *CH* p. 228)

Jerrold's presses home the point made by both Whipple (the 'power' of *Wuthering Heights* 'is power thrown away') and by the *Atlas* (the writer 'seems not to turn [his strength] to the best advantage') by making it explicit that it is a moral intention which is lacking:

■ What may be the moral which the author wishes the reader to deduce from his work, it is difficult to say . . . to speak honestly, we have discovered none but mere glimpses . . . There seems to us great power in this book but a purposeless power, which we feel a great desire to see turned to better account.[3] □

(*CH* p. 228)

The experience of reading these reviews is of being shuttled back and forth between praise and censorious blame, as if the writers themselves could not reconcile their impressions. This is true even of the most intelligent of the American reviewers, George Washington Peck. He begins, like so many of the others, with a statement of bafflement:

■ its power is so predominant that it is not easy . . . to analyse one's impressions . . . We have been taken and carried through a new region, a melancholy waste, with here and there patches of beauty . . . fierce passions . . . extremes of love and hate, and with sorrow that none but those who have suffered can understand. This has not been accomplished with ease, but with an ill-mannered contempt for the decencies of language, and in a style which might resemble that of a Yorkshire farmer who . . . [has taken] lessons of a London footman. □

Warning lady readers, he goes on:

■ The book is original; it is powerful; full of suggestiveness. But still it is *coarse* . . . such a general roughness and savageness in the soliloquies and dialogues . . . as never should be found in a work of art . . . It would indicate that the writer was not accustomed to the society of gentlemen, and . . . rather gloried, in showing it. □

(*CH* pp. 235–6)

Like the *Examiner* and the *New Monthly*, Peck assumes that what is unpleasant is somehow not realistic; he questions the 'naturalness' of the emotion expressed in Catherine's speeches in Chapter 9, arguing that no real person would reason, as Catherine does, that marrying one man is the best way to keep another. This 'coarse' conception cannot be excused on the grounds of Catherine's innocence, he argues, since

■ The physical condition of our bodies, the changes which take place on arriving at an age proper for marriage, do not allow of the ignorance which our author requires us to suppose in his heroine . . . especially after Heathcliff's absence and return, when she is the wife of Linton and about to become a mother . . . Could Mrs Linton . . . desire his presence . . . unless . . . she meant to be untrue to her husband? . . . □

(CH p.239)

The 'coarseness', it seems, consists not in the sensuality of the text but in its inexplicable lack of sensuality:

■ there is in these characters an absence of all that natural desire which should accompany love. They are abstract and bodiless. Their love is feline; it is tigerish.

Yet the work is carried on with such power that it excites a sense of shame to turn back to many of its most 'thrilling' scenes, and reflect that we were able to read them with so little disgust . . . The children know too much about their minds and too little about their bodies; they understand at a very early age all the intellectual and sentimental part of love, but the 'bloom of young desire' does not warm their cheeks. The grown-up characters are the mere tools of fixed passions. Their actions and sayings are like those of monomaniacs or persons who have breathed nitrous oxide. □

(*CH* pp. 239–40)

This bewilderment suggests a perverse fascination which Peck is unable to evaluate:

■ Yet with all this faultiness, *Wuthering Heights* is, undoubtedly, a work of many singular merits . . . It lifts the veil and shows boldly the dark side of our depraved nature . . . It goes into the under-current of passion, and the rapid hold it has taken of the public shows how much truth there is hidden unde its coarse extravagance. □

(*CH* p. 240)

■ Nothing like it has ever been written before; it is to be hoped . . . for the sake of good manners, nothing will be hereafter. Let it stand by itself, a coarse, original, powerful book . . . It will live a short and brilliant life and then die and be forgotten. □

(*CH* p. 241)

Grudgingly generous, Peck reveals that the quality he cannot stomach in the book is its defiance:

■ if the rank of a work of fiction is to depend solely on its naked imaginative power, then this is one of the greatest novels in the language . . . But . . . the writer . . . must have been designedly original. He must have set to his work with some such feeling towards the world, as he would probably think well expressed by the words, 'There! take *that*, and see how you like it!' □

(CH pp. 241–2)

The only appreciation of the pseudonymous novel wholehearted enough to please Charlotte poignantly appeared only after Emily's death. This was by the young poet Sydney Dobell, who took the opposite line from Peck on the moral 'coarseness' of Catherine Earnshaw's character (Dobell insisted that Wuthering Heights was an early work by Currer Bell):

■ Catherine Earnshaw – at once so wonderfully fresh, so fearfully natural . . . what can surpass the strange compatibility of her simultaneous loves; the involuntary art with which her two natures are so made to coexist, that in the very arms of her lover we dare not doubt her purity . . .

one looks back at the whole story as to a world of brilliant figures in an atmosphere of mist; shapes that . . . burn their colours into the brain, and depart into the enveloping fog. It is the unformed writing of a giant's hand; the 'large utterance' of a baby god. □

(CH pp. 278–9)

Emily Brontë

After Emily's death in 1848, Charlotte felt absolved from her promise to preserve her pseudonym; she added a 'Biographical Notice' to the second edition of *Wuthering Heights* in 1850, revealing for the first time the details of her sister's life and death. Charlotte laments that Emily, despite 'a secret power and fire that might have informed the brain and kindled the veins of a hero . . . had no worldly wisdom . . . An interpreter ought always to have stood between her and the world . . .' (p. 366).

In the 'Editor's Preface' which also accompanied this edition of *Wuthering Heights*, Charlotte tried to be that interpreter:

■ I have just read over 'Wuthering Heights', and, for the first time, have obtained a clear glimpse of what are termed (and, perhaps, really are) its faults; have gained a definite notion of how it appears to other people – to strangers who knew nothing of the author; who are unacquainted with the locality where the scenes of the story are laid; to whom the inhabitants, the customs, the natural characteristics of the outlying hills and hamlets in the West-Riding of Yorkshire are things alien and unfamiliar.

To all such 'Wuthering Heights' must appear a rude and strange production. The wild moors of the north of England can for them have no interest; the language, the manners, the very dwellings and household customs of the scattered inhabitants of those districts, must be to such readers in a great measure unintelligible, and – where intelligible – repulsive. Men and women who, perhaps, naturally very calm, and with feelings moderate in degree, and little marked in kind, have been trained from their cradle to observe the utmost evenness of manner and guardedness of language, will hardly know what to make of the rough, strong utterance, the harshly manifested passions, the unbridled aversions, and headlong partialities of unlettered moorland hinds and rugged moorland squires, who have grown up untaught and unchecked, except by mentors as harsh as themselves . . .

With regard to the rusticity of 'Wuthering Heights', I admit the charge, for I feel the quality. It is rustic all through. It is moorish, and wild, and knotty as a root of heath. Nor was it natural that it should be otherwise; the author being herself a native and nursling of the moors. Doubtless, had her lot been cast in a town, her writings, if she had written at all, would have possessed another character. Even had chance or taste led her to choose a similar subject, she would have treated it otherwise. Had Ellis Bell been a lady or a gentleman accustomed to what is called 'the world', her view of a remote and unreclaimed region, as well as of the dwellers therein, would have differed greatly from that actually taken by the homebred country girl. Doubtless it would have been wider – more comprehensive: whether it would have been more original or more truthful is not so certain. As far as the scenery and locality are concerned, it could scarcely have been so sympathetic: Ellis Bell did not describe as one whose eye and taste alone found pleasure in the prospect; her native hills were far more to her than a spectacle; they were what she lived in, and by, as much as the wild birds, their tenants, or as the heather, their produce. Her descriptions, then, of natural scenery, are what they should be, and all they should be.

Where delineation of human character is concerned, the case is different. I am bound to avow that she had scarcely more practical knowledge of the peasantry amongst whom she lived, than a nun has of the country people who sometimes pass her convent gates. My sister's disposition was not naturally gregarious; circumstances favoured and fostered her tendency to seclusion; except to go to church or take a walk on the hills, she rarely crossed the threshold of home. Though her feeling for the people round was benevolent, intercourse with them she never sought; nor, with very few exceptions, ever experienced. And yet she knew them: knew their ways, their language, their family histories; she could hear of them with interest, and talk of them with detail, minute, graphic, and accurate; but *with* them, she rarely exchanged a word. Hence it ensued that what her mind had gathered of the real concerning them, was too exclusively confined to those tragic and terrible traits of which, in listening to the secret annals of every rude vicinage, the memory is sometimes compelled to receive the impress. Her imagination, which was a spirit more sombre than sunny, more powerful than sportive, found in such traits material whence it wrought creations like Heathcliff, like Earnshaw, like Catherine. Having formed these beings, she did not know what she had done. If the auditor of her work when read in manuscript, shuddered under the grinding influence of natures so relentless and implacable, of spirits so lost and fallen; if it was complained that the mere hearing of certain vivid and fearful scenes banished sleep by night, and disturbed mental peace by day, Ellis Bell would wonder what was meant, and suspect the complainant of affectation. Had she but lived, her mind would of itself have grown like a strong tree, loftier, straighter, wider-spreading, and its matured fruits would have attained a mellower ripeness and sunnier bloom; but on that mind time and experience alone could work; to the influence of other intellects, it was not amenable.

Having avowed that over much of 'Wuthering Heights' there broods 'a horror of great darkness';[4] that, in its storm-heated and electrical atmosphere, we seem at times to breathe lightning, let me point to those spots where clouded daylight and the eclipsed sun still attest their existence. For a specimen of true benevolence and homely fidelity, look at the character of Nelly Dean; for an example of constancy and tenderness, remark that of Edgar Linton. (Some people will think these qualities do not shine so well incarnate in a man as they would do in a woman, but Ellis Bell could never be brought to comprehend this notion: nothing moved her more than any insinuation that the faithfulness and clemency, the long-suffering and loving-kindness which are esteemed virtues in the daughters of Eve, become foibles in the sons of Adam. She held that mercy and forgiveness are the divinest attributes of the Great Being who made both man and woman, and that what clothes the Godhead in glory, can disgrace no form of feeble humanity.) There is a dry saturnine humour in the delineation of old Joseph, and some glimpses of grace and gaiety animate the younger Catherine. Nor is even the first heroine of the name destitute of a certain strange beauty in her fierceness, or of honesty in the midst of perverted passion and passionate perversity.

Heathcliff, indeed, stands unredeemed; never once swerving in his arrow-straight course to perdition, from . . . [his first arrival] to . . . [his death]. [Charlotte here quotes from the novel.]

Heathcliff betrays one solitary human feeling, and that is *not* his love for Catherine; which is a sentiment fierce and inhuman: a passion such as might boil and glow in the bad essence of some evil genius; a fire that might form the tormented centre – the ever-suffering soul of a magnate of the infernal world: and by its quenchless and ceaseless ravage effect the execution of the decree which dooms him to carry Hell with him wherever he wanders. No; the single link that connects Heathcliff with humanity is his rudely confessed regard for Hareton Earnshaw – the young man whom he has ruined; and then his half-implied esteem for Nelly Dean. These solitary traits omitted, we should say he was child neither of Lascar nor gipsy, but a man's shape animated by demon life – a Ghoul – an Afreet.[5]

Whether it is right or advisable to create beings like Heathcliff, I do not know: I scarcely think it is. But this I know; the writer who possesses the creative gift owns something of which he is not always master – something that at times strangely wills and works for itself . . . Be the work grim or glorious, dread or divine, you have little choice left but quiescent adoption . . . If the result be attractive, the World will praise you, who little deserve praise; if it be repulsive, the same World will blame you, who almost as little deserve blame.

'Wuthering Heights' was hewn in a wild workshop, with simple tools, out of homely material. The statuary found a granite block on a solitary moor: gazing thereon, he saw how from the crag might be elicited a head, savage, swart, sinister; a form moulded with at least one element of grandeur – power. He wrought with a rude chisel, and from no model but the vision of his meditations. With time and labour, the crag took human shape; and there it stands colossal, dark, and frowning, half statue, half rock: in the former sense, terrible and goblin-like; in the latter, almost beautiful, for its colouring is of mellow grey, and moorland moss clothes it; and heath, with its blooming bells and balmy fragrance, grows faithfully close to the giant's foot. □

(*WH* pp. 367–71)

Charlotte Brontë's 'Preface' has had enormous influence on critics of later generations. Her version of the involuntary creative process persisted from Matthew Arnold's memorial poem, 'Haworth Churchyard' (1855) to Peter Kosminsky's 1992 film, *Emily Brontë's Wuthering Heights*, with its introductory sequence showing Emily 'inspired' by an old house on the moors. Charlotte's unease about Heathcliff also persists, so that Miriam Allott is still debating 'The Rejection of Heathcliff?' in 1958. In 1964 Philip Drew concludes that Charlotte was essentially right about Emily.

The immediate readers of the 1850 edition, however, reacted less to the 'Preface' than to the 'Biographical Notice', which revealed for the first time that the 'brutal' author was a woman. As G. H. Lewes puts it:

■ Curious enough it is to read *Wuthering Heights* and *The Tenant of Wildfell Hall*, and to remember that the writers were two retiring, solitary, consumptive girls! Books, coarse even for men, coarse in language and coarse in conception, the coarseness apparently of violence and uncultivated men – turn out to be the productions of two girls living almost alone, filling their loneliness with quiet studies, and writing these books from a sense of duty . . . [6] □

(*CH* p. 292)

The Economist (1851) now dwells on the 'beautiful picture of three young women, living in a remote place, animated by a heroic desire for distinction by useful and honourable labours' – a marked change from its earlier prim disapproval.

Nicola Thompson, in her 1996 analysis of the early reception of *Wuthering Heights*, concludes that:

■ the new awareness of Ellis Bell's way of life, innocence, and regional isolation led to an increased sympathy with her novel, a tendency to excuse the author from normal standards of literary and female propriety . . . *Wuthering Heights* was not judged as severely in 1850 as it had been in 1847 and 1848. □

(p. 58)

This change, however, had its drawbacks. One reaction to the female authorship of *Wuthering Heights* is that reviewers no longer confessed to its spellbinding power. Whereas the first reviewers had cast themselves as Wedding Guest to Ellis Bell's Ancient Mariner, these later readers begin to place *Wuthering Heights* in the gothic category peculiarly associated with women, to which the masculine reviewer can profess knowing superiority. The *Eclectic Review* now finds 'little more power . . . than . . . the ghost stories which made our granddames tremble' (*CH* p. 298). Dante Gabriel Rossetti, in 1854, describes *Wuthering Heights* as 'a fiend of a book, an incredible monster, combining all the stronger female tendencies from Mrs Browning to Mrs Brownrigg. The action is laid in Hell, – only it seems places and people have English names there'. Like the *Eclectic* reviewer, Rossetti distances himself from the novel's power by associating it with a notorious female villain, Mrs Brownrigg, a midwife who was hanged for murder in 1767. As Nicola Thompson puts it:

■ the sense of 'mastery' that Culler identifies as part of finishing a book . . . eluded the reviewers until 1850. With the 'Biographical Notice' and 'Preface' provided by Charlotte . . . the tone of the reviewers changes from one of bewilderment to confidence, even to condescension. □

(p. 45)

In 1857 a new spate of reviews followed Elizabeth Gaskell's *Life of Charlotte Brontë*, which gave an eloquent account of the sisters' sufferings, made even more poignant by the knowledge that even Charlotte was now dead. In the light of this extended biography, some journals made a marked turn-about in attitude. The *North American Review*, which in 1848 had pictured the author of *Wuthering Heights* as taking 'a morose satisfaction in developing a full and complete science of human brutality' (*CH* p. 247), was now, in 1857, able to see Emily as 'a very extraordinary woman', showing

■ germs . . . which, placed under more favourable circumstances, must have developed into nobility and grandeur . . . Few who read the Brontë novels when they first appeared could have suspected, in ever so faint a degree, the strangeness of the private history which lay concealed behind the friendly shelter of those oracular names. □

(pp. 308, 316)

Like *The Economist*, the *North American* reviewer now accepts that the writers' circumstances excuse their apparent 'coarseness' and is ingenuous about his dependence on knowledge of the author for judgement of the writing:

■ The materials were not selected by them but thrust upon them by circumstances clamorous for utterance . . . And looking at these novels in the strong daylight cast upon them by our study of the hearts and brains in which they had their birth, – no longer mere creations of an imagination which leaves a cheery social circle at its will, to retire to the study and indulge its untrammelled powers, able to return at any moment to healthful and happy influences from without, – they come to us as the very outpourings of pent-up passion, the cry of unfettered hearts, the panting of hungry intellects, restrained by the iron despotism of adverse and unconquerable circumstance. □

(p. 316)

The journal which had condemned *Wuthering Heights* as compounded of 'nightmares and dreams, through which devils dance and wolves howl' (*CH* p. 248), now uses the same imagery to explain and excuse, rather than to accuse and condemn:

■ it is only in the author that the key to such an extraordinary story can be found . . . It calls for no harsh judgement as a moral utterance; for its monstrosity removes it from the range of moralities altogether, and can no more be reduced to any practical application than the fancies which perplex a brain in a paroxysm of nightmare. □

(pp. 327–8)

So inevitably is the work perceived as the product of its author that no apology is deemed necessary for this change of judgement:

■ The world . . . would gladly offer [the Brontë family] a more kindly tribute than it could conscientiously have given while ignorant of so much which now reveals the virtues, the struggles, and the sufferings of the sisters in that desolate Haworth parsonage. □

(p. 329)

The change is particularly marked in relation to Emily: W. C. Roscoe now claims that 'in force of genius, in the power of conceiving and uttering intensity of passion, Emily surpassed her sister Charlotte' (*CH* p. 348). Although he repeats the hyperbolic abuse of earlier reviewers ('frightful excesses of degrading vices . . . snarling hypocrisy . . . idiotic imbecility'), he also recognises that 'her rude titanic story "rich with barbaric gems and crusted gold"' is 'caught up, as it were, into the highest heaven of imagination . . . fused together as by fire; and the reader has neither power nor inclination to weigh probabilities or discuss defects' (pp. 350, 349). Sir John Skelton singles out the story of Catherine, whose scene with the feathers 'is as sad and true as the "coronet flowers" of Ophelia' (p. 338).

There are also, however, plenty of reviewers in the 1850s and 60s who are not prepared to 'make allowances' for Emily. For the *Christian Remembrancer*, the 'secret' revealed by Gaskell's *Life* is Emily's love for *animals*: *Wuthering Heights* is 'Life in the Kennel' (p. 367)! *Bentley's Miscellany* refutes Charlotte's 'rustic' explanation:

■ The truth is, there are no such people as Catherine Earnshaw and Heathcliff in Yorkshire, or anywhere else . . . The reader would feel disgust and detestation, only that he soon feels that the chief characters are out of their senses, – a circumstance of which the Authoress was not aware. □

(p. 449)

Peter Bayne, in an extensive essay (1857), still sees the book as powerful but wrong. Like Peck and later critics, Bayne struggles to explain the novel in psychological terms, as a result of a 'fixed idea' or monomania, but ultimately cannot absolve the author of moral responsibility. *Wuthering Heights* contains 'evidence of powers it were perhaps impossible to estimate, and mental wealth which we might vainly attempt to compute' (*CH* p. 322).

■ But, after all, we must pronounce what has been left us by this wonderful woman, unhealthy, immature, and worthy of being avoided. *Wuthering Heights* . . . belongs to the horror school of fiction, and is involved in its unequivocal and unexcepting condemnation ... Works like those of Edgar Poe and this *Wuthering Heights* must be plainly declared to blunt, to brutalize, and to enervate the mind. □

(*CH* p. 325)

E. S. Dallas, also in 1857, finds in *Wuthering Heights* a 'deadly fatalism': 'The whole gloomy tale is in its idea the nearest approach that has been made in our time to the pitiless fatality which is the dominant idea of Greek tragedy' (*CH* pp. 360–1). Leslie Stephen, in 1877, still finds it 'a kind of baseless nightmare, which we read with . . . more pain than pleasure or profit' (p. 421).

Shakespeare's Younger Sister

As time passes, moral indignation somewhat abates. An article in *Galaxy* (1873) argues that *Wuthering Heights* does not 'deserve the wholesale condemnation and unqualified abuse which have been heaped upon it. Though a brutal, it is not a sensual book; though coarse, it is not vulgar; though bad, it is not indecent' (*CH* pp. 392–3). From this grudging beginning, the refusal to recognise *Wuthering Heights* as the work of a female author gives way to a mythologising of Emily Brontë. George Barnet Smith can still write in 1873 that *Wuthering Heights* is 'perhaps one of the most unpleasant books ever written: but', he goes on, 'we stand in amaze at the almost incredible fact that it was written by a slim country girl who would have passed in a crowd as an insignificant person'. His praise recoups the 1857 praises of Skelton and Roscoe with a new note of hyperbole; even the excesses of *Wuthering Heights* seem to become virtues worthy of comparison with Shakespeare:

■ Emily Brontë . . . has written a book which stands as completely alone in the language as does the *Paradise Lost* or the *Pilgrim's Progress* . . . *Wuthering Heights* . . . shows a massive strength which is of the rarest description. Its power is absolutely Titanic: from the first page to the last it reads like the intellectual throes of a giant . . . In Heathcliff, Emily Brontë has drawn the greatest villain extant, after Iago. He has no match out of Shakespeare . . . We challenge the world to produce another work in which the whole atmosphere seems so surcharged with suppressed electricity, and bound in with the blackness of tempest and desolation . . . while we cannot defend it altogether possibly as it stands, we should regret never having seen it, as one of the most extraordinary and powerful productions in the whole range of English Literature. □

(pp. 65–8)

This critic, ignoring the *furore* which accompanied the publication of *Wuthering Heights*, opts for a myth of unrecognised genius: 'whilst she lived the world made no sign of recognition of her strangely weird powers' (p.66).

T. Wemyss Reid, on the other hand, in 1877, writes that 'the Brontë novels continued to sell largely for some time after Charlotte's death' although '*Wuthering Heights* . . . is now practically unread'. Reid combines the forgiving stance of the 1850s with the fascination of the 1840s. *Wuthering Heights* is, he says,

■ the work of one who, in everything but years, was a mere child, and its great and glaring faults are to be forgiven as one forgives the mistakes of childhood. But how vast was the intellectual greatness displayed in this juvenile work! The author seizes the reader . . . holds him thrilled, entranced, terrified . . . and leaves him at last . . . shaken and exhausted as by some great effort of the mind. Surely nowhere in modern English fiction can more striking proof be found of the possession of 'the creative gift' in an extraordinary degree than . . . in *Wuthering Heights*. From what unfathomed recesses of her intellect did this shy, nervous, untrained girl produce such characters . . . ? . . . They come forth with all the vigour and freshness, the living reality and impressiveness, which can belong only to the spontaneous creations of genius. They are no copies, but living originals, owing their lives to her own travail and suffering. □

(*CH* pp.400–401)

This 'repulsive and almost ghastly' book is, Reid concludes, comparable with Shakespeare's *Titus Andronicus* (*CH* p.399).

Peter Bayne, who had struggled to acknowledge the power of *Wuthering Heights* in 1857, returned to the task in 1881. In this, the period of Hardy's early novels, Bayne finds that 'the burden of *Wuthering Heights* is the potency of evil – its potency to pervert good'. This 'strange and appalling thesis to be expounded by an English girl!' makes *Wuthering Heights* even bleaker than the most renowned tragedies of world literature – the *Iliad*, the great Greek tragedies or *Lear*. In them the tragedy rises from sin or folly, 'but in *Wuthering Heights* the root of pain and misery is goodness, and the world in which we move seems God-forsaken'. Although Bayne is not prepared to see this raw vision as a strength, he does not, like Reid, patronise Emily's 'juvenile' powers:

■ the best that can be said for the book is that it is the product of marvellous genius that never freely and genially expanded . . . that seems to have watched, and wailed, and waited for God, and yet never *once* saw His eye light up the 'wildering clouds'. □

The novel's 'execution', however, 'is singularly mature':

■ The author never seems for one moment to lose her self-possession and self-command. Had Shakespeare written *Lear* before he was thirty, and died, we should have had a right to believe that he took a pessimistic view of life. □

(pp. 426–8)

The single greatest change of direction in the Victorian evaluation of *Wuthering Heights* came with A. Mary F. Robinson's biography, *Emily Brontë*, in 1883, which lifted the discussion of Emily's work out of the moral-realist frame and into that of the aesthetic and feminist movements. Robinson was herself a poet and a friend of Swinburne. Like Reid, she presents *Wuthering Heights* within the myth of neglected genius:

■ a few brave lines of welcome from Sydney Dobell, one fine verse of Mr Arnold's, one notice from Mr Reid, was all the praise that had been given to the book by those in authority. Here and there a mill-girl in the West Riding factories read and re-read the tattered copy from the lending library; here and there some eager, unsatisfied, passionate child came upon the book and loved it, in spite of chiding . . . or some strong-fibred heart felt without a shudder the justice of that stern vision of inevitable, inherited ruin following the chance-found child of foreign sailor and seaport mother. But these readers were not many: even yet the book is not popular. □

(p. 2)

Robinson's emotional writing establishes *Wuthering Heights* as the voice of the silenced, the comrade of the dispossessed. As a champion of the cause of women, she emphasised the damage done by Emily's brother, Branwell, to his sisters' peace of mind. To ignore Branwell's story of debauch and degradation would be, she says,

■ to leave untold the patience, the courage, the unselfishness which perfected Emily Brontë's heroic character; and to have left her burdened with the calumny of having chosen to invent the crimes and violence of her *dramatis personae*. Not so, alas! They were but reflected from the passion and sorrow that darkened her home; it was not perverse fancy which drove that pure and innocent girl into ceaseless brooding on the conquering force of sin and the supremacy of injustice. □

(p. 6)

Robinson's version of Emily is, however, no meek Angel in the House, but a 'dissenter'. For the first time, a critic recognised that a writer need not be judged by pre-existing rules but can force her readers to recognise their injustice:

■ Never was a nature more sensitive to the stupidities and narrowness of conventional opinion, a nature more likely to be found in the ranks of the opposition; and with such a nature indignation is the force that most often looses the gate of speech. The impulse to reveal wrongs and sufferings as they really are, is overwhelmingly strong; although the revelation itself be imperfect. What, then, would this inexperienced Yorkshire parson's daughter reveal? The unlikeness of life to the author-ised pictures of life; the force of evil, only conquerable by the slow-revolving process of nature which admits not the eternal duration of the perverse; the grim and fearful lessons of heredity . . . the all-penetrating kinship of living things . . . the sure and universal peace of death. □

(pp. 157–8)

The 'grim and fearful lessons of heredity' were most obviously those of Darwin or Lamarck, and the modern critic Stevie Davies supports this supposition, arguing that Emily's Belgian essays, 'The Cat' and 'The Butterfly', display proto-Darwinian awareness of the struggle for survival (1994 pp. 104–9). Robinson's imagery, however, is likely to draw some of its force from the feminist agitation for the repeal of the Contagious Diseases Acts, which, in the early 1880s, had exposed the fact that men could, with impunity, spread disease among their wives and children. Believing that Emily was brought up as a Calvinist, Robinson transforms the language of predestination into that of hereditary doom:

■ From this doctrine of reward and punishment she learned that for every unchecked evil tendency there is a fearful expiation; though she placed it not indeed in the flames of hell, but in the perverted instincts of our own children. Terrible theories of doomed incurable sin and pre-destined loss warned her that an evil stock will only beget contamination: the children of the mad must be liable to madness; the children of the depraved, bent towards depravity; the seed of the poi-son-plant springs up to blast and ruin. □

Applying this theory to Heathcliff, she concludes, 'From thistles you gather no grapes' (pp. 158–9).

Unlike the male critics who were inclined to see Emily as a child, and were incredulous that an inexperienced girl could have written such a book, Robinson, like the earlier poet Sydney Dobell, argued that these qualities, which set her apart from the world, were in fact her strength:

■ none but a personally inexperienced girl could have treated the subject with the absolute and sexless purity which we find in 'Wuthering Heights'. How *infecte*, commonplace, and ignominious would Branwell, relying on his own recollections, have made the thwarted passion of a violent adventurer for a woman whose sickly husband both despise! That purity as of polished steel, as cold and harder than ice, that freedom in dealing with love and hate, as audacious as an infant's love for the bright flame of fire, could only belong to one whose intensity of genius was rivalled by the narrowness of her experience. □

(pp. 163–4)

Robinson's book is a biography, and her contribution to *Wuthering Heights* criticism, in an age when literature was judged as inseparable from its author, was to change the image of the author. Charlotte's image of Emily as rustic recluse was refined by Robinson into a modern Joan of Arc: chaste, courageous, combative.

Swinburne's review of Mary Robinson's biography, however, treats *Wuthering Heights* as a work of art – a 'poem' in fact. Where current popular taste accepted 'accumulated horrors' in place of tragedy, in *Wuthering Heights*, 'we breathe the fresh dark air of tragic passion and presage' (p. 439). Allowing that 'Heathcliff's treatment of his victims make[s] the reader feel . . . as though he were reading a police report or even a novel by some French "naturalist" of the latest and brutallest order' (p. 443), he argues that this effect is 'transfigured' by its 'purity and passionate straightforwardness':

■ The love which devours life itself, which devastates the present and desolates the future with unquenchable and raging fire, has nothing less pure in it than flame or sunlight; and this passionate and ardent chastity is utterly and unmistakably spontaneous and unconscious. Not until the story is ended . . . does the reader even perceive the simple and natural absence of any grosser element, any hint or suggestion of a baser alloy in the ingredients of its human emotion than in the splendour of lightning or the roll of a gathered wave . . . not a grain in it of soiling sand, not a waif of clogging weed. As was the author's life, so is her book in all things: troubled and taintless, with little of rest in it, and nothing of reproach. It may be true that not many will ever take it to their hearts: it is certain that those who do like it will like nothing very much better in the whole world of poetry or prose. □

(pp. 443–4)

This eulogy appropriates Emily Brontë for the aesthetic movement, where vividness in the representation of the moment as it passes is more important than moral earnestness.

The critics of the last decades of the century were self-consciously professional in their literary evaluations; their object is not to pronounce moral judgement but to place Emily Brontë in a literary tradition. Thus Walter Pater uses a scene from *Wuthering Heights*, with its 'passionate' characters 'woven on a background of delicately beautiful, moorland scenery' to epitomise 'the spirit of romanticism'. Angus Mackay's 1898 essay includes numerous comparisons between Emily Brontë and Shakespearean figures, and his conclusion sums up a growing consensus that if we consider 'the imagination displayed in *Wuthering Heights* – its power, its intensity, its absolute originality – it is scarcely too much to say of Emily that she might have been Shakespeare's younger sister' (p. 217; *CH* p. 446).

It was, however, a woman critic, Mary Augusta Ward, who, in her Introduction to the Haworth edition of *Wuthering Heights* (1900), first placed Emily Brontë in a complex literary tradition. Mary Ward, herself a respected novelist, was the niece of Matthew Arnold and familiar with literary and philosophical debate. Peter Collister, in his 1985 study of Ward, stresses her 'Arnoldian range of reference' which aligns her Introduction with high culture and 'sets it apart from the bulk of Victorian thinking on the Brontës' (p. 414). The feminist critic Beth Sutton-Ramspeck (1990), on the other hand, stresses the fact that Ward writes as a woman, and thus differently from both the male avant-garde and the reviewers. For Sutton-Ramspeck, Ward appears as a precursor of modern feminist critical strategies. This is unexpected, since 'her best known political role was as leader and prolific polemicist for the anti-suffrage movement in Britain'. Nevertheless, Sutton-Ramspeck aims to show

■ that her writings on the Brontës are feminist in three different ways: first, in celebrating her female literary precursors, she defends them against trivializing and devaluing readings by such powerful male critics as Henry James, Leslie Stephen, and Matthew Arnold; second, in her critical methods – her biographical and 'reader response' approaches – Ward implicitly rejects these critics' essentially androcentric paradigms of proper ('objective') critical procedure; and third, both Ward's resistance to male literary authority and her own critical practice adumbrate contemporary feminist critical approaches. Ward stands as one of our own critical foremothers. □

(pp. 55–6)

Henry James, who effected a major shift in the way that novels were read in the twentieth century, objected to the Victorian tendency to confuse the lives and works of the Brontës, which, he says, produced

■ the most complete intellectual muddle . . . ever achieved, on a literary question, by our wonderful public . . . Literature is an objective, a projected result; it is life that is the unconscious, the agitated, the strug-gling, floundering cause. But the fashion has been, in looking at the Brontës, so to confound the cause with the result that we cease to know, in the presence of such ecstasies, what we have hold of or what we are talking about. They represent, the ecstasies, the high-water mark of sentimental judgment. □

(p. 64)

Mary Ward, whose treatment is largely biographical, seems to invite this criticism. Sutton-Ramspeck, however, argues that Ward is right in focus-ing on women writers' 'special perceptions', especially of love: 'feminists have generally questioned the absolute separation of literature from author and reader', and share with Ward the sense that biography can tell us 'what it means to be a woman writer, a woman struggling against patri-archal barriers' (pp. 61, 63).

Leslie Stephen is another late-Victorian critic whose 'advice', Sutton-Ramspeck argues, Ward ignores. Stephen's criticism is based on the assumption that '"Though criticism cannot boast of being a science, it ought to aim at something like a scientific basis"'; the critic's task is thus '"to classify the phenomena with which he is dealing as calmly as if he were ticketing a fossil in a museum"' (Sutton-Ramspeck p. 64). In contrast, Sutton-Ramspeck argues, Mary Ward responded to works of literature

■ as living subjects to which other living subjects actively, emotionally responded. If 'intellectual muddle', so scorned by Henry James, means seeking connections between the woman writer, the woman character, and the woman reader, then Mary Ward was distinctly muddled, but hers is the kind of connection-forging that feminists have come to see as a welcome corrective to a masculinist 'autonomy' that is merely separa-tion and control . . .

Just as more recent feminists have learned that the personal is polit-ical – that truths of the individual experience reveal wider social truths about power and privilege – so Mary Ward insisted that, in literature, the personal is 'poetical'. □

(p. 72)

Sutton-Ramspeck's article gives a useful insight into the development of late-nineteenth-century criticism towards a 'science of the text', and shows how a critical movement regarded as 'radical' or 'avant-garde' for one section of the community may not be so for others – in this case women. I have to say, however, that I do not think that her argument holds good for Emily Brontë. Both she and Ward tend to speak of 'the Brontës' in general, and many of her examples of the personal basis of 'the Brontës" writing are actually drawn from Charlotte's work.

When Mary Ward speaks specifically of Emily, her analysis moves decidedly away from the personal; *Wuthering Heights* 'has much more than a mere local or personal significance. It belongs to a particular European moment' (*CH* p.455). It

■ is a book of the later Romantic movement, betraying . . . the Romantic tendency to invent and delight in monsters, the *exaltation du moi*, which has been said to be the secret of the whole Romantic revolt against classical models and restraints; the love of violence in speech and action, the preference for the hideous in character and the abnormal in situation – of all these there are abundant examples in *Wuthering Heights*. □

(*CH* pp.456–7)

This literary placing enables Mary Ward to arrive at an informed judgement which is aesthetic – even impersonal – in its basis:

■ the peculiar force of Emily's work lies in the fact that it represents the grafting of a European tradition upon a mind already richly stored with English and local reality, possessing at command a style at once strong and simple, capable both of homeliness and magnificence. □

(*CH* pp.457–8)

Giving *Wuthering Heights* an ancestry including 'Christopher North', James Hogg, De Quincey, Carlyle, Scott, Lockhart, Wordsworth, Southey, Coleridge, Goethe and Hoffmann, Ward shows a modern conceptualisation of the text as rooted in other texts, rather than 'the authority of experience'. Explicitly refusing the Victorian assumption that the text is a line of communication from author to reader – that 'it is only in the author that the key to such an extraordinary story can be found'[7] – Ward argues that in *Wuthering Heights*,

■ the artist remains hidden and self-contained; the work, however morbid and violent . . . has always that distinction which belongs to high talent working solely for its own joy and satisfaction, with no thought of a spectator, or any aim but that of an ideal and imaginative whole . . . She has that highest power – which was typically Shakespeare's power . . . – the power which gives life, intensest life, to the creatures of imagination, and, in doing so, endows them with an independence behind which the maker is forgotten . . . □

(*CH* p.456)

CHAPTER TWO

The Rise and Fall of the Author: Humanism, Formalism, Deconstruction

Humanism

I ENDED CHAPTER one with Mary Ward's statement in 1900 that in *Wuthering Heights* 'the artist remains hidden and self-contained' (*CH* p. 456), and this perception fittingly stands at the turn of the century which ushered in the Modernist movement. From our perspective at the end of that century, 'Modernism' is Janus-faced. Compared with the moral and realist preoccupations of the Victorians, Modernism is distinguished by its focus on art as opposed to the artist – its belief in *impersonality* as the test of artistic quality. Compared, on the other hand, with Postmodernism, and its ideas of the split subject, decentred text and infinite deferral of meaning, Modernism appears aligned with Humanism in its continuing belief in individual consciousness as the origin of meaning and value. The clue to this apparent paradox is that the Modernist artist is still seen as the *creator* (rather than the Postmodernist 'producer') of works of art, but that the concept of 'creation' is pushed to a level of intensity which transcends the merely personal to achieve a vision which appeals beyond the time and place of its production. 'Universality' and 'timelessness' become the highest terms of praise. Malcolm Bradbury writes that 'now human consciousness and especially *artistic* consciousness could become more intuitive, more poetic; art could now fulfil *itself*' (p. 25). In this new atmosphere, Emily Brontë, unlike most Victorian writers, offered herself as a kindred spirit. As Heather Glen puts it:

■ the intensely private, self-enclosed figure of Emily Brontë has come to stand for a peculiar creative individuality and independence . . . None of the explanatory schemata whereby her sisters may be seen as representative – as governesses, as women struggling for economic independence or for larger spheres of activity, as spinsters racked with the 'need of being loved' – seems quite appropriate to her. 'The sphynx of literature', a nineteenth-century reviewer called her. □

(p. 1)

During the early years of the twentieth century, Emily's reputation steadily overtook Charlotte's, whose work was seen to be tied by her very realism to the circumstances of its production. Even a critic like May Sinclair, whose motivation was ultimately feminist, uses the current terms of 'transcendent' humanism to praise Emily Brontë for representing not just the surface, but the underlying order of things, a focus which lifts her work from the local to the universal:

■ love of life and passionate adoration of the earth, adoration and passion fiercer than any pagan knew, burns in *Wuthering Heights* . . . we are plunged apparently into a world of most unspiritual lusts and cruelties; into the very darkness and thickness of elemental matter; a world that would be chaos, but for the iron Necessity that brings its own terrible order. □

(p. 210)

The absence of physical passion which for Peck in 1848 simply meant a lack of realism (*CH* pp. 239–40) is for Sinclair evidence of a more elevated state of mind:

■ never was a book written with a more sublime ignoring of the physical . . . the passion that consumes Catherine and Heathcliff, that burns their bodies and destroys them, is nine-tenths a passion of the soul. It taught them nothing of the sad secrets of the body. □

(pp. 214–15)

Virginia Woolf, in an essay written in 1916, takes a very similar stance and, like Swinburne and Mary Ward, the 'aestheticists' of the *fin de siècle*, she expresses the elevation of Emily's writing as a 'poetic' quality:

■ *Wuthering Heights* is a more difficult book to understand than *Jane Eyre*, because Emily was a greater poet than Charlotte. When Charlotte wrote she said with eloquence and splendour and passion 'I love', 'I hate', 'I suffer'. Her experience, though more intense, is on a level with our own. But there is no 'I' in *Wuthering Heights*. There are no governesses. There are no employers. There is love, but it is not the love of men and women. Emily was inspired by some more general conception. The impulse which urged her to create was not her own suffering or her own injuries. She looked out upon a world cleft into gigantic disorder and felt within her the power to unite it in a book. That gigantic ambition is to be felt throughout the novel – a struggle, half thwarted but of superb conviction, to say something through the mouths of her characters which is not merely 'I love' or 'I hate', but 'we, the whole human race' and 'you, the eternal powers . . . ' the sentence remains unfinished. It is not strange that it should be so; rather it is astonishing that she can make us feel what she had it in her to say at all. It surges up in the half-articulate words of Catherine Earnshaw . . . It breaks out again in the presence of the dead . . . It is this suggestion of power underlying the apparitions of human nature and lifting them up into the presence of greatness that gives the book its huge stature among other novels. ☐

By this appeal to the universal, Woolf is able to answer the Victorian objection to Emily's lack of realism by asserting the existence of a higher truth:

■ But it was not enough for Emily Brontë to write a few lyrics, to utter a cry, to express a creed . . . She must take upon herself a more laborious and a more ungrateful task. She must face the fact of other existences, grapple with the mechanism of external things, build up, in recognisable shape, farms and houses and report the speeches of men and women who existed independently of herself. And so we reach these summits of emotion not by rant or rhapsody but by hearing a girl sing old songs to herself . . . ; by watching the moor sheep crop the turf . . . We are given every opportunity of comparing *Wuthering Heights* with a real farm and Heathcliff with a real man. How, we are allowed to ask, can there be truth or insight or the finer shades of emotion in men and women who so little resemble what we have seen ourselves? But even as we ask it we see in Heathcliff the brother that a sister of genius might have seen; he is impossible we say, but nevertheless no boy in literature has a more vivid existence than his. So it is with the two Catherines; never could women feel as they do or act in their manner, we say. All the same, they are the most lovable women in English fiction. It is as if she could tear up all that we know human beings by, and fill these unrecognisable transparences with such a gust of life that they transcend reality. Hers, then, is the rarest of all powers. She could free life from its dependence on facts; with a few touches indicate the spirit of a face so that it needs no body; by speaking of the moor make the wind blow and the thunder roar. ☐

If, for the Victorians, it was obvious that *Wuthering Heights* was an immoral and uncivilised book, so, by the 1920s, it was just as obvious that it was a metaphysical work. It was Lord David Cecil, Professor of English

Literature at Oxford, who 'canonised'[1] *Wuthering Heights* by his famous chapter in *Early Victorian Novelists* (1934). Taking the same elegiac tone as Sinclair and Woolf, Cecil is more analytical about what Sinclair had described as 'the iron Necessity that brings its own terrible order', and suggests a structure of meaning for the novel which generations of readers have grasped with relief.

■ Like Blake, Emily Brontë is concerned solely with those primary aspects of life which are unaffected by time and place. Looking at the world, she asks herself not, how does it work? what are its variations? – but what does it mean? None of the other Victorian novelists are concerned with such a question. And the fact that she is so occupied makes Emily Brontë's view of life essentially different from theirs. For it means that she sees human beings, not as they do in relation to other human beings, or to human civilisations and societies and codes of conduct, but only in relation to the cosmic scheme of which they form a part. Mrs Brown appears not as to Jane Austen in relation to Mr Brown, or as to Scott in relation to her ancestors, or as to Trollope in relation to her place in the social structure, or as to Proust in relation to herself; but in relation to time and eternity, to death and fate and the nature of things. Nature plays a much larger part in Emily Brontë's books than it does in most novelists'. On the other hand those individual and social aspects of life which fill their canvasses do not appear on hers. Her great characters exist in virtue of the reality of their attitude to the universe; they loom before us in the simple epic outline which is all that we see of man when revealed against the huge landscape of the cosmic scheme. □

(pp. 150–1)

Cecil presents the poet-writer as inspired, adopting the metaphysics of the Romantic movement to express the Modernist approval of 'moments of vision', with its concomitant acceptance that obscurity is almost a guarantee of profundity:

■ She was – once more like Blake – a mystic. She had on certain occasions in her life known moments of vision – far and away the most profound of her experiences – in which her eyes seemed opened to behold a transcendental reality usually hidden from mortal sight. And it is in the light of these moments of vision that she envisages the world of mortal things; they endow it with a new significance; they are the foundation of the philosophy on which her picture of life rests. What precisely this philosophy was she never tells us in explicit terms. She was an artist, not a professor. Moreover, founded as it was on sporadic flashes of vision, she seems never to have made it wholly clear even to herself. And any attempt to state it explicitly reveals it as full of dark places and baffling inconsistencies of detail. However, its main features are clear enough. ☐

And here Cecil elaborates the 'storm and calm' structure which has become one of the most widely accepted of all readings of *Wuthering Heights*:

■ The first is that the whole created cosmos, animate and inanimate, mental and physical alike, is the expression of certain living spiritual principles – on the one hand what may be called the principle of storm – of the harsh, the ruthless, the wild, the dynamic; and on the other the principle of calm – of the gentle, the merciful, the passive and the tame.

Secondly, in spite of their apparent opposition these principles are not conflicting. Either – Emily Brontë does not make clear what she thinks – each is the expression of a different aspect of a single pervading spirit; or they are the component parts of a harmony. They may not seem so to us. The world of our experience is, on the face of it, full of discord. But that is only because in the cramped conditions of their earthly incarnation these principles are diverted from following the course that their nature dictates, and get in each other's way. They are changed from positive into negative forces; the calm becomes a source of weakness, not of harmony, in the natural scheme, the storm a source not of fruitful vigour, but of disturbance. But when they are free from fleshly bonds they flow unimpeded and unconflicting; and even in this world their discords are transitory. The single principle that ultimately directs them sooner or later imposes an equilibrium.

Such convictions inevitably set Emily Brontë's view of human life in a perspective fundamentally different from that presented to us by other English novelists. For they do away with those antitheses which are the basis of these novelists' conceptions. The antithesis between man and nature to begin with: Emily Brontë does not see animate man revealed against inanimate nature, as Mrs Gaskell does. She does not even see suffering, pitiful, individual man in conflict with unfeeling, impersonal, ruthless natural forces, like Hardy. Men and nature to her are equally living and in the same way. To her an angry man and an angry sky are not just metaphorically alike, they are actually alike in kind; different manifestations of a single spiritual reality. ☐

(pp. 151–3)

The 'storm and calm' thesis has implications for the novel's moral interpretation:

■ Again, and more important, Emily Brontë's vision of life does away with the ordinary antithesis between good and evil. To call some aspects of life good and some evil is to accept some experiences and to reject others. But it is an essential trait of Emily Brontë's attitude that it accepts all experience. Not that she is an optimist who believes that the pleasant parts of life are its only real aspects. The storm is as much part of her universe as the calm. Indeed, she is peculiarly aware of the storm: she makes out the harsh elements of life to be as harsh as they can be. Her characters set no bridle on their destructive passions; nor do they repent of their destructive deeds. But since these deeds and passions do not spring from essentially destructive impulses, but impulses only destructive because they are diverted from pursuing their natural course, they are not 'bad'. Further, their fierceness and ruth-lessness have, when confined to their true sphere, a necessary part to play in the cosmic scheme, and as such are to be accepted. Emily Brontë's outlook is not immoral, but it is pre-moral. It concerns itself not with moral standards, but with those conditioning forces of life on which the naive erections of the human mind that we call moral standards are built up. □

(pp. 154–5)

It also explains the 'supernatural' elements in the novel:

■ Finally, Emily Brontë does away with the most universally accepted of all antitheses – the antithesis between life and death. She believes in the immortality of the soul. If the individual life be the expression of a spiritual principle, it is clear that the mere dissolution of its fleshly integument will not destroy it. But she does more than believe in the immortality of the soul in the orthodox Christian sense. She believes in the immortality of the soul *in this world*. The spiritual principle of which the soul is a manifestation is active in this life; therefore, the disembod-ied soul continues to be active in this life. Its ruling preoccupations remain the same after death as before. Here she is different from other Victorian novelists: and, as far as I know, from any novelists of any time. Emily Brontë does not see human conflict as ending with death. Catherine Earnshaw dreams that she goes to heaven, but is miserable there because she is homesick for Wuthering Heights, the native country of her spirit. Nor is this a parable: it is a sort of prophecy. For when in fact she comes to die, her spirit does take up its abode at Wuthering Heights. And not just as an ineffective ghost: as much as in life she exerts an active influence over Heathcliff, besieges him with her passion.

Thus the supernatural plays a different part in *Wuthering Heights* from that which it does in other novels. Most novelists, intent on trying to give a picture of life as they know it, do not bring in the supernatural at all. Those who do, either use it as a symbol, not to be believed liter-ally, like Nathaniel Hawthorne – or like Scott, as an extraneous anomaly at variance with the laws of nature. With Emily Brontë it is an expression of those laws. It is, in truth, misleading to call it super-natural: it is a natural feature of the world as she sees it. □

(pp. 158–9)

Cecil goes on to show that the 'cosmic scheme' allows us to see order in the construction of *Wuthering Heights*, where previous critics had only seen confusion:

■ If *Wuthering Heights* gives a confused impression the confusion lies only in our own minds – and not Emily Brontë's. We are trying to see it in the wrong focus. When we shift our focus to reconsider *Wuthering Heights* in the light of her particular vision, its apparent confusion vanishes. From a murky tangle lit by inexplicable flashes, it falls into a coherent order.

The setting is a microcosm of the universal scheme as Emily Brontë conceived it. On the one hand, we have Wuthering Heights, the land of storm; high on the barren moorland, naked to the shock of the elements, the natural home of the Earnshaw family, fiery, untamed children of the storm. On the other, sheltered in the leafy valley below, stands Thrushcross Grange, the appropriate home of the children of calm, the gentle, passive, timid Lintons. Together each group, follow-ing its own nature in its own sphere, combines to compose a cosmic harmony. It is the destruction and re-establishment of this harmony which is the theme of the story. It opens with the arrival at Wuthering Heights of an extraneous element – Heathcliff. He, too, is a child of the storm; and the affinity between him and Catherine Earnshaw makes them fall in love with each other. But since he is an extraneous element, he is a source of discord, inevitably disrupting the working of the natural order. He drives the father, Earnshaw, into conflict with the son, Hindley, and as a result Hindley into conflict with himself, Heathcliff. The order is still further dislocated by Catherine, who is seduced into uniting herself in an 'unnatural' marriage with Linton, the child of calm. The shock of her infidelity and Hindley's ill-treatment of him now, in its turn, disturbs the natural harmony of Heathcliff's nature, and turns him from an alien element in the established order, into a force active for its destruction. He is not therefore, as usually supposed, a wicked man voluntarily yielding to his wicked impulses. Like all Emily Brontë's characters, he is a manifestation of natural forces acting involuntarily under the pressure of his own nature. But he is a natural force which has been frustrated of its natural outlet, so that it inevitably becomes destructive; like a mountain torrent diverted from its channel, which flows out on the surrounding country, laying waste whatever may happen to lie in its way. Nor can it stop doing so, until the obstacles which kept it from its natural channel are removed. □

(pp. 164–5)

Cecil now summarises the plot, showing how each feature fits this overall premise, until we arrive at Heathcliff's death.

■ His death removes the last impediment to re-establishment of harmony. Hareton and Catherine settle down happy and united at Thrushcross Grange. Wuthering Heights is left to its rightful possessors, the spirits of Heathcliff and the first Catherine. The wheel has come full circle; at length the alien element that has so long disturbed it has been assimilated to the body of nature; the cosmic order has been established once more. □

On the basis of this analysis Cecil feels confident to re-establish *Wuthering Heights* on the stage of world literature:

■ This analysis is enough to show how wide of the mark the usual criticisms of *Wuthering Heights* are. It is not incoherent. On the contrary, its general outline is as logical as that of a fugue. Nor is it an improbable story. On the plane on which it is composed its every incident is the inevitable outcome of the situation. Still less is it remote from the central issues of human life. It may seem so, because it presents the world from an angle in which the aspects which bulk biggest to most novelists are hidden from its view. But those aspects with which it is concerned are nearer to the heart of life than those explored by any other Victorian novelist. Even the varied world-panorama of *Vanity Fair* seems trivial beside this picture of a sparsely-populated country village, revealed, as it is, against the background of the eternal verities. For in it Emily Brontë has penetrated beneath those outward shows of experience which are the subject-matter of Thackeray and his contemporaries, to the ultimate issues which are generally looked on as the subject-matter of tragedy or epic. Like *Hamlet* and the *Divine Comedy*, *Wuthering Heights* is concerned with the primary problems of men and destiny. Like *Paradise Lost* it sets out 'to justify the ways of God to Man'. No novel in the world has a grander theme. □

(pp. 167–8)

In his final words, Cecil oddly echoes Mary Robinson's claim, in 1883, that only someone remote from the world could achieve 'that purity as of polished steel' (p. 164); the echo suggests again that there is an unbroken line from the 'aesthetic' appreciations of the *fin de siècle* to this transcendent humanism of the Modernist period:

■ ironically enough, her circumstances were the secret of her success. It was they that enabled her to maintain the consistent integrity of her imagination. Since she had no ready-made conventions to help her, since she always had to invent them for herself, her form is appropriate to her conception, as it could never have been if she had tried to mould her inspiration to fit the accepted Victorian formulas . . . the form she evolves in *Wuthering Heights* fits it perfectly. So perfectly, indeed, that if we knew nothing about it we should never guess it to be the unique work of a lonely genius, but the culminating achievement of a whole literary civilisation. Against the urbanised landscape of Victorian fiction it looms up august and alien, like the only surviving monument of a vanished race. □

(Cecil pp. 192–3)

Cecil's reading of the novel has become an orthodoxy surviving in classrooms to the present day. In the 1940s and 1950s we hear Cecil's rhapsodic tone from one critic after another, especially, it seems, from women. From Edith Sitwell:

■ The life of this woman of genius is like that of the wind and the rain, knowing no incidents and but few landmarks . . . She was not a creature of this warm human life, her home was not built with hands; □

Laura Hinkley:

■ in that deep, glowing forge of imagination she could fuse her own traits with others and shape them to other ends; □

(p. 205)

Phyllis Bentley:

■ we feel raised to the level of sombre grandeur and intensity which the book displays; we feel set free, it is true, in body, soul and spirit – but free not from ourselves, only to be more of whatever grandeur our selves have to offer. □

(p. 111)

Derek Traversi, in a famous centenary essay (1949), takes on both the tone of Cecil's chapter and his dualistic argument; reproduced in Boris Ford's immensely influential *Pelican Guide to English Literature* (1958), Traversi's essay became a 'standard' reading available to generations of students. Where other Victorian novels deal with character development and interaction, Traversi writes of the characters of *Wuthering Heights* that,

■ purged of all accidental qualities, indivisible in essence and too self-consistent to undergo change, their function is that of elements which can only, in their relations with the similar entities around them, destroy or suffer destruction. The result is a unique imaginative creation which, largely ignoring the moral and social assumptions of the contemporary novel, aspires rather to the severe simplicity of ancient tragedy. □

(p. 261)

Melvin R. Watson, in a remarkable centenary survey of 'Wuthering Heights and the Critics' (1948–9), singles out Cecil's essay as 'the most complete, thorough, and penetrating analysis and interpretation of Wuthering Heights to date' (p. 262). W. J. Harvey uses Wuthering Heights to demonstrate how the novel can confront huge issues such as reality, time, identity, freedom, essence and existence, while David Daiches, in his influential Introduction to the 1965 Penguin edition of Wuthering Heights, also takes up Cecil's argument that

■ The most powerful, the most irresistible, and the most tenacious of forces that reside in the depths of human nature have no relation with the artificial world of civilization and gentility, but they do have a relation to the elemental forces at work in the natural world. □

(V p. 109)

As late as 1980, Anne Leslie Harris's essay on 'Psychological Time in Wuthering Heights' comes essentially to the same conclusion as Cecil: 'the children's world of union and oneness . . . is regained beyond chronological time – in the midst of natural time, yet not subject to cyclical decay' (p. 117) – in other words, 'The wheel has come full circle; at length the alien element that has so long disturbed it has been assimilated to the body of nature; the cosmic order has been established once more' (Cecil p. 167).

Formalism

Cecil's notion of the transcendent genius, who is not locked into the circumstances of her own life but can 'see through' surfaces to underlying structures, shows us the 'humanist' face of the new emphasis on 'impersonality' in art. He continues the stance taken up in the 1880s by Algernon Swinburne (CH p. 439–40), who tried to distinguish Emily's intensity of genius by calling Wuthering Heights 'a poem'. Once Emily was seen primarily as a 'poet' rather than a social interpreter, critics began to look for evidence of virtue or quality in her text not in its supposed 'message' but in its form; the word 'poetic' suggests not only inspiration but highly crafted writing.

As early as 1850, Sydney Dobell had argued that 'the *thinking-out*' of Emily Brontë's scenes 'is the masterpiece of a poet, rather than the hybrid creation of the novelist' (CH p. 280), and for Abercrombie also (1924)

Wuthering Heights 'is throughout clearly the work of a poet' (A p. 106). By 1934 Cecil could conclude:

■ Style, structure, narrative, there is no aspect of Emily Brontë's craft which does not brilliantly exhibit her genius. The form of *Wuthering Heights* is as consummate as its subject is sublime. So far from being the incoherent outpourings of an undisciplined imagination, it is the one perfect work of art amid all the vast varied canvasses of Victorian fiction. □
(p. 192)

Somewhat inconsistently, however, Cecil's transcendent humanism required that the creative genius of the artist should not be *too* 'thought-out'. Just as, for Milton, Shakespeare seemed to 'warble his native wood-notes wild',[2] so for Cecil, Emily Brontë

■ speaks as the bird sings, instinctively, carelessly, ignorantly: and at times she is both clumsy and amateurish . . . her freshness combines with this very clumsiness to invest her work with an untutored enchanting grace . . . Emily Brontë achieves that rarest of literary triumphs: she writes an old language so that it seems like a new one. □
(pp. 190–1)

Cecil speaks of the rhythm of Emily Brontë's prose as 'unfailingly beautiful; a varied, natural, haunting cadence, now buoyantly lilting, now surging like the sea' (p. 191), and his language seems to link him to the aesthetic movement – with, for instance, Swinburne, who in 1883 saw in Emily's writing 'the roll of a gathered wave' (*CH* p. 443); but aestheticism itself was becoming more rigorous. Vernon Lee, the close friend (possibly lover) of Mary Robinson, Emily Brontë's first biographer, had in 1913 written an analysis of aestheticism in *The Beautiful*. In *The Handling of Words* (1922), however, she indicates how Cecil's 'humanist' Modernism could be tilted towards 'formalism' by focusing on the reader, 'without whose active response, whose output of experience, feeling and imagination, the living phenomenon, the only reality, of Literary Art cannot take place' (pp. vii–viii). In 1936 Irene Cooper Willis used Vernon Lee's methods of stylistic analysis in her reading of *Wuthering Heights*.[3]

It was not, however, Vernon Lee's statement of the case which was to have a decisive effect in shifting critical attitudes, but the institutionalised academics of North America, who developed the strategy of reading later known as the 'New Criticism'. I. A. Richards' *Principles of Literary Criticism* (1924) and *Practical Criticism* (1929) insisted that eulogy and 'appreciation' of literature should be replaced by close and analytic reading of 'the words on the page'. The focus was shifting, *via* the reader, from the artist to the work of art – to Cleanth Brooks's *Well-Wrought Urn* (1947) or W. K. Wimsatt's

Verbal Icon (1954). Formalism, especially in America, produced two main strands of enquiry: into the language, especially the imagery, of texts, and into their structure.

The American Mark Schorer was the first to investigate patterns of imagery in *Wuthering Heights*, in 1949. By citing R.P. Blackmur and Henry James's 'house of fiction', and advocating attention to detail, Schorer identifies himself as a crusading 'new critic', inheritor of James's anti-biographical, anti-sentimental stance.[4] Interestingly, where the Aestheticists had claimed 'poetic' status for *Wuthering Heights* to distinguish it from the social novel, the New Critic removes the distinction altogether:

■ If the novel, as R.P. Blackmur recently proposed, is now to enjoy the kind of attention from criticism that for the past twenty years has been the privilege of poetry, criticism must begin with the simplest assertion: fiction is a literary art. It must begin with the base of language, with the word, with figurative structures, with rhetoric as skeleton and style as body of meaning. A beginning as simple as this must overcome corrupted reading habits of long standing; for the novel, written in prose, bears an apparently closer resemblance to discursive forms than it does to poetry,[5] thus easily opening itself to first questions about philosophy or politics, and, traditionally a middle-class vehicle with a reflective social function, it bears an apparently more immediate relation to life than it does to art, thus easily opening itself to first questions about conduct. Yet a novel, like a poem, is not life, it is an image of life; and the critical problem is first of all to analyse the structure of the image. Thus criticism must approach the vast and endlessly ornamented house of fiction with a willingness to do a little at a time and none of it finally, in order to suggest experiences of meaning and of feeling that may be involved in novels, and responsibilities for their style which novelists themselves may forget. □

(p.539)

Schorer's chosen approach is through imagery:

■ To choose, more or less at random and without premeditated end, one novel by each of only three novelists, and to examine in each only one element in the language, the dominant metaphorical quality – this, positively, is to work piecemeal, and merely to suggest. I emphasize not *metaphor* but *quality*, intending not only the explicit but the buried and the dead metaphors, and some related traits of diction generally, that whole habit of value association suggested in Scott Buchanan's phrase, the 'matrix of analogy'. □

(pp.539–40)

Despite his modest disclaimers about the scope of his enquiry, Schorer begins his analysis of *Wuthering Heights* with some sweeping assumptions:

■ *Wuthering Heights*, as I understand it, means to be a work of edification: Emily Brontë begins by wishing to instruct her narrator, the dandy, Lockwood, in the nature of a grand passion; she ends by instructing herself in the vanity of human wishes . . . What her metaphors signify is the impermanence of self and the permanence of something larger. □

(p. 545)

In accordance with Wimsatt and Beardsley's 1946 essay, 'The Intentional Fallacy' (1946), Schorer demonstrates that attention to the metaphors of the novel can reveal meanings which were not consciously available to the author.[6] Schorer proceeds in a methodical way to list metaphors and incidental references which derive from definable 'matrices' or sources: 'To exalt the power of human feeling, Emily Brontë roots her analogies in the fierce life of animals and in the relentless life of the elements – fire, wind, water'. Quoting Emily Brontë's explanation of the word 'wuthering', and her description of the slanting fir trees, Schorer shows how this landscape is explicitly applied to character in the second half of the novel, when Heathcliff says, 'Now, my bonny lad, you are *mine*! And we'll see if one tree won't grow as crooked as another, with the same wind to twist it!' Schorer goes on, however, to argue that

■ this analogy provides at least half the metaphorical base of the novel.
Human conditions are like the activities of the landscape, where rains *flood*, blasts *wail*, and the snow and wind *whirl wildly* and *blow* out lights. A serving woman *heaves* 'like a sea after a high wind'; a preacher '*poured* forth his zeal in a *shower*'; Mrs Dean *rushes* to welcome Lockwood, 'exclaiming *tumultuously*'; spirits are 'at high-water mark'; Linton's soul is as different from Heathcliff's 'as a moonbeam from lightning, or frost from fire'; abuse is *lavished* in a *torrent*, or *pours forth* in a *deluge*; illnesses are '*weathered* . . . through'; 'sensations' are felt in a *gush*; 'your veins are *full* of *ice water*; but mine are *boiling*'; hair *flies*; bodies *toss* or *tremble* like reeds, tears *stream* or *rain down* among ashes; discord and distress arise in a *tumult*; Catherine Linton 'was *struck* during a *tempest* of passion with a kind of fit' and '*flew off* in the *height* of it'.
Faces, too, are like landscapes: 'a *cloud* of meditation' hangs over Nelly Dean's '*ruddy* countenance'; Catherine had 'a suddenly *clouded* brow; her humour was a mere *vane* for constantly varying caprices'; 'the surface of' the boy Heathcliff's 'face and hands was dismally *beclouded*' with dirt; later, his face '*brightened* for a moment; then it was *overcast* afresh'. 'His forehead . . . *shaded* over with a heavy *cloud*'; and 'the *clouded*

windows of hell', his eyes, 'flashed'. Hareton, likewise, grows 'black as a *thunder-cloud*'; or *darkens* with a frown. The older Catherine experienced whole *'seasons* of gloom', and the younger Catherine's 'heart was *clouded* . . . in double *darkness*'. Her 'face was just like the *landscape – shadows* and *sunshine* flitting over it in rapid succession; but the *shadows* rested longer, and the *sunshine* was more transient'. Sometimes 'her eyes are *radiant* with *cloudless* pleasure', and at the end, Hareton shakes off 'the *clouds* of ignorance and degradation', and his *'brightening* mind *brightened* his features'. □

(pp. 545–6)

In the same way, Schorer lists metaphors deriving from fire, from earth and from wild animals:

■ Most of the animals are wild. Hareton's 'whiskers encroached *bearishly* over his cheeks', and Heathcliff denies the paternity of 'that *bear*'. Hareton had been 'cast out like an unfledged *dunnock*', and Heathcliff is a 'fierce, pitiless, *wolfish* man'. He is also 'a *bird* of bad omen' and 'an evil *beast*', prowling between a 'stray *sheep*' 'and the fold, waiting his time to spring and destroy'. He has a *'ferocious* gaze' and a *savage* utterance; he *growls* and *howls* 'like a beast', and is many times named 'a brute', 'a beast', 'a brute beast'. He struggles like a *bear*, he has *sharp cannibal teeth* which *gleam* 'through the dark', and *'basilisk* eyes . . . *quenched* by sleeplessness'. He *gnashes* his teeth and *foams* like a *mad dog*. He is 'like a *bull*' to Linton's *'lamb*', and only at the very end, the exhausted end, 'he breathed as fast as a *cat*'. □

(p. 547)

For the *Christian Remembrancer* in 1857, the recognition that Emily Brontë's 'heroines *scratch*, and *tear*, and *bite*, and *slap* . . . The men . . . roll, and grapple, and struggle, and throttle, and clutch, and tear, and trample' (*CH* p. 368), was evidence of her moral degradation. For Schorer the point is to do with the necessities of language: Emily Brontë's characteristic verbs not only have a certain quality but also suggest a certain outcome. They

■ are verbs of violent movement and conflict, both contributing to a rhetorical texture where everything is at a pitch from which it can only subside. The verbs *demand* exhaustion, just as the metaphors *demand* rest. And there is an antithetical chorus in this rhetoric, a contrapuntal warning which, usually but not only in the voice of Nelly Dean, says 'Hush! Hush!' all through the novel . . . At the end, everything *is* hushed. And the moths *fluttering* over Heathcliff's grave and 'the soft wind *breathing* through the grass' that grows on it have at last more

power than he, for all his passion. These soft and fragile things paradoxically endure. ☐

(Schorer p. 548)

Even Heathcliff's passion wears itself out, and

■ the story of his life has been a moral teething for the author.
Lockwood is instructed in the nature of a grand passion, but he and
Emily Brontë together are instructed in its final fruits: even roaring
fires end in a bed of ashes. Her metaphors instruct her, and her
verbs. . . . At the end, the voice that drones on is the perdurable voice of
the country, Nelly Dean's. No more than Heathcliff did Emily Brontë
quite intend that homespun finality. Like the older Catherine, Emily
Brontë could have said of her book, 'I've dreamed in my life dreams
that have stayed with me ever after, and changed my ideas: they've
gone through and through me, like wine through water, and altered the
colour of my mind'. Her rhetoric altered the form of her intention. It is
her education; it shapes her insight. ☐

(pp. 549–50)

Schorer's conclusion thus endorses Cecil's reading, that the novel
comes to rest in a restitution of a natural order; but Schorer does not
imply, like Cecil, that this shaping is to be attributed to Emily's 'genius'.
Where Cecil writes that 'drenched in the magical rejuvenating elixir of
her temperament, the most faded clichés of letters gleam and shimmer
with all the palpitating life that animated them on the day of their
creation' (p. 191), Schorer is able to show that those 'faded clichés' carry
their own associational logic, which asserts itself irrespective of 'the
author's intention'.[7]

In 1952, only three years after Schorer's essay, another American
critic, Dorothy Van Ghent, published an even more influential essay
focused on two specific patterns of imagery in *Wuthering Heights*. This was
'The Window Figure and the Two Children Figure in *Wuthering Heights*'.
Like Cecil, Van Ghent sees the 'strangeness' of *Wuthering Heights* as lying
in 'the perfect simplicity with which it presents its elemental figures
almost naked of the web of civilized habits, ways of thinking, forms of
intercourse, that provides the familiar background of other fiction'
(p. 154). Also like Cecil, she sees a dualistic structure in the novel; but
whereas for Cecil the duality is within the 'elemental' schema and suscep-
tible to 'natural' resolution, for Van Ghent, it is the narrative frame
provided by Nelly and Lockwood which means that 'this nakedness is not
quite complete'. The friction between the elemental and social ways of
seeing life creates, she argues, an unavoidable difficulty in accepting any
single reading of the text, including Cecil's 'cosmic harmony' argument.

In the new spirit of technical enquiry, however, Van Ghent is prepared to
investigate phenomena in detail:

■ Let us try to diagram these technical aspects of the work, for the compositional soundness of *Wuthering Heights* is owing to them. We may
divide the action of the book into two parts, following each other
chronologically, the one associated with the earlier generation
(Hindley and Catherine and Heathcliff, Edgar and Isabella Linton), the
other with the later generation (young Cathy and Linton and Hareton).
The first of these actions is centered in what we shall call a 'mythological romance' – for the astonishingly ravenous and possessive,
perfectly amoral love of Catherine and Heathcliff belongs to that realm
of the imagination where myths are created. The second action,
centered in the protracted effects of Heathcliff's revenge, involves two
sets of young lives and two small 'romances': the childish romance of
Cathy and Linton, which Heathcliff manages to pervert utterly; and the
successful assertion of a healthy, culturally viable kind of love between
Cathy and Hareton, asserted as Heathcliff's cruel energies flag and
decay. Binding the two 'actions' is the perduring figure of Heathcliff
himself, demon-lover in the first, paternal ogre in the second. Binding
them also is the framing narrational convention or 'point of view': the
voices of Nelly Dean and Lockwood are always in our ears; one or the
other of them is always present at a scene, or is the confidant of someone who was present; through Lockwood we encounter Heathcliff at
the beginning of the book, and through his eyes we look on Heathcliff's
grave at the end. Still another pattern that binds the two actions is the
repetition of what we shall call the 'two children' figure – two children
raised virtually as brother and sister, in a vibrant relationship of charity
and passion and real or possible metamorphosis. The figure is
repeated, with variation, three times, in the relationships of the main
characters. Of this we shall speak again later. The technical continuities
or patterning of the book could, then, be simplified in this way [see
Diagram 1 overleaf]:

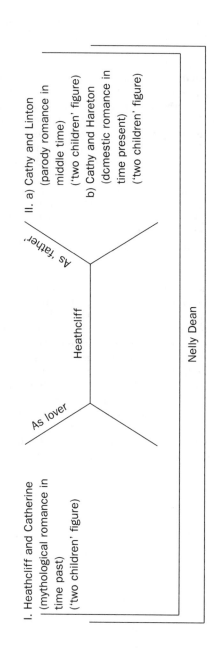

I. Heathcliff and Catherine
(mythological romance in time past)
('two children' figure)

As lover

Heathcliff

As 'father'

II. a) Cathy and Linton
(parody romance in middle time)
('two children' figure)
b) Cathy and Hareton
(domestic romance in time present)
('two children' figure)

Nelly Dean

Lockwood

Diagram 1

What, concretely, is the effect of this strict patterning and binding? What does it 'mean'? The design of the book is drawn in the spirit of intense compositional rigor, of *limitation*; the characters act in the spirit of passionate immoderacy, of *excess*. Let us consider this contrast a little more closely. Essentially, *Wuthering Heights* exists for the mind as a tension between two kinds of reality: the raw, inhuman reality of anonymous natural energies, and the restrictive reality of civilized habits, manners, and codes. The first kind of reality is given to the imagination in the violent figures of Catherine and Heathcliff, portions of the flux of nature, children of rock and heath and tempest, striving to identify themselves as human, but disrupting all around them with their monstrous appetite for an inhuman kind of intercourse, and finally disintegrated from within by the very energies out of which they are made. It is this vision of a reality radically alien from the human that the ancient Chinese landscape paintings offer also. But in those ancient paintings there is often a tiny human figure . . . very definite in the giant surrounding indefiniteness. The effect is one of contrast between finite and infinite, between the limitation of the known and human, and the unlimitedness of the unknown and the nonhuman. So also in *Wuthering Heights*: set over against the wilderness of inhuman reality is the quietly secular, voluntarily limited, safely human reality that we find in the gossipy concourse of Nelly Dean and Lockwood, the one an old family servant with a strong grip on the necessary emotional economies that make life endurable, the other a city visitor in the country, a man whose very disinterestedness and facility of feeling and attention indicate the manifold emotional economies by which city people particularly protect themselves from any disturbing note of the ironic discord between civilized life and the insentient wild flux of nature in which it is islanded. This second kind of reality is given also in the romance of Cathy and Hareton, where book learning and gentled manners and domestic charities form a little island of complacence. The tension between these two kinds of reality, their inveterate opposition and at the same time their *continuity* one with another, provides at once the content and the form of *Wuthering Heights*. We see the tension graphically in the diagram given above. The inhuman excess of Heathcliff's and Catherine's passion, an excess that is carried over into the second half of the book by Heathcliff's revenge, an excess everywhere present in language[8] – in verbs and modifiers and metaphors that seethe with a brute fury – this excess is held within a most rigorous pattern of repeated motifs and of what someone has called the 'Chinese box' of Nelly Dean's and Lockwood's interlocutions. The form of the book, then – a form that may be expressed as a tension between the impulse to excess and the impulse to limitation or economy – *is* the content. The form, in short, is the book itself. Only in the fully wrought, fully realized, work of art does form so exhaust the possibilities of the material that it identifies itself with these possibilities. □

(pp. 155–8)

Van Ghent, therefore, sees the patterns of imagery as part of the structure of the whole novel. She goes on to discuss the relationship between Catherine and Heathcliff and the fact that our first encounter with this relationship comes through Lockwood's dream, and particularly the window through which he drags the ghost-child's hand:

■ The window-pane is the medium, treacherously transparent, separating the 'inside' from the 'outside', the 'human' from the alien and terrible 'other'. Immediately after the incident of the dream, the time of the narrative is displaced into the childhood of Heathcliff and Catherine, and we see the two children looking through the window of the Lintons' drawing room . . . □

and she goes on to quote from Chapter 6 . . .

■ Here the two unregenerate waifs look *in* from the night on the heavenly vision of the refinements and securities of the most privileged human estate. But Heathcliff rejects the vision: seeing the Linton children blubbering and bored there (*they* cannot get *out*!), he senses the menace of its limitations; while Catherine is fatally tempted. She is taken in by the Lintons, and now it is Heathcliff alone outside looking through the window. □

(p. 161)

Captured, in fairy-tale manner, by the Linton world, Catherine yields to her destiny; later she resists it tormentedly and finds her way out of it by death. Literally she 'catches her death' by throwing open the window in Chapter 12.

■ On the night after her burial, unable to follow her (though he digs up her grave in order to lie beside her in the coffin from which the side panels have been removed), [Heathcliff] returns to the Heights *through the window* – for Hindley has barred the door – to wreak on the living the fury of his frustration. It is years later that Lockwood arrives at the Heights and spends his uncomfortable night there. Lockwood's outcry in his dream brings Heathcliff *to the window*, Heathcliff who has been caught ineluctably in the human to grapple with its interdictions long after Catherine has broken through them. The treachery of the window is that Catherine, lost now in the 'other', can look through the transparent membrane that separates her from humanity, can scratch on the pane, but cannot get 'in', while Heathcliff, though he forces the window open and howls into the night, cannot get 'out'. When he dies, Nelly Dean discovers the window swinging open, the window of that old-fashioned coffin-like bed where Lockwood had had the dream. Rain has been pouring in during the night, drenching the dead man. □

Nelly describes his death in Vol. 2, Chapter 20, and Van Ghent goes on:

■ Earlier, Heathcliff's eyes have been spoken of as 'the clouded windows of hell' from which a 'fiend' looks out. All the other uses of the 'window' that we have spoken of here are not figurative but perfectly naturalistic uses, though their symbolic value is inescapable. But the fact that Heathcliff's eyes refuse to close in death suggests the symbol in a metaphorical form (the 'fiend' has now got 'out', leaving the window open), elucidating with simplicity the meaning of the 'window' as a separation between the daemonic depths of the soul and the limited and limiting lucidities of consciousness, a separation between the soul's 'otherness' and its humanness. □

(pp. 161–3)

Van Ghent's argument has been incorporated into many subsequent readings, and image-hunting is now a standard method of reading texts.[9] It reaches an interesting extension in a recent video study-guide by 'Literary Images', which,

■ Filmed on location in the village of Haworth and on the Yorkshire moors, . . . looks closely at the major themes and images of the novel. We find, for instance, the elements of earth, air, fire and water, which have their origin in the landscape which Emily knew and loved.
    Here too are the 'barrier' images of windows, doors and gates . . . The landscape . . . is still there . . . and this video has captured it in all its detail – 'the elemental rocks beneath' . . . Cathy's rustling 'heaven', the moths on the heather and the harebells of the last paragraph. □

Thus, by way of the formalist attention to the words on the page, we are guided right back to the authorial source. Formalism has not, then, superseded humanism but is often overlaid upon it. 'The author' does not die easily.

My division of 'formalism' into studies of imagery and studies of structure is quite artificial: 'structure' figures largely in Van Ghent's essay, for instance. 'Structure' is a large word, however, and can be used to refer to a number of different features in a text. The aspect of *Wuthering Heights* which has generated the most persistent debate is what I shall call 'narrative structure'; namely, the allocation of parts of the story to different voices, which has the incidental effect of dislocating the time scheme.

Victorian reviewers, like the *Examiner* (1848), assumed that the author had a duty to make 'his' meaning clear, and complained that 'it is not easy to disentangle the incidents and set them forth in chronological order. The tale is confused' (*CH* p. 221). The Aestheticists were divided on this issue. Vernon Lee saw the fact that 'Emily Brontë gave the narrative to several different people' as 'a fault of construction' inherited from Brontë's literary models, such as Hoffmann. It is also, she says, a fault common 'with beginners' (p. 200). May Sinclair, despite her passionate defence of Emily Brontë, also thinks *Wuthering Heights* 'probably the worst-constructed tale that ever was written' (p. 231).[10] Swinburne (1883), however, argues that *Wuthering Heights* has been unfairly singled out: critics have been so vigorous in their objections, he says, that 'it might be supposed that the rules of narrative observed by all great novelists were of an almost legal or logical strictness and exactitude' (*CH* p. 442). Other critics were more positive in their defence. T. W. Reid (1877) praises 'the workmanship' of *Wuthering Heights*, noting that 'every date fits into its place, and so does every incident' (*CH* p. 402). Ironically, however, it was a lawyer, C. P. Sanger, who came forward in 1926 to argue that 'the structure of *Wuthering Heights*' did indeed conform to 'an almost legal or logical strictness and exactitude with regard to probability of detail' (Swinburne, *CH* p. 442). The questions Sanger sets out to answer are:

■ How is the tale to be kept together? How are we to be made to feel the lapse of time without being pestered by dates? How far did the authoress accurately visualise the ages of the characters in the different incidents, the topography, and so on? And how did Heathcliff succeed in getting the property? □

In the course of answering these questions, Sanger incidentally makes visible some now well-known features of the novel's structure:

■ The most obvious thing about the structure of the story which deals with three generations is the symmetry of the pedigree. Mr and Mrs Earnshaw at Wuthering Heights and Mr and Mrs Linton at Thrushcross Grange each have one son and one daughter. Mr Linton's son marries Mr Earnshaw's daughter, and their only child Catherine marries successively her two cousins – Mr Linton's grandson and Mr Earnshaw's grandson. See the following pedigree [Diagram 2]:

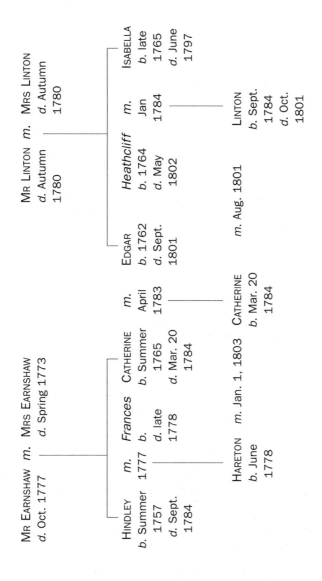

Diagram 2

In actual life I have never come across a pedigree of such absolute symmetry . . . It is a remarkable piece of symmetry in a tempestuous book. ☐

(pp. 8–9)

Like so many things that seem obvious once pointed out, this structure is now a commonplace of criticism, and Lord David Cecil, for instance, refers to Sanger as one source of his structural argument based on 'two houses' (p. 163).

Sanger now subjects the novel to forensic examination, painstakingly reconstructing a linear chronology from passing details about seasons, birthdays and so on; a topography from passing references to distances and directions; and, most surprising of all, unearthing an accurate knowledge of property law underlying Heathcliff's revenge. He concludes:

■ There is, so far as I know, no other novel in the world which it is possible to subject to an analysis of the kind I have tried to make. This in itself makes the book very unusual. ☐

(p. 19)

For Sanger, the whole intricate structure 'demonstrates the vividness of the author's imagination' (p. 20). Emily Brontë is thus triumphantly vindicated. In 1930 H.W. Garrod could still complain that *Wuthering Heights* showed 'an insufficient acquaintance with the craft of fiction' (A p. 118), but on the whole Sanger's book stands as a watershed between critics who could condescend to Emily Brontë and those who had to take her construction seriously.[11] Ironically, Edward Chitham's 1998 book, *The Birth of Wuthering Heights*, with its detailed analysis of the phases of the novel's construction, shows that Emily probably began the novel without a plan, and that the time-scheme was probably a late addition (pp. 158–62).

Knowing that a structure underlies apparent confusion does not, moreover, remove the impression. If, as E.M. Forster asks in 1927, 'she had a clear idea . . . Then why did she deliberately introduce muddle, chaos, tempest?' His own answer is interesting: 'Because . . . she was a prophetess: because what is implied is more important to her than what is said'. In 1930, the same year as Garrod's adverse judgement, William Empson published *Seven Types of Ambiguity*, arguing that the 'machinations of ambiguity' is 'among the very roots of poetry'.[12] The idea that ambiguity is a positive rather than a negative quality in writing has been immensely fruitful in all kinds of literary criticism, including the discussion of narrative structure.

As usual, the new theories merely codified ideas which had already been expressed in other words: the poet Alice Meynell comments in 1911 on the elusive quality of a text which cannot be traced back to the author

(A p. 105). By 1946, however, G. D. Klingopulos is much more confident in writing that 'Emily Brontë could not have written as an omniscient author without being compelled to adopt an omniscient attitude . . . to explain what she could not explain' (p. 286), and Rebecca West, in 1954, claims that in the device of the two narrators, 'Emily Brontë was showing dazzling technical competence. She was, indeed, solving a most difficult problem of the novelist's art'. By 1957, Carl R. Woodring voices the new orthodoxy that the narrative voices are part of a deliberate structure of oppositions (pp. 297–8), and in 1962 Bertil Romberg cites *Wuthering Heights* as his example of the 'virtuoso effects' which can be produced by 'first-person narrators in Chinese boxes' (compartments enclosed by other compartments – Lockwood's narrative containing Nelly's, which includes Heathcliff's, and so on) (pp. 65–6).

In 1998, Edward Chitham argues persuasively that Nelly may have been a late addition to Emily's narrative plan (Ch. 13). During the 1950s, however, a running debate developed in *Nineteenth-Century Fiction* on the exact role of the narrators. John K. Mathison (1956) argues that 'Nelly is an admirable woman whose point of view, I believe, the reader must reject', so that the reader is 'forced into an active participation in the book' (p. 106). Carl Woodring (1957) appears to shift the ground only slightly by seeing Nelly and Lockwood as not only narrators but actors in the plot (pp. 301, 304). This shift, however, moves the focus from the aesthetic question of structure to the moral question of responsibility, and James Hafley makes a spectacular contribution to this debate in 1958 by arguing that Nelly Dean is 'The Villain in *Wuthering Heights*'. According to Hafley, Nelly is both ambitious and resentful of her lack of status in the family, and uses her privileged access to people's emotional weaknesses to manipulate events so that she is left effective mistress of Thrushcross Grange. Hafley's essay has seemed to some critics to epitomise what Margaret Lane (1968) called the '"How-Absurd-Can-You-Get" School' of criticism (p. 190), and it is singled out by Q. D. Leavis (1969) as an example of 'sustained sophistry', the product 'of an age which conceives literary criticism as either a game or an industry, not as a humane study' (pp. 229, 263).

In 1965, John Fraser wrote a more reasoned answer to Hafley, arguing that it is too easy to attack people in difficult moral circumstances. Fraser's conclusion combines a Victorian-sounding commitment to moral responsibility with a Modernist recognition of the ambiguity of evidence: 'the world that Emily Brontë presents in the novel is one in which . . . there are no unquestionable social and moral norms', in which

■ people exist for one another in terms of momentary encounters, unsatisfactory signals, fragmentary reports and recollections, and loose working hypotheses whose insufficiency may at any moment be exposed by the staggering gesture or the sudden autobiographical revelation of passions and perplexities that one had barely guessed at and even now cannot adequately comprehend. □

(p. 235)

John Hagan's 1967 essay, 'Control of Sympathy in *Wuthering Heights*', opens the issues out further, engaging not only with Cecil but with Arnold Kettle, whose essay will be discussed in chapter five. For Hagan, the problem with *Wuthering Heights* is that it requires us both to sympathise with and to condemn its protagonists even though 'Catherine after Heathcliff's return', for instance, is 'a histrionic, vindictive harridan – an ego-maniac and a paranoic on the verge of insanity' (pp. 307, 309). Hagan insists, however, that, as in Euripedes, this 'cruelty is not innate' but 'is the consequence of their extreme suffering' (p. 310). Hagan argues that sympathy is maintained by the *timing* of various scenes – for instance, Catherine's poignant 'feather' scene which follows her outrageous statement of intention to 'break their hearts' (p. 320).

In Hagan's essay we can see a reaction against both the 'transcendent' humanism of Cecil and those aspects of formalism which D. Crompton in 1960 called 'playing hunt-the-slipper with theme and symbol' (p. 360). Hagan's suggestion turns to manifesto, however, in Q. D. Leavis's 1969 essay, 'A Fresh Approach to *Wuthering Heights*'. Together with her husband, F. R. Leavis, Q. D. Leavis had been associated with the English journal *Scrutiny*, which set up a moral school of criticism in opposition to the prevailing (American) formalism. Leavis complains that the project of formalism is, precisely, to worship the 'verbal icon', to find ever new ways in which the work is perfect, rather than confronting its actual qualities. Leavis thus sets herself to examine the structure of *Wuthering Heights* because this seems to her its *weakest* point.

■ The difficulty of establishing that a literary work is a classic is nothing compared to the difficulty of establishing *what kind* of a classic it is – what is in fact the nature of its success, what kind of creation it represents. One has only to read the admiring critics of *Wuthering Heights*, even more the others, to see that there is no agreed reading of this novel at all. Desperate attempts to report a flawless work of art lead to a dishonest ignoring of recalcitrant elements or an interpretation of them which is sophistical. □

Leavis's pragmatic approach to the construction of the novel demands the reappearance of the intentional author; a real writer who constructed the novel through time, working with pre-existing materials, rather like Vernon Lee's adolescent writer. Edward Chitham reconstructs just such a working writer from a variety of sources in *The Birth of Wuthering Heights* (1998). In 1969, however, Leavis focuses on the words on the page.

■ Of course, in general one attempts to achieve a reading of a text which includes all its elements, but here I believe we must be satisfied with being able to account for some of them and concentrate on what remains. It is better to admit that some of the difficulties of grasping what is truly creative in *Wuthering Heights* are due to the other parts – to the author in her inexperience having made false starts, changing her mind (as tone and style suggest) probably because of rewriting from earlier stories with themes she had lost interest in and which have become submerged, though not assimilated, in the final work. Another source of confusion to the reader is that she tried to do too much, too many different things (a common trouble in first novels and in most Victorian novels) and that some of these interfere with her deeper intentions – though of course this is also one source of the richness of this novel and we wouldn't care to sacrifice many of these, I think. The novel has all the signs of having been written at different times (because in different styles) and with varying intentions; we must sort these out in order to decide what *is* the novel. In spite of the brilliantly successful time-shifts and what has been called, not very happily, the 'Chinese box' ingenuity of construction, it certainly isn't a seamless 'work of art', and candour obliges us to admit ultimately that some things in the novel are incompatible with the rest, so much so that one seems at times to find oneself in really different novels. □

(pp. 229–30)

Edward Chitham's 1998 reconstruction of the phases of the novel's composition shows that, although Emily Brontë's 'first thoughts' may not have been quite as Leavis supposed, the process was more as she describes than the instant perfection implied by the formalists. Leavis proceeds to 'clear out of the way the *confusions* of the plot' which she attributes to several 'false start[s]' – for instance, that 'clearly, Heathcliff was originally the illegitimate son and Catherine's half-brother, which would explain why, though so attached to him . . . Catherine never really thinks of him as a possible lover' (p. 231). Leavis also finds traces of a fairy-tale plot (father brings home gifts) and a 'social' plot:

■ There are various signs that the novelist intended to stress the aspect of her theme represented by the corruption of the child's native goodness by Society . . . But this originally naive and commonplace subject – the Romantics' image of childhood in conflict with society – becomes something that in this novel is neither superficial nor theoretic because the interests of the responsible novelist gave it . . . a new insight, and also a specific and informed sociological content. The theme is here very firmly rooted in time and place and richly documented: we cannot forget that Gimmerton and the neighbourhood are so bleak that the oats are always green there three weeks later than anywhere else, and that old Joseph's Puritan preachings accompany his 'overlaying his large Bible with dirty bank-notes, the produce of the day's transactions' at market; and we have a thoroughly realistic account of the life indoors and outdoors at Wuthering Heights as well as at the gentleman's residence at the Grange. In fact, there would be some excuse for taking this, the pervasive and carefully maintained sociological theme which fleshes the skeleton, for the real novel. This novel, which could be extracted by cutting away the rest, was deliberately built, to advance a thesis, on the opposition between Wuthering Heights and Thrushcross Grange, two different cultures of which the latter inevitably supersedes the former. The point about dating this novel as ending in 1801 (instead of its being contemporary with the Brontës' own lives) – and much trouble was taken to keep the dates, time-scheme and externals such as legal data, accurate[13] – is to fix its happenings at a time when the old rough farming culture based on a naturally patriarchal family life, was to be challenged, tamed and routed by social and cultural changes that were to produce the Victorian class consciousness and 'unnatural' ideal of gentility. □

(pp. 237–8)

■ But if we were to take the sociological novel as the real novel and relegate the Heathcliff-Catherine-Edgar relationship and the corresponding Cathy-Linton-Hareton one, as exciting but ex-centric dramatic episodes, we should be misconceiving the novel and slighting it, for it is surely these relationships and their working out that give all the meaning to the rest. For instance, though Cathy has in the second half to unlearn, very painfully, the assumptions of superiority on which she has been brought up at the Grange, this is only part of her schooling; it is only incidental to the process by which we see her transcend the psychological temptations and the impulses which would have made her repeat her mother's history; and this is not a question of sociology or social history but is timeless. □

(p. 239)

From our perspective it is difficult to recall the novelty of what Leavis next says; we need to remember that for Allott and many previous critics, 'Heathcliff *is* the story',[14] while for Leavis:

■ the focus of the first half of the novel is most certainly Catherine, and it is her case that is the real moral centre of the book. This case is examined with wonderful subtlety and conveyed in a succession of brilliantly managed dramatic scenes with complete impersonality. □

(p. 240)

Like Hagan (pp. 313–14), Leavis complains that this focus on human experience has been obscured by previous critics:

■ It is very unfortunate that the brief, and on the whole misleading, 'metaphysical' parts of *Wuthering Heights* should have been not only overrated but universally seized on as a short cut to the meaning, the significance of the novel. □

(p. 242)

The following pages examine Catherine's story in some detail, including an extended comparison with Henri-Pierre Roché's novel, *Jules et Jim* (1953), which also shows a woman with two lovers.

■ The plight of Catherine Earnshaw is thus presented as at once a unique personal history, a method of discussing what being a woman means, and a tragedy of being caught between socially incompatible cultures, for each of which there is much to be said for and against . . . That Emily Brontë intended to create a coherent, deeply responsible novel whose wisdom should be recognized as useful we can have no doubt. □

(pp. 260–1)

We might notice here that, by judicious excision, Leavis has recreated not only the novel but the novelist in her own image, a 'deeply responsible' novelist committed to moral usefulness. Leavis's position represents a resurgence of humanism in a formalist age:

■ I would make a plea, then, for criticism of *Wuthering Heights* to turn its attention to the human core of the novel, to recognize its truly human centrality. How can we fail to see that the novel is based on an interest in, concern for, and knowledge of, real life? We cannot do it justice, establish what the experience of reading it really is, by making analyses of its lock and window imagery, or by explaining it as being concerned with children of calm and children of storm, or by putting forward such bright ideas as that '*Wuthering Heights* might be viewed at long range as a variant of the demon-lover motif' (*The Gates of Horn*, H. Levin) or that 'Nelly Dean is Evil'[15] – these are the products of an age which conceives literary criticism as either a game or an industry, not as a humane study. To learn anything of this novel's true nature we must put it into the category of novels it belongs to – I have specified *Women in Love* and *Jules et Jim* and might add *Anna Karenina* and *Great Expectations* – and recognize its relation to the social and literary history of its own time. The human truths *Wuthering Heights* is intended to establish are, it is necessary to admit, obscured in places and to varying degrees by discordant trimmings or leftovers from earlier writings or stages of its conception; for these, stylistic and other evidence exists in the text. Nor could we expect such complexity and such technical skill to have been achieved in a first novel otherwise; it is necessary to distinguish what is genuine complexity from what is merely confusion. That there is the complexity of accomplished art we must feel in the ending, ambiguous, impersonal, disquieting but final. □

(pp. 263–4)

Lord David Cecil and Q. D. Leavis are still among the most popular critics of *Wuthering Heights*, and the reason must be that their readings appeal to our need to 'make sense' of what we read by arriving at a single, inclusive meaning. Where Cecil offers us a message of philosophical unity, Leavis offers us a moral coherence; but each does this by emphasising some aspects of the text at the expense of others.

Formalist critics who regard themselves as committed to the words on the page are not, however, prepared to jettison parts of the text and are thus obliged to make a virtue of its ambiguity. The difference between Cecil and these later critics can be seen particularly in their analysis of the novel's closure. For Cecil, the end of the novel restores a cosmic peace in which the opposing forces of storm and calm are reconciled in 'a single pervading spirit' (p.152); for later critics, from Dorothy Van Ghent onwards, ambiguity remains the 'message' of the novel. Albert J. Guerard, for instance, in his 1960 'Preface' to *Wuthering Heights*, does not believe, like Cecil, that the end of *Wuthering Heights* gives us reconciliation, but he accounts for the popularity of Cecil's reading by pointing out that the dream of reconciliation remains active in the text. Where Cecil believes in the truth of cosmic harmony, Guerard sees the 'dream' of unity as a 'fantasy' (V pp. 68, 67). For such critics, the author's 'perfection' lies in her ability to represent the dream and the dilemma we all share.

This is clearly a larger question than one of literary criticism, and one of the best statements of its philosophical context is that by the Harvard critic J. Hillis Miller in *The Disappearance of God* (1963). Miller places *Wuthering Heights* in the 'ambient present' represented by the Romantic movement (p. vii). One aspect of this change was the growth of a historical sense, and with it a sense 'of the arbitrariness of any belief' (p. 10): 'culture in all its forms is the insubstantial foam upon a great sea of shapeless matter' (p. 11). (Here it is inevitable for the Brontë scholar to recall Emily Brontë's poem:

■ Vain are the thousand creeds
   That move men's hearts, unutterably vain,
   Worthless as withered weeds
   Or idlest froth amid the boundless main . . . [16]) □

Miller goes on: 'The change from traditional literature to a modern genre like the novel can be defined as a moving of once objective worlds of myth and romance into the subjective consciousness of man' (p. 12) (and so Emily Brontë's poem substitutes for the old creeds a paean to the individual life:

- O God within my breast
  Almighty ever-present Deity
  Life, that in me hast rest
  As I Undying Life, have power in Thee.). □

The huge emphasis placed on 'the author' by critics such as Cecil was not, therefore, 'natural' or inevitable but was a historical phenomenon deriving from the Romantic movement:

- The romantics still believe in God, and they find his absence intolerable . . . All the traditional means of mediation have broken down, and romanticism therefore defines the artist as the creator or discoverer of hitherto unapprehended symbols, symbols which establish a new relation, across the gap, between man and God. The artist is the man who goes out into the empty space between man and God and takes the enormous risk of attempting to create in that vacancy a new fabric of connections between man and the divine power. □

(pp. 13–14)

(So Emily Brontë represents herself as this glorious venturer:

- No coward soul is mine
  No trembler in the world's storm-troubled sphere
  I see Heaven's glories shine
  And Faith shines equal arming me from Fear.) □

The Victorians, 'though their situations are more desperate, . . . attempt, like the romantics, to bring God back to earth as a benign power inherent in the self, in nature, and in the human community' (p. 15).

Miller argues that 'the violence of Emily Brontë's characters is a reaction to the loss of an earlier state of happiness' (p. 170). 'All suffering', he goes on, 'derives ultimately from isolation. A person is most himself when he participates most completely in the life of something outside himself. This self outside the self is the substance of a man's being'. Emily Brontë's poems and *Wuthering Heights* 'suggest three possible entities with which the self may be fused: nature, God, and another human being' (p. 172); Catherine's relation with Heathcliff is described in Ch. 9 in the same terms as the soul's to God in 'No Coward Soul' (pp. 172–3).[17]

'I *am* Heathcliff' sounds positive, but, Miller argues, demonstrates what he calls

■ Emily Brontë's dialectic of love: when you have it you cannot know that you have it, and to know it is to destroy it. It can only be known retrospectively, by exiles who look back in longing at the lost kingdom of joy. Cathy's explicit analysis of her relation to Heathcliff comes only after she has separated herself from him, and is about to marry Edgar Linton. □

(p. 176)

Miller's account of the novel's ending curiously recalls Cecil's images: 'the tremendous storm raised by the separation of the two lovers . . . has been appeased at last and calm has returned' (p. 205). The difference between Cecil and Miller, however, is that Miller does not merely endorse the wish for unity but is able to place it historically as a post-Romantic cultural phenomenon:

■ God has been transformed from the transcendent deity of extreme Protestantism . . . to an immanent God, pervading everything, like the soft wind blowing over the heath. This new God is an amiable power who can, through human love, be possessed here and now. The break-through into God's world of Heathcliff and Cathy has not only made possible the peaceful love of Hareton and the second Cathy; it has also made institutionalized religion unnecessary. The love of Heathcliff and Cathy has served as a new mediator between heaven and earth, and has made any other mediator for the time being superfluous. □

(p. 211)

One aspect of a historicised reading was to locate in time not only the novel but the process of reading it. Critics of the 1970s became self-conscious about the relativity of their own positions. Mark Kinkead-Weekes (1970) argues that 'We must not attempt to "unify" the conflicting visions by trying to make one prevail; but try instead to encompass the whole landscape' (p. 94), just as the author 'does not resolve, she encompasses, ensuring vision through both eyes' (p. 95). David Sonstroem (1971), however, opposes the idea that the artist has an encompassing 'vision'. He argues that the 'Limits of Vision' in *Wuthering Heights* are what the novel is 'about':

■ Emily Brontë does not pretend to an overarching vision, and that is her point. The stumbling shortsightedness that she depicts in her characters and induces in her reader is in fact her own experience of the world and the burden of her message. She does not expect the reader to embrace any world view, not even the attractively Romantic, elemental, animistic one implicit in the relationship between Heathcliff and Catherine. She expects the reader rather to experience with them the sense of it looming intangibly and uncertainly just beyond their ken, even as it is naggingly gainsaid, crossed by ineradicably foregrounded considerations. In a word, she presents wuthering as basic to almost all human experiences. □

(pp. 60–1)

Sonstroem's position was not, however, readily adopted. Behind titles like John Hagan's 'The Control of Sympathy' (1967) and Gideon Shunami's 'The Unreliable Narrator' (1973) lies Wayne C. Booth's influential book, *The Rhetoric of Fiction* (1961). Although Booth's approach is formalist, he still sees the devices of literary technique as 'the author's means of controlling his reader' (Preface). The British critic Keith Sagar (1976) feels that the reader's task is to respond to this control by reuniting the disparate meanings of the text:

■ If we can keep them all in mind simultaneously, noting how the novel throws one or another into prominence or twists them together, we shall see how marvellously coherent it is, like printing when all the colours are overlaid in perfect register. □

(p. 137)

Sagar is not dismayed by Miller's argument; if Miller's reading exposes 'cosmic' harmony as a metaphysical illusion, he argues, this throws even more weight on the author, like Emily Brontë, who can hold ideas together: 'Her stage spans, like a cosmic rack, the space between the necessary and the possible' (p. 159).

In the 1970s the formalist commitment to ambiguity thus pushes critics in two directions. On the one hand there is a proliferation of readings, all more or less based on 'the words on the page', which suggest that there is no definitive meaning for the text. On the other hand there is the notion of the author who 'contains' the work of art. Although Mark Schorer, writing in 1949, recognised that language had a logic of its own which controlled the author rather than being controlled by her, this insight became lost in the prevailing deference to the author's mastery.

The critic who wrote most lucidly about this point of critical time is Frank Kermode. Kermode's 1975 chapter on *Wuthering Heights* was originally written in response to T. S. Eliot's paper, 'What is a Classic?', delivered to the Virgil Society in 1944, and is thus located within the tradition of the Greek and Latin classics taught in the old British universities. On the other hand, he is alert to 'the new French criticism' – to Claude Lévi-Strauss, Roland Barthes and other 'structuralists' (p. 130).

'Structuralism' is a term derived ultimately from the linguistic theories of Ferdinand de Saussure early in the twentieth century. De Saussure argued that meanings are not to be found 'in' units of language (such as words), but in the distinctions between them. Within any given language system, we are used to distinguishing between the arbitrary meanings assigned, say, to 'dog' as opposed to 'god', or 'bog', 'dig' or 'dug'. Meaning is thus dependent on differentiation or opposition, and this idea was extended by the structuralist anthropologist Claude Lévi-Strauss, who noticed that almost every aspect of social existence is 'coded' by distinctions which have social significance. Thus all societies distinguish between male and female, old and young, locals and foreigners, those available and non-available for marriage, and so on. On a mythological plane, significant meanings derive from oppositions between winter and summer, day and night, famine and plenty. Cecil's 'storm and calm' is quite in line with this general system of binary oppositions from which all our meanings derive, and so are Van Ghent's oppositions of 'inside' and 'outside'. The difference between these critics, who work with what are sometimes called 'archetypes', and the structuralists who also work with binary oppositions, is that the structuralists see these systems of meaning as to a large extent controlling rather than being controlled by the 'imagination' of a gifted writer.

Anthropological structuralism is particularly concerned with kinship patterns, and Kermode also begins his study of *Wuthering Heights* with an analysis of its proper names and patterns of family alliance, beginning from the names which Lockwood reads scratched on the window-sill.

■ Charlotte Brontë remarks, from her own experience, that the writer says more than he knows, and was emphatic that this was so with Emily. 'Having formed these beings, she did not know what she had done'. Of course this strikes us as no more than common sense; though Charlotte chooses to attribute it to Emily's ignorance of the world. A narrative is not a transcription of something pre-existent. And this is precisely the situation represented by Lockwood's play with the names he does not understand, his constituting, out of many scribbles, a rebus for the plot of the novel he's in.[18] The situation indicates the kind of work we must do when a narrative opens itself to us, and contains information in excess of what generic probability requires.

Consider the names again; of course they reflect the isolation of the society under consideration, but still it is remarkable that in a story whose principal characters all marry there are effectively only three surnames, all of which Catherine assumes. Furthermore, the Earnshaw family makes do with only three Christian names, Catherine, Hindley, Hareton. Heathcliff is a family name also, but parsimoniously, serving as both Christian name and surname; always lacking one or the other, he wears his name as an indication of his difference, and this persists after death since his tombstone is inscribed with the one word *Heathcliff*. Like Frances, briefly the wife of Hindley, he is simply a sort of interruption in the Earnshaw system.

Heathcliff is then as it were between names, as between families (he is the door through which Earnshaw passes into Linton, and out again to Earnshaw). He is often introduced, as if characteristically, standing outside, or entering, or leaving, a door. He is in and out of the Earnshaw family simultaneously; servant and child of the family (like Hareton, whom he puts in the same position, he helps to indicate the archaic nature of the house's society, the lack of sharp social division, which is not characteristic of the Grange). His origins are equally betwixt and between: the gutter or the royal origin imagined for him by Nelly; prince and pauper, American or Lascar, child of God or devil. This betweenness persists, I think: Heathcliff, for instance, fluctuates between poverty and riches; also between virility and impotence. To Catherine he is between brother and lover; he slept with her as a child, and again in death, but not between latency and extinction. He has much force, yet fathers an exceptionally puny child. Domestic yet savage like the dogs, bleak yet full of fire like the house, he bestrides the great opposites: love and death (the necrophiliac confession), culture and nature ('half-civilized ferocity') in a posture that certainly cannot be explained by any generic formula ('Byronic' or 'Gothic').

He stands also between a past and a future; when his force expires the old Earnshaw family moves into the future associated with the civilized Grange, where the insane authoritarianism of the Heights is a thing of the past, where there are cultivated distinctions between gentle and simple – a new world in the more civil south. It was the Grange that first separated Heathcliff from Catherine, so that Earnshaws might eventually live there. Of the children – Hareton, Cathy, and Linton – none physically resembles Heathcliff; the first two have Catherine's eyes (XXXIII) and the other is, as his first name implies, a Linton. Cathy's two cousin-marriages, constituting an endogamous route to the civilized exogamy of the south[19] – are the consequence of Heathcliff's standing between Earnshaw and Linton, north and south; earlier he had involuntarily saved the life of the baby Hareton. His ghost and Catherine's, at the end, are of interest only to the superstitious, the indigenous now to be dispossessed by a more rational culture.

If we look, once more, at Lockwood's inscriptions, we may read them thus [see Diagram 3 overleaf]:

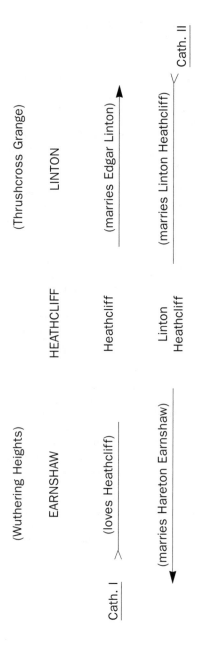

Diagram 3

N.B. Heathcliff stands between Earnshaw and Linton as having Earnshaw origins but marrying Isabella Linton. He could also be represented as moving from left to right and right to left – into the Linton column, and then back to the Earnshaw when he usurps the hereditary position of Hareton. Hareton himself might be represented as having first been forced out of the Earnshaw column into the intermediate position when Heathcliff reduces him to a position resembling the one he himself started from, a savage and inferior member of the family. But he returns to the Earnshaw column with Cath. II. Finally they move together (without passing through the intermediate position, which has been abolished) from left to right, from Wuthering Heights to Thrushcross Grange.

Earnshaws persist, but they must eventually do so within the Linton culture. Catherine burns up in her transit from left to right. The quasi-Earnshaw union of Heathcliff and Isabella leaves the younger Cathy an easier passage; she has only to get through Linton Heathcliff, who is replaced by Hareton Earnshaw, Hareton has suffered part of Heathcliff's fate, moved, as it were, from Earnshaw to Heathcliff, and replaced him as son-servant, as gratuitously cruel; but he is the last of the Earnshaws, and Cathy can both restore to him the house on which his name is carved, and take him on the now smooth path to Thrushcross Grange. □

(pp. 122–4)

So far Kermode has been 'reading' the events of the novel in terms of the passage of the characters through various family identities. He now goes on to consider the dreams in the novel. From Lockwood's dream, he passes to Catherine's and then to the 'vision' that Nelly has by the sign-post of the child Hindley who 'turns into' Hareton who in turn 'turns into' Heathcliff.

■ This is very like a real dream in its transformations and displacements. It has no simple narrative function whatever, and an abridgement might leave it out. But the confusion of generations, and the double usurpation of Hindley by his son and Heathcliff, all three of them variants of the incivility of the Heights, gives a new relation to the agents, and qualifies our sense of all narrative explanations offered in the text. For it is worth remarking that no naturalistic explanation of Nelly's experience is offered; in this it is unlike the treatment of the later vision, when the little boy sees the ghost of Heathcliff and 'a woman', a passage which is a preparation for further ambiguities in the ending. Dreams, visions, ghosts – the whole pneumatology of the book is only indeterminately related to the 'natural' narrative.[20] And this serves to muddle routine 'single' readings, to confound explanation and expectation, and to make necessary a full recognition of the intrinsic plurality of the text.

Would it be reasonable to say this: that the mingling of generic opposites – daylight and dream narratives – creates a need, which we must supply, for something that will mediate between them? If so, we can go on to argue that the text in our response to it is a provision of such mediators, between life and death, the barbaric and the civilized, family and sexual relations. The principal instrument of mediation may well be Heathcliff: neither inside nor out, neither wholly master nor wholly servant, the husband who is no husband, the brother who is no brother, the father who abuses his changeling child, the cousin without kin. And that the chain of narrators serve to mediate between the barbarism of the story and the civility of the reader – making the text itself an intermediate term between archaic and modern – must surely have been pointed out.

What we must not forget, however, is that it is in the completion of the text by the reader that these adjustments are made; and each reader will make them differently. Plurality is here not a prescription but a fact. There is so much that is blurred and tentative, incapable of decisive explanation; however we set about our reading, with a sociological or a pneumatological, a cultural or a narrative code uppermost in our minds, we must fall into division and discrepancy; the doors of communication are sometimes locked, sometimes open, and Heathcliff may be astride the threshold, opening, closing, breaking. And it is surely evident that the possibilities of interpretation increase as time goes on. The constraints of a period culture dissolve, generic presumptions which concealed gaps disappear, and we now see that the book, as James thought novels should, truly 'glories in a gap', a hermeneutic gap in which the reader's imagination must operate, so that he speaks continuously in the text. For these reasons the rebus – *Catherine Earnshaw, Catherine Heathcliff, Catherine Linton* – has exemplary significance.[21] It is a riddle that the text answers only silently; for example it will neither urge nor forbid you to remember that it resembles the riddle of the Sphinx – what manner of person exists in these three forms? – to which the single acceptable and probable answer involves incest and ruin . . .

I have not found it possible to speak of *Wuthering Heights* in this light without, from time to time, hinting – in a word here, or a trick of procedure there – at the new French criticism. I am glad to acknowledge this affinity, but it also seems important to dissent from the opinion that such 'classic' texts as this – and the French will call them so, but with pejorative intent – are essentially naive, and become in a measure plural only by accident. The number of choices is simply too large; it is impossible that even two competent readers should agree on an authorized naive version . . . It is true, as I have said, that time opens them up; if readers were immortal the classic would be much closer to changelessness; their deaths, do, in an important sense, liberate the texts. But to attribute the entire *potential* of plurality to that cause (or to the wisdom and cunning of later readers) is to fall into a mistake. The 'Catherines' of Lockwood's inscription may not have been attended to, but there they are in the text, just as ambiguous and plural as they are now. What happens is that methods of repairing such indeterminacy change; and, as Wolfgang Iser's neat formula has it, 'the repair of indeterminacy' is what gives rise 'to the generation of meaning'.[22] ☐

(pp. 129–31)

Having considered the question of 'plural' readings in theory, Kermode then goes on to consider some actual readings of *Wuthering Heights*; in particular he engages with Q. D. Leavis's 1969 essay, 'A Fresh Approach to *Wuthering Heights*' (discussed above). The difference between his approach and hers, he argues, is that she tries to assert that she has the 'right' reading:

■ A reading such as that with which I began . . . is of course extremely selective, but it has the negative virtue that it does not excommunicate from the text the material it does not employ; indeed, it assumes that it is one of the very large number of readings that may be generated from the text of the novel. They will of course overlap, as mine in some small measure does with that of Mrs Leavis.

And this brings me to the point: Mrs Leavis's reading is privileged; what conforms with it is complex, what does not is confused; and pre-sumably all others would be more or less wrong, in so far as they treated the rejected portions as proper objects of attention. On the other hand, the view I propose does not in any way require me to reject Mrs Leavis's insights. It supposes that the reader's share in the novel is not so much a matter of knowing, by heroic efforts of intelligence and div-ination, what Emily Brontë really meant . . . as of responding creatively to indeterminacies of meaning inherent in the text and possibly enlarged by the action of time. □

(pp. 133–4)

Having distinguished himself from the humanist-formalist school, Kermode then turns his attention to the structuralists. Referring particu-larly to Roland Barthes, he describes, in terms similar to Miller's *Disappearance of God*, how the historical secularisation of knowledge 'multiplies the world's structures of probability', creating a pluralism of meaning which 'denies the authoritative or authoritarian reading that insists on its identity with the intention of the author' (p. 138). Harking back to Charlotte Brontë's comment, with which these extracts from Kermode began, he is now able to give it a new meaning:

■ When we say now that the writer speaks more than he knows we are merely using an archaism; what we mean is that the text is under the absolute control of no thinking subject, or that it is not a message from one mind to another.

The classic, we may say, has been secularized by a process which recognizes its status as a literary text; and that process inevitably plu-ralized it, or rather forced us to recognize its inherent plurality. We have changed our views on change. We may accept, in some form, the view proposed by Michel Foucault, that our period-discourse is controlled by certain unconscious constraints, which make it possible for us to think in some ways to the exclusion of others. However subtle we may be at reconstructing the constraints of past *epistèmes*, we cannot ordinarily move outside the tacit system of our own; it follows that except by extraordinary acts of divination we must remain out of close touch with the probability systems that operated for the first readers of the *Aeneid* or of *Wuthering Heights*.[23] And even if one argues, as I do, that there is clearly less epistemic discontinuity than Foucault's crisis-philosophy proposes, it seems plausible enough that earlier assumptions about continuity were too naive. The survival of the classic must therefore depend upon its possession of a surplus of signifier; as in *King Lear* or *Wuthering Heights* this may expose them to the charge of confusion, for they must always signify more than is needed by any one interpreter or any one generation of interpreters. We may recall that, rather in the manner of Mrs Leavis discarding Heathcliff, George Orwell would have liked *King Lear* better without the Gloucester plot, and with Lear having only one wicked daughter – 'quite enough', he said.

If, finally, we compare this sketch of a modern version of the classic with the imperial classic . . . we see on the one hand that the modern view is necessarily tolerant of change and plurality whereas the older, regarding most forms of pluralism as heretical, holds fast to the time-transcending idea of Empire. Yet the new approach, though it could be said to secularize the old in an almost Feuerbachian way, may do so in a sense which preserves it in a form acceptable to changed probability systems. For what was thought of as beyond time, as the angels . . . were beyond time, inhabiting a fictive perpetuity, is now beyond time in a more human sense; it is here, frankly vernacular, and inhabiting the world where alone, we might say with Wordsworth, we find our happiness – our felicitous readings – or not at all. The language of the new Mercury may strike us as harsh after the songs of Apollo; but the work he contemplates stands there, in all its native plurality, liberated not extinguished by death, the death of writer and reader, unaffected by time yet offering itself to be read under our particular temporal disposition. 'The work proposes; man disposes'. Barthes's point depends upon our recalling that the proverb originally made God the disposer. The implication remains that the classic is an essence available to us under our dispositions, in the aspect of time. So the image of the imperial classic, beyond time, beyond vernacular corruption and change, had perhaps, after all, a measure of authenticity; all we need to do is bring it down to earth. □

(pp. 139–41)

The addition of a historical sense to structuralist ideas is often taken as the distinguishing mark of *post*structuralism; whereas structuralists, especially in anthropology, look for patterns which transcend time and place, poststructuralists recognise that systems of meaning are constantly in movement, and that cultural meanings are always relative. Frank Kermode's explanation of the state of *Wuthering Heights* criticism in 1975 includes both the structuralist awareness of how signification works through binary oppositions and the poststructuralist consciousness that 'meaning' is produced anew by every group of readers. Nevertheless, his conclusion betrays a nostalgia for the inclusive perfection of the old-style 'classic'. His essay thus stands at the border between formalist pluralism and the kind of poststructuralism called 'deconstruction'.

Deconstruction

In 1982, almost twenty years after *The Disappearance of God*, J. Hillis Miller returns to *Wuthering Heights* in *Fiction and Repetition*, an equally influential book which now espouses a deconstructionist stance. Miller's new discussion of *Wuthering Heights* begins by posing it as a hermeneutic puzzle:

■ Charlotte's prefaces establish the rhetorical stance which has been characteristic of criticism of this novel. This stance involves dismissing most previous criticism and claiming one has oneself solved the enigma, cracked the code. □

(p. 47)

He goes on to give a summary of some well-known readings of the text including those by Frank Kermode, Margaret Homans, Leo Bersani and Terry Eagleton,[24] and concludes that although each one is coherent in itself, each is incompatible with the others (p. 50). He then adopts the 'rhetorical stance' described above, declaring, 'all these interpretations are, I believe, wrong'. Unlike his predecessors, however, he does not claim to have 'cracked the code':

■ My argument is that the best readings will be the ones which best account for the heterogeneity of the text, its presentation of a definite group of possible meanings which are systematically interconnected, determined by the text, but logically incompatible . . . The secret truth about *Wuthering Heights* . . . is that there is no secret truth. □

(p. 51)

He proceeds by citing passages from *Wuthering Heights* in which Lockwood reads the names on the window-sill, fears to lose his way in the snow, and sees the three headstones at the end. Each of these, Miller argues, 'seems to ask to be taken as an emblem of the whole novel . . . Each such passage leads to a different formulation of the structure of the whole . . . Each such reading implicitly excludes other passages which do not fit' (p. 56). Although they are 'presented in paired oppositions' (such as the alternative lovers on the headstones), 'the reader is nowhere given access to the generative unity from which the pairs are derived' – for instance, we never see the initial childhood bonding between Catherine and Heathcliff which generates subsequent expressions of loss: 'what is lost in the case of *Wuthering Heights* is the "origin" which would explain everything' (pp. 60–1). Miller then instances how paired oppositions tend to subdivide further, proliferating echoes, and ending with Heathcliff's bewilderment at finding that 'everything' equals 'no thing' – Catherine's absence.

■ Each passage stands for another passage . . . Such a movement is a constant passage from one place to another without ever finding the original literal text of which the others are all figures . . . It is something which has always already occurred and been forgotten. □

(p. 67)

■ The sense of 'something missing' is an effect of the text itself . . . created by figures of one sort or another – substitutions, equivalences, representative displacements . . . controlled by the invitation to believe that some invisible or transcendent cause, some origin, end, or underlying ground, would explain all the enigmatic incongruities of what is visible. □

(p. 68)

Miller's reading echoes Kermode's tentative proposition: 'would it be reasonable to say this: that the mingling of generic opposites – daylight and dream narratives – creates a need, which we must supply, for something that will mediate between them?' (Kermode p. 129). Miller's reading is, however, 'deconstructive', because it insists on the impossibility of that mediation – 'there is no secret truth' (p. 51). In this he is following a general principle about the possibilities of meaning developed by the French philosopher Jacques Derrida. Derrida extends the structuralist idea that meaning is not inherent in single units of language but in the distinctions between them, arguing that words can thus only ever be defined in terms of other words, producing an endless chain or 'deferral' of meaning, which creates its own illusion of a final, or ultimate, truth – a 'transcendental signified' – which can never actually be arrived at. The urge to discover 'harmony', 'unity', 'coherence' in the text is, therefore, an effect of the text; but the text cannot produce these qualities. Deconstruction is, then, a linguistic explanation for 'the disappearance of God'. Conscious knowledge of the system of binary oppositions, which keeps the chain of meaning in motion, effectively disqualifies God as anything other than, precisely, 'ineffable' (that which cannot be spoken) – an effect of textual gesturing toward what is 'beyond', 'outside', 'other'.

Within literary criticism, this way of thinking also rules out the idea of the author as the point of origin of meaning. The Romantics used the deity as a metaphor for the 'ineffable' power of the imagination; Coleridge's 'infinite I AM', and Emily Brontë's 'God within my breast'. The Victorians felt unable to 'read' the text without knowledge of its author. Formalists see the author as encompassing plurality. The reason why there is such resistance to deconstruction is that it removes this final comfort and leaves us subject to what David Sonstroem (above) called 'conceptual wuthering' (p.61); the recognition that the author is not, as Catherine Earnshaw imagines she will be after death, 'incomparably beyond and above you all' (*WH* p.160), but down here with the rest of us struggling to create an illusion of presence where language can only ever stand in the place of absence.

Deconstructive reading can, therefore, be bleak, as in the American critic Carol Jacobs's '*Wuthering Heights*: At the Threshold of Interpretation' (1979). Jacobs's essay starts, like Kermode's, with the inscription over the door of Wuthering Heights. For Kermode, 'it is quite clear'

■ that everybody read and reads this . . . as a sort of promise of something else to come. It is part of what is nowadays called a 'hermeneutic code'; something that promises, and perhaps after some delay provides, explanation. □

(Kermode p.119)

For Jacobs, however, the 'hermeneutic promise' is only of infinite deferral, and will not, even 'perhaps', provide explanation: 'in *Wuthering Heights* one dreams of finding its center only to find that the center is a dream' (p.99). The system of concentric narrative voices contributes to the notion that there is a 'centre' and an 'outside' to the story, but the distinction between the 'fictional' content of Lockwood's story and the 'real' frame also proves to be a false one. Lockwood 'explains' his dream, for instance, by reference to 'reality' – what he read before he went to sleep – but 'reality' itself is a series of texts – the diary, the Bible. 'Inside' and 'outside', both shown to be textual, thus implicitly displace one another, so that it becomes impossible to say which is 'central' and which 'marginal'.

Jacobs is here drawing on Jacques Derrida's 'logic of the supplement', which challenges the neat binary oppositions of structuralism by pointing out that such oppositions always contain hidden value-judgements which create a hierarchy, so that, for instance, we value the 'centre' more highly than the 'margin'. Derrida's 'deconstructive method' asks us first to reverse the hierarchy and notice the importance of the unvalued 'other' quality, and then to upset the opposition altogether by realising that it is not 'natural' but constructed by the system of values in which it is placed. What seems to be 'supplementary' to the 'centre' always proves to be essential (so that you can't conceive of light without dark or male without female). The overall effect of deconstruction is to show that there is no 'scientific' way of arriving at the 'truth' about anything. What appear to be 'truths' are socially-endorsed value-judgements.

Jacobs therefore objects to Kermode's reading which organises the 'plurality' of the text into orderly explanations. His 'structural' reading of the name-patterns rests on repetitions which are all, she says, 'imperfect', and in the end merge into one another as '"the entire world"' becomes 'endless signs for Cathy' (p. 106). What readers have always registered as an anarchic quality in the text is here identified as a refusal of orderly systems of binary opposition and a pushing of the mechanisms of meaning to the (impossible) point where 'everything' equals 'one thing only' – a point incompatible with rational thought and conceivable only in a state of mania.

Jacobs argues that

■ What is in question here is not only a particular ending to the tale of *Wuthering Heights* but the sense of an ending altogether, which is to say an ending with sense, one that puts to rest all wandering and all generation of contradictory forces. □

(p. 117)

She is here referring to Kermode's earlier book, *The Sense of an Ending* (1967), where he argues that we need 'the sense of an ending' in fiction as a stable place from which we can look back to 'make sense' of what has gone before. To some extent the quarrel between deconstructionists and those like Kermode, who retain links with an older notion of literary criticism as a 'humane study', is to do with what literature and criticism, is *for*. If, like the Leavises, you believe that literature should 'teach you how to live', then such stable vantage-points are indeed necessary. If, like Derrida and Jacobs, you take literary criticism as part of a philosophical exploration of the possibilities of meaning, then all such resting-places are temporary and expedient.

Like Jacobs, John T. Matthews begins his 1985 essay, 'Framing in *Wuthering Heights*', at a threshold.

■ *Wuthering Heights* is a novel preoccupied with the idea of boundary. In vast variations of single-mindedness, it haunts the sites of division – between self and other, individual and family, nature and culture, mortality and immortality . . . [and here Matthews refers to Dorothy Van Ghent and to J. Hillis Miller's *The Disappearance of God*] It is not surprising, then, that Emily Brontë should be drawn to a formal expression of

her concern with boundaries by enclosing her 'central' story in an outlying narrative episode. What is the relation of the story *itself* – the
chronicle of Earnshaw-Linton transactions crowned by Catherine and
Heathcliff's love – to the story's *other* in its frame – Nelly Dean's enter-
taining account to her convalescent master Lockwood? Brontë means
us to cross this question repeatedly in her deployment of the frame, in
part because *Wuthering Heights* broods both at its centre and in its margins on the problem of articulation. As in its structure, the novel's
imagery and diction are saturated to the same purpose by the rhetoric of
framing. Dorothy Van Ghent and others have written insightfully on
the prominence of doors and windows as representations of the mind's
and spirit's grasp of interior and exterior. We will come to see, in addition, that the narrative frame is required by the incapacity of the central
lovers to utter their relation. Perpetually frustrated, they cannot articulate the relation that would bind them, and so they leave a gap to be
framed and filled by the loquacity of the narrators. Accordingly, Brontë
brings into play a subtle and wide-spread terminology of framing that
sounds almost all of its senses: to frame is to set off, to encompass, to
edge, but also to invent, to lie, even – in the idiomatic 'frame-off' – to
cease, to leave off, to escape. Likewise, a frame may be a border, but
also one's state of mind, skeletal build, or bodily condition. Brontë
invites us to entertain the agreements between these kinds of framing
as she considers how establishing a ground for the story's figure is
indistinguishable from inventing the story 'itself'. Disclosure is enclosure. The discreteness of the frame wavers under the labor of setting off
the story. ☐

(pp. 26–7)

Matthews's essay thus repeats the focus on textuality and the impossibility of escape from language which we saw in Jacobs's essay, and a
footnote acknowledges the pervasive influence of Derrida in this paper –
especially Derrida's graphically titled 'Living On: *Border Lines*' (1979).[25]
According to Derrida's logic of the supplement (discussed above in relation to Jacobs), the relation between 'core' and 'frame' is intimate:

■ If, as so many readers are willing to have it, Catherine and
Heathcliff's passion involves a yearning for self-possession by means of
the passage through the other, . . . [here Matthews refers us again to the
Disappearance of God] then central to that passion is the sense of lack, of
an interiority yearning for completion by (or through) its exterior. The
structure of the core story is a synecdoche for the novel's structure,
then,[26] since the existence of the frame narrative signals that the central
story lacks self-sufficiency, just as each of the lovers defines love as
lack. The central story's compromised self-sufficiency actually constitutes

its unity by calling forth the encircling frame. A silence, a reticence, some stunted power of speech in the lovers' relation requires the supplement of Nelly's telling and Lockwood's writing. The frame's preliminary nature requires completion by the central story it serves, but the self-insufficiency of the enframed story returns us to the required frame. This conceptual cycle is doubled by our actual reading experience of the novel, since we sink past the circumstances of the narrating scene only to rise back into the frame at the conclusion. □

(p. 29)

In a long footnote, Matthews explains that his 'focus on the alterity of selfhood differs from both Miller's and Bersani's treatments by concentrating on the prominence of the border or the space between the lovers' desire' (p. 60).[27] Like Miller, however, Matthews argues that the 'original moment' of Catherine and Heathcliff's childhood union is never represented:

■ The so-called fullness of childhood innocence rarely if ever appears in *Wuthering Heights*; it is a virtual condition made palpable by the incessant flights and breakings out of the two children as they seek 'to have a ramble at liberty' (*WH* p. 45), liberty meaningful only in the context of tyranny. Even the paradisiacal state of unity, then, is already a curative ghost called forth by what was an intolerable present. The remembered wholeness of childhood is the memory of a dream that was to have redeemed what was already lost. Nelly's account of the earliest phases of Heathcliff's and Catherine's positions in the family (the fourth and following chapters) invariably demonstrates that separation is the condition of their attraction, displacement the location of their alliance, exile the origin of their union. □

(pp. 32–3)

The lovers are not only constrained by social prohibitions as children, but as adults they conform more or less voluntarily to social expectations of gentility and decorum – even Heathcliff is not only gentlemanly in manners but proceeds within the law.

■ Brontë's strategy is folded, then, in a way too readily ignored by readers who want to identify the contents of the opposing wings of *Wuthering Heights*. The realms of nature and culture, person and family, and male and female, for example, bear features which seem to divide them on the basis of intrinsic content; but the force of Brontë's writing simultaneously evacuates the contents by showing that each realm is at once the outer zone defining the other and also the required, essential, central, interior supplement to the other's lack. The namelessness of

Catherine and Heathcliff's relationship accents this situation and helps explain the odd pointlessness of the characters' schemes for satisfaction. Many critics imply that Catherine and Heathcliff simply miss or renounce possibilities for contentment available to them out there – as if with Heathcliff grinning at her side, Catherine might have had the roof removed from the Heights and set up an authentically natural household, with Nelly serving them supper on the moors. I have sought to show instead how their longing cannot abide the congealment of representation. □

(pp. 35–6)

Denied either a point of origin, or a point of destination, the lovers are caught in restless motion:

■ This incessant reversal of interior and exterior, origin and destination, governs virtually all of the lovers' movements. Heathcliff is constantly coming in from the outside (from Liverpool, the stable, the moors, the Grange, the American war for independence, the conditions of dispossession and subservience, the position of Catherine's brother or servant), only to be driven, or to drive himself, back outside. Likewise, Catherine stands at windows looking out upon freedom, but once out (in nature, in childhood, in heaven), she longs to return inside. □

(p. 39)

The bulk of Matthews's substantial article deals in detail with these movements of reversal in both 'frame' and 'core' stories, showing how each is defined by the other:

■ In the interval of their narrative, Nelly and Lockwood both occupy manners of being otherwise inadmissible by them. Through their exacting conventionality, Nelly and Lockwood evoke the spectral satisfactions and transgressions that haunt the repressive order of society. Catherine and Heathcliff's love is the ghost of the prohibitions that structure society: it has the air of unspeakably natural passion, even incest, the spaciousness of escape from tyrannous convention, the heedlessness of self-abandon, the dark allure of disease and deathliness. Toward this representation of an existence beyond the numbing containments of their lives, the narrators grope as they pass into the story. And yet the mysterious 'ideal' of Catherine and Heathcliff's passion fails finally to sustain its perfect otherness. Inexorably the script of the framers' hands grows legible in the novel's palimpsest:[28] the subversiveness of passion in the core story – whether we focus on the romantic or social facet of that passion – reverts into subservience to convention, representation, reason, health. The central love is stained, then, from the outset by the strains of its creators' imaginations. Catherine and Heathcliff end up reinforcing the dictates of class, family, the law and mortality. What they seem to defy they actually verify. And it is in this swerve towards a holier, sanctioned frame that Lockwood and Nelly escape (with) themselves, for the survival of the narrators at the cost of their protagonists defines the triumph of framing this fiction. 'Imaging' transcendence, innocence, regression, and naturalness – the zone projected by the novel's fantasy of a perfected society – imaging them is losing them and accepting their loss. When critics speak of Brontë's vision of a world in which authentic values might hold sway, [and he refers here to Gilbert and Gubar and to Terry Eagleton, whose essays will be discussed in chapter five], they comply with the very process that Brontë unsettles in *Wuthering Heights*. Brontë shows that – helpless as we are to stop longing for a corrective transformation of our present circumstances – those circumstances determine the very nature of the ideal. The oppressions of society not only compromise our present, they condition the dreams of its reversal and defeat. The 'subversive' exterior ends up being seen as the representation of the spectral interior, a conflation of outside and inside that we have noted in every region of the novel. All that beckons us as the beyond is the blank inverse of what is within. Brontë sees that these versions of personal and social desire are the shapes of their own repression, pressing in to keep the configuration of the boundary in force. □

(p. 54)

Matthews then shows how the notion of 'framing' operates at every level of the novel.

■ Each of the lovers seeks to supplement an interior lack by representing it as an other who becomes the 'all in all'. The lack in each, then, constitutes the unifying lock of their love; each frames and is enframed by the other. At the next remove, the unity of the core story is secured by a lack to be filled by the frame story. The lovers' inability to grasp a form, a word, for their attachment requires the labors of their tellers; yet we have seen that the lack in the core is also the lack of the frame story, since the authors conjure up the emanations of their own and society's discontents. *Wuthering Heights* does not offer us a regulated structural whole; rather, it displays mutually embracing structures that despair of perfected unity while simulating its effect . . .

The point of my analysis is not to displace one center of *Wuthering Heights* in order to substitute another; I am not arguing that the frame narrative is 'actually' the more important part of the novel, nor that readers must begin with it and see it as the origin of the work's meaning.

Instead, I have sought to follow the novel's own leading as it proceeds through the passages of representation, constantly turning us back at the point we take to be the center of significance, our attainment of the 'penetralium'. For Brontë shows us how the nature of narrative is all frame and framing, the articulation of thresholds meaningful as they conduct our passing through them, and not our passing by or over them. Throughout the novel, doors bear words, and words serve as doors. Lockwood notices at the outset that the threshold to Wuthering Heights demands reading [and here Matthews refers back to Frank Kermode, whose 'hermeneutic promise' is discussed by Jacobs above]. And toward the end Hareton signals his crossing (back) into literacy by reading his (ancestor's) name inscribed on the lintel: 'he moved off to open the door, and, as he raised the latch, he looked up to the inscription above'. Words promise to be the portals to what we desire and imagine. They offer access to what we do not possess: the perfected self, the object of longing, the exiled regions of the mind. Yet Nelly only once agrees to 'leaving the door of communication open' (*WH* p.71); more often she insists on keeping doors closed. Though language promises to conduct us to what it signifies, it can only keep us moving in the passages of communication. □

(pp. 56–7)

Matthews ends by widening his comment from the novel to its critical reception, touchingly repeating, in this sophisticated reading, the images of enchantment used by the earliest Victorian readers. For Matthews, then, 'keeping moving' bears a positive rather than a negative connotation:

■ Since the readers and tellers of the story all are only passing through, any passage might be taken as introductory to any other, any frame actually the enframed. We step immediately into Lockwood's story, which also is to be taken as the novel's 'central' subject. It is this incessant dissolving of figure into ground and back that I contend organizes our spellbinding admiration for *Wuthering Heights* and our remarkable inability to agree on what it means. □

(p. 57)

It might seem that deconstruction is such a 'new' and, perhaps, arrogant approach that its effect would be to outlaw all previous readings (Miller, for instance, declares roundly that 'all these interpretations are, I believe, wrong' (*Repetition* p. 51)). The distinguished critic Patricia Parker, however, in 'The (Self-)Identity of the Literary Text: Property, Proper Place, and Proper Name in *Wuthering Heights*' (1987), demonstrates how deconstructive techniques demand to be combined with traditional scholarship. Since the upshot of deconstruction is that there is no reality outside language, it is precisely the range of (literary) language which becomes the working ground for such critics. Parker shares Matthews's admiration for the text, and argues that 'the relation between the text of something called (for better or for worse) "literature" and something called (for better or for worse) "theory" is anything but a *sens unique* [one-way passage]' (p. 7). 'Literature' often anticipates 'theory', which is in any case related to earlier philosophical insights.

■ For Derrida, the self-identity of the text is intimately linked to *propriété* in its widest sense. What must be emphasized, however, is that the complex of terms related to the 'proper', a complex to which recent criticism has again called our attention, also engaged the Enlightenment, precisely in connection with the problem of identity. By considering the relation of property, proper place, and proper name in Lockwood's text to the question of its unified identity, we return to . . . the Lockean principle of individuation, its relation to discrete chronological sequence or line and to the boundary-marking of individual identity through what Locke termed the 'appropriation' of the proper name. In the process, I shall suggest that the two sides of the debate over *Wuthering Heights* – between formalist critics who emphasize its narrative structures and Marxist or sociological critics who emphasize its involvement with the laws of private property – converge in this novel precisely on the question of 'property' in its most radical or fundamental sense.

Property and proper name are connected, first, in the figure of Lockwood himself: it is he who owns or masters his own text – as Hobbes says of the connection between Author and Owner (*Leviathan*, I.xvi) – and lends his name as the single unifying presence of a narrative which repeatedly calls attention to the importance of proper place, property, propriety, and proper name. The emphasis on place or position in Lockwood's text is everywhere: in the plot founded on the relation between the two houses, Wuthering Heights and Thrushcross Grange; in the sense of speech as placing characters by region or social class; and in Joseph's pharisaical insistence on the Sabbath as an inviolable place in time. This is joined by a more specific focus on ownership, possession, and property, from Heathcliff's opening 'Thrushcross Grange is my own, sir' (I, 45), his reference to his own son as 'property' (XX, 242), Lockwood's uncertainty about who is the 'favoured possessor' of the female figure he encounters at the Heights (II, 55), and Earnshaw's finding the orphan Heathcliff without an 'owner' (IV), to the principal exchange of the plot, in which Heathcliff acquires the very property from which he had been excluded . . . [29] [and she continues to cite the quarrel between the young Lintons over ownership of the dog, and the bulldog which bites Catherine in defence of property at Thrushcross Grange].

'Property' in the sense of the establishment of boundaries – and the prohibition of trespass fundamental to a society based on the laws of private possession – appears as well in the frequency in the novel of images such as windows, thresholds, and gates which mark the boundaries between places, or between inside and outside. From the opening chapter, the novel's establishment of boundaries or dividing walls is intimately linked with the language of its narrator, whose syntax raises barriers even as he pushes through the gate which keeps him from the Heights ('I do myself the honour of calling as soon as possible, after my arrival, to express the hope that I have not inconvenienced you by my perseverance in soliciting the occupation of Thrushcross Grange'), and whose convoluted speech contrasts pointedly with the abruptness of Heathcliff's replies and the Heights' own unmediated entrance ('One step brought us into the family sitting-room, *without any introductory lobby, or passage*'). Lockwood, indeed, presents himself in a series of episodes involving the interposition of barriers: his rebuffing of the young girl whose attentions he had initially encouraged, his interposing of a 'table' between himself and the dog whose fury he himself provoked (I), his piling up of books to keep out a ghostly 'Catherine Linton' (III) and rubbing her wrist against the broken glass of a partition which no longer divides. These apotropaic gestures provide our first introduction to the narrator who will both request and relate the housekeeper's story from the framed and mediated distance of Thrushcross Grange. In the midst of the chaos he himself has caused by baiting the dogs, Lockwood assimilates them to the biblical 'herd of possessed swine', and his hastening to interpose a table between himself and the fury he has raised proleptically enacts the function of the narrative which ensues, the casting out or distancing of demons too menacing to the enlightened mind, in a novel whose mediating perspectives and multiple narrations themselves both conjure and frame.[30]

Lockwood's text, however, is remarkable for its emphasis not only on proper place, property, and boundary lines but also on trespass, transgression, or crossing, or on boundary lines which themselves become thresholds. ☐

(pp. 161–3)

– and there follows a characteristically dense sequence of examples. Parker then takes up the question of proper names, referring back to Frank Kermode's treatment of this issue (discussed above). Names are indicators both of proper place and of transgression, as in the various dream sequences of the novel, and the repeated or echoing names belonging to different people.

■ *Wuthering Heights* refuses to let the reader forget that both the chrono-logical sense of time and the linear habit of reading depend upon sequence, on events maintaining a syntax, or proper sense of place. But Lockwood's encounter with the swarming and spectral 'letters', the undercutting of the rational explanation of his first dream (merely a 'fir-tree') in the uncanny return of the second, Nelly's crossroads apparition, chapter XII's preposterous recalls [this plural noun refers to Catherine's delirious memories where she imagines herself a child again at the Heights] . . . are all episodes in which things refuse to keep their proper place. Tropes such as metaphor (Catherine's defiant 'I *am* Heathcliff' or the sheer parataxis of the juxtaposed 'Catherines') and *hysteron proteron* (the figure of reversal which Puttenham called 'The Preposterous') unsettle the careful boundaries and spaced linearity of Lockwood's text and reveal its own strategies of closure or enclosure as precisely that . . . [31] □

(p. 174)

The novel's ending abounds in unsettling appearances:

■ The curious absence of names in the description of the returning 'ramblers' Lockwood hastens at this ending to 'escape' creates, if only for a moment, the illogical possibility that these ramblers are not the solid, second-generation Cathy and Hareton but the ghostly Catherine and Heathcliff, whom the country folk insist still 'walk'. □

(p. 175)

Parker's conclusion, supported by a long and detailed examination of the text, is that its 'identity' is 'as Derrida would say, always already inhabited by difference'.

■ The identity of the literary text, both as unity and as a self-identity, guaranteed by the narratorial subject who offers the novel we read as his book, is in *Wuthering Heights* radically undermined: the text remains perpetually, and frustratingly, other to itself, forever inhabited by its own ghosts. The haunting of the narratorial text by something which escapes both identification and placing cannot simply be explained by recourse to the distinction between narrator and effaced author, to the substitution of one proper name – or kind of mastery – for another. Indeed, we feel in reading Emily Brontë's novel the pertinence of at least one of her sister's prefatory remarks: 'the writer who possesses the creative gift owns something of which he [*sic*] is not always master – something that at times strangely wills and works for itself'. Critics of *Wuthering Heights* as diverse as Fredric Jameson and Frank Kermode have remarked on its unsettling sense of automatism, a staple feature of the gothic as a mode which foregrounds the unsettling mobility of *things*. Brontë's novel, whose 'characters' are both the embodiments of a genealogical history and the unsettling graphic letters of chapter III, suggests that something as apparently modern as the notion of a text writing itself may have a peculiarly gothic pedigree. And the recurrence of the figure of the 'specter' or 'ghost' in contemporary narrative theory may return us to the ghost narratives of the period we call post-Enlightenment – if we understand that 'post', as we now do that of 'post'-structuralist, as still caught within the very structures it dismantles or undermines. *Wuthering Heights* calls into question not only private property but the very idea of the 'proper'; its violation is not only of moral proprieties but of novelistic ones. In the terms of one of its own most persistent figures, it demands a reading which seeks to raise more demons than it casts out. □

(pp. 176–7)

CHAPTER THREE

Psychoanalysis: Uncovering the Unconscious

IN CHAPTER two, I tried to suggest the overall shape of the critical movements within which *Wuthering Heights* has been read during the
twentieth century. Within, and echoing, this overall shape, there have,
however, been particular strands of approach which repay separate attention. One of these is psychoanalysis.

Several Victorian critics, including Sydney Dobell and Peter Bayne
(1857) saw that *Wuthering Heights* could be read as a study in abnormal
psychology. Freudian theory, however, gives a more pointed vocabulary
and a more technical explanation for obsessive and divided mentalities.
Since psychoanalysis is a therapeutic practice aimed at restoring functional 'wholeness' to real individuals, the earliest psychoanalytic critics
applied it to the author rather than the fictional characters, as if by understanding her 'illness' we could better understand her 'message'. Such
critics often speak in terms of 'repression'. Freud argues that repression is
a necessary mechanism by which 'uncivilised' infants 'forget' and stow
away in the unconscious those primitive desires – such as lust, greed and
rage – which are incompatible with socialised behaviour. He thought that
children achieve this necessary repression by encountering what he calls
the 'reality principle', which governs what is possible in terms of social co-
existence. 'Repression' is, however, often read as the deliberate
oppression of one person by another, particularly within the family, and
interwar studies such as Romer Wilson's assume that the Brontë sisters
were 'repressed' by an authoritarian father. Patrick Brontë's supposed
authoritarianism, now decisively discredited by Juliet Barker's biography,
was then widely accepted, as shown by a *Punch* cartoon in 1935, where
the three sisters comment on their father's departure from the dinner table:

- ■   Anne: He's gone.
      Emily: Thank God!

Charlotte: His dinner barely tasted.
                Just like our lives – hard, underdone and wasted. □

Freud argued that repressed desires could reappear in socially acceptable or 'sublimated' forms, and this understanding produced a lurid, though psychoanalytically orthodox, extreme in Emilie and Georges Romieu's 1931 reading, which attributed to the Brontë sisters 'infinite aspirations' to match their unparalleled repression:

■ A thirst that shall be appeased by no beauty, by no love, by no happiness. Nothing. Such desires exceed human realizations. The waiting lips will never receive the charity of one kiss. No lover will spring to their side or will press them against a heart that beats only for them. Their arms embrace only the void, and no form emerges for them to press frenziedly to their ripening breasts – unless it be the form of a dream – or a dog.
    Blessed misery!
    Deep within life will burn with an unexampled heat – unappeased. The white page is the needful outlet; thereupon in words of flame they will write an immortal utterance. □

(p. 10)

Taboos

Freud's theory also provides ways of reconciling individual psychology with larger structures such as those described by Cecil. Freud's account of the socialisation of children through the family is supported by references to ancient literature and to the habits of diverse cultures, and thus claims to identify a structure which underlies what it is to be human. To this extent, Freudian psychoanalysis can be seen as an aspect of structuralism, and the ideas in his *Totem and Taboo* (1918) were certainly adopted by structuralist anthropologists such as Claude Lévi-Strauss. A flourishing branch of *Wuthering Heights* criticism derives from this, focused on the taboos against incest and intra-family violence which Freud posits as basic to social co-existence. Eric Solomon, in 1959, was the first to suggest that the peculiar atmosphere of *Wuthering Heights* was attributable to incest. Wade Thompson's 'Infanticide and Sadism in *Wuthering Heights*' (1963) is a more developed study, in which he argues that because the children in *Wuthering Heights* are motherless, they find themselves engaged in the primal struggles for survival in an unusually direct way:

■ Without the care of their mothers, the children find themselves in a fierce struggle for survival against actively hostile adults who seem obsessed with the desire to kill or maim them. From Lockwood's early dream of pulling the wrist of the ghostchild Catherine along a jagged window ledge, to Heathcliff's presiding with delight over the death of his overgrown child, the novel plays a multitude of insistent variations on the ghastly theme of infanticide. □

(p. 69)

■ In summary, then, the world of *Wuthering Heights* is a world of sadism, violence, and wanton cruelty, wherein the children – without the protection of their mothers – have to fight for very life against adults who show almost no tenderness, love, or mercy. Normal emotions are almost completely inverted: hate replaces love, cruelty replaces kindness, and survival depends on one's ability to be tough, brutal, and rebellious. □

(p. 71)

In this context, Thompson argues, it appears odd that Catherine longs to be a child again, but the explanation is that 'as a child Catherine is endowed with a kind of masculine power that only the most hardened adults usually possess' (p. 71). The tragedy of *Wuthering Heights* is thus one of failure to achieve normal gendered socialisation:

■ The disintegration of Catherine's personality begins with the Thrushcross Grange episode. She fails to see that her entrance into puberty requires a radical change in her relation with Heathcliff . . . Even after her marriage, she is tough and masculine in the presence of Heathcliff . . . The source of her strength, however, is Heathcliff. Without him, she gradually finds herself unable to endure pain or to keep her self-possession, and her temper becomes uncontrollable . . . As she grows older, pain becomes intolerable . . . The girl who could once hold off a whole household of angry adults now loses all self-possession . . .

In the brief life of Catherine, then, there is a complete reversal of roles. As a child she is an adult; even her sauciness is grounded in inner strength. As an adult she becomes a child, and the pain of living proves intolerable. 'I wish I were a girl again', she cries pathetically, 'half savage and hardy and free; and laughing at injuries, not maddening under them'. She remembers that she was once strong and knows that she is strong no longer. Logically enough, therefore, in her ghostly state, she assumes the role, not of a lovely lady in the lonely moors calling for her lover (which would surely be the 'romantic' expectation), but of a little girl come back 'home'. □

(p. 72)

The Catherine-Heathcliff relationship is revealed as 'regressive':

■ While Catherine's return in the role of a child fulfils her yearning to regain her childhood strength, it also betrays the fact that only as a child was she ever able to love Heathcliff. After puberty, she is never able to transform her childish passion for identity ('I am Heathcliff', she says – but one does not mate with one's self, with one's kind) into a passion for the union of opposites. Her marriage to Linton, a weak, respectable, undemanding person, is essentially an escape from the demands of adult sexuality, and she sees no betrayal of Heathcliff in the escape. To her, Heathcliff is, and always will be, her wild 'childhood' lover; Linton is her respectable 'adult' lover, and the two are perfectly compatible. She is never jealous of Heathcliff and cannot understand his jealousy of her; she simply thinks of her 'love' for him as entirely different from her 'love' for Linton.

Indeed she is correct. The 'love' she can offer Heathcliff is precisely the love she offered him as a child – tough, masculine 'identity', born in pain, expressed in pain – but nothing like normal adult love: no eroticism, no sex, no pleasure, no satisfaction. *Her* 'love' is expressed through pain, hate, and relentless recrimination. Hair-pulling and pinching are her modes of physical expression. Surely no more sexless and abnormal scene can be imagined than the final love scene between herself and Heathcliff: 'I shouldn't care what you suffered. I care nothing for your sufferings. Why shouldn't *you* suffer?' she says to him. And he can only respond in kind: 'Is it not sufficient for your infernal selfishness, that while you are at peace I shall writhe in the torments of hell?' They can meet only in pain and distress: 'should a word of mine distress you hereafter, think I feel the same distress underground'. □

(pp. 72–3)

Since Catherine cannot meet the needs of adult sexuality, Heathcliff takes revenge by imposing adult sexuality on the children of the second generation. Thompson notes that his essay was written partly to invalidate readings such as Melvin R. Watson's 'Tempest in the Soul', which sees love as triumphant over all odds in the novel. In stark contrast, Thompson argues:

■ The great love story of *Wuthering Heights*, then, begins in perversity and ends in perversity. The 'love' between Catherine and Heathcliff grows under the terrible threat of infanticide, never undergoes a metamorphosis into maturity, and so culminates in revenge on the next generation. The only escape is death; and both Catherine and Heathcliff deeply yearn to die ... In the end, the shepherd boy sees 'Heathcliff and a woman' (no longer a child) now roaming freely and happily about the moors. But such a consummation could never come in life. Life is pain, hate, and perversity. It is a tribute to Emily Brontë's uncanny poetic powers that she has deceived generations of readers into believing that they were reading a beautiful, romantic, and indeed glorious love story. □

(pp. 73–4)

William R. Goetz's 'Genealogy and Incest in *Wuthering Heights*' (1982) derives explicitly from Claude Lévi-Strauss's distinction between the 'raw' and the 'cooked'.[1] According to Lévi-Strauss, all cultures have rules for distinguishing between (unsocialised) infants and adults, between (barbaric) strangers and friends, between (inedible) raw food and cooked, and Goetz reads the contrast between Wuthering Heights and Thrushcross Grange as that between the 'raw' and the 'cooked'. The tightly limited 'society' within the novel produces an 'elementary' structure of kinship in which there is only one eligible mate for Catherine and Isabella, and the first-generation plot, in which each finds a mate from the opposite house, thus acts out 'the rule which, according to Lévi-Strauss, stands at the basis of all culture: the renunciation of incest' (p. 363). Goetz points out, however, that the raw–cooked contrast exists both diachronically (Wuthering Heights is ousted by Thrushcross Grange) and synchronically (the houses continue to co-exist). This means that the second-generation plot

■ does not chronicle anything so simple as the victory of culture over nature, or of the Victorian world over the Romantic one. Rather, it shows in retrospect that the entire story has been composed of a series of moments that *seem* to make a step in the direction from nature to culture, but never arrive at a final term or goal. The novel shows that the 'progress' from nature to civilization is one that must be won anew, or simply repeated, from generation to generation; nature and culture are not the two chronological poles of a linear history, but the two co-present sides of a process that is never concluded. □

(p. 373)

Desires

Critics were slow to psychoanalyse the characters of *Wuthering Heights*. May Sinclair in 1912 could see that Catherine's suffering is partly due to her ignorance of sexuality, but she uses non-Freudian language (p.215), and Coleman Kavanagh, in 1920, could still talk of the characters as if they were allegorical figures of 'despair' or 'pride'. As late as 1949, Melvin R. Watson uses quite conventional language to describe Heathcliff's 'Tempest in the Soul'.

Thomas Moser, in 1962, was the first to make a straightforwardly Freudian analysis of *Wuthering Heights* in 'What Is the Matter with Emily Jane?'. Moser's thesis is that

■ over a century ago Emily Brontë dramatized what Freud subsequently called the id. She discovered and symbolized in Heathcliff and, to a lesser extent, in Cathy that part of us we know so little about, . . . the child that lurks within everyone . . . The primary traits which Freud ascribed to the id apply perfectly to Heathcliff: the source of psychic energy; the seat of the instincts (particularly sex and death); the essence of dreams; the archaic foundation of personality – selfish, asocial, impulsive . . .

The basic childishness of Cathy and Heathcliff and their impulse to lose themselves in the world of external nature need no analysis . . . But Heathcliff as the embodiment of sexual energy requires detailed explanation not only because critics have largely ignored this role but also because Emily Brontë apparently tried to disguise the truth from herself. The large body of evidence suggesting that Emily Brontë felt Heathcliff to be pure sexual force lies just beneath the surface, in a series of scenes involving Heathcliff, Cathy, and, in most cases, an ineffectual male. Each scene dramatizes a dispute of some sort over entrance through a door or window. Heathcliff always wins, and the images suggest that the victory is a sexual conquest. □

(pp. 4–5)

After examining a number of such scenes, Moser concludes that 'whether she "knew" it or not, Emily Brontë was writing a passionate paean to Eros. The novel moves relentlessly toward its necessary end – the complete physical union of Cathy and Heathcliff' (p. 12). For Moser, the failure of the 'thin-blooded' second-generation characters lies in the fact that the younger Catherine's relationships are with 'boys' who 'desire, not union with an equal, but unsexed bliss with a mother' (p. 13). Charlotte must have been right, he argues, and Emily did not know what she was doing when she created Catherine and Hareton:

■ Surely the authentic Emily Brontë does not believe that real love can be exemplified by this couple, so oblivious to the primitive forces that underlie life. The authentic Emily Brontë who wrote the masterpiece we return to is the creator of Heathcliff, vibrating with energy, and Cathy, scorning the pusillanimous Edgar to cry across the moors to her demon lover. □

(p. 19)

It was perhaps inevitable that Moser's paean to vibrant masculinity was written by a man. Feminist critics are, on the whole, more sober in their use of Freudian theory. In *Women, the Longest Revolution* (1966), Juliet Mitchell points out that the narrow focus of Emily Brontë's novel replicates Freud's focus on the family as an explanatory mechanism for the growth of individual psyches:

■ Emily Brontë's society was so small that she was able to grasp nearly everything about it. Within these narrow confines she explored the depths. If the family is to be a society, intensity must make up for extensiveness; depth for breadth. In one sense, it is this limiting context that is the cause of the cosmic quality so often commented on in *Wuthering Heights*. The universe has become the family, and a microcosm has become the cosmos. □

(p. 128)

Emily Brontë's subjects, like Freud's, were 'infancy, adolescence, early childhood and death' (p. 128). In the story of Catherine Earnshaw, 'Emily Brontë, uncluttered with diverse experience, could trace through an almost complete life cycle' (p. 141). Mitchell's chapter on *Wuthering Heights* is subtitled 'Romanticism and Rationality', and it is this (Freudian) insistence on an unbroken personal development which she sees as the 'rational' element which combines with the apparently anarchic 'Romantic' elements of *Wuthering Heights*. The focus on childhood

■ allows Emily Brontë to explain all her characters, while presenting them with romantic and ontological intensity. Thus, contrary to received critical notions, there are no mysteries in *Wuthering Heights*. The nature and actions of every character in the drama are fully intelligible because they are always related to the total biographical development of the person and, above all, to what we now know to be the most critical phase of life: childhood. □

(pp. 143–4)

Helen Moglen, in her 1971 essay, 'The Double Vision of *Wuthering Heights*: A Clarifying View of Female Development', also reads *Wuthering Heights* as based on the continuous linear development of a female mind, but she sees Catherine Linton as completing the maturing process which Catherine Earnshaw fails to achieve (p. 398). Rebecca West had already in 1954 seen the elder Catherine as suffering 'in the grip of an emotion which cannot come to fruition for abstract and absolute reasons. What she wants is to be with Heathcliff as they were in childhood . . . The man Heathcliff is of no use to her; she does not even like him' (p. 264). Moglen explains this by quoting from Norman O. Brown's (Freudian) *Life Against Death*:

■ 'this early blossoming of the erotic life must succumb to repression when it finally confronts the reality-principle. But though it is repressed, this early experience of love stays with us as the immortal dream of love, as an indestructible demand of human nature, as the source of our restless discontent.'[2] □

(p. 405)

As Freudian theory fragmented between relatively dissident disciples, so there are studies of *Wuthering Heights* from a variety of post-Freudian positions by Mary Burgan, Bernard Paris, Philip Wion and Barbara Schapiro. Anne Williams, in her 1991 essay, '"The Child is *Mother* of the Man"'(1991), shows how Freud's theory of the Oedipal crisis can be adapted, by way of Lacan, to suit feminist readers:

■ How can love so definitively express itself as hate and violence? Why does it so sublimely ignore social realities? How can Cathy assert at once that she '*is*' Heathcliff and that it would 'degrade' her to marry him? And why should such patently 'unrealistic' characters remain so perennially moving to generations of readers?

. . . I believe that the appeal of their story can be understood by recognizing that this love represents not merely childish immaturity (as Q.D. Leavis has argued), but the stage of development psychoanalysts call the pre-Oedipal. This period precedes separation from the mother, acquisition of language (including the structures for ordering reality that language imposes), and self-consciousness. Communication at this stage is a communion which has no need of words. The later Oedipal Crisis demands that the child grasp a culture and language effecting separation from, and repression of, the mother (and all culture associated with her). This theory also supposes that the child, exiled from the 'paradise' of wordless communication, non-identity, and gratified desires, will ever after yearn to rediscover that prior state, which becomes a powerful unconscious motive for all subsequent action. □

(pp. 84–5)

When Catherine describes the conflicting attractions of Edgar and Heathcliff, using imagery drawn from dreams and nature, Williams argues, she

■ is describing, from the female point of view, the situation Freud called the Oedipal crisis – in the broadest terms, one's coming to terms with the relative power and value culture accords the two sexes and the qualities associated with them. The 'healthy' son supposedly learns to renounce the mother and align himself with the father. Freud speculated that the daughter, recognizing her 'castration', learns to shun the mother and transfer her affections from her father to her husband, through whom she gains whatever power culture accords her as a woman accepting male superiority.

Brontë tells a different story. Culture, she says, tragically separates not only a woman's head from her heart . . . It also cuts her off from the energy and active power culture attributes to the male . . . □

(p. 88)

■ What Freud called 'castration', then, is not female submission to her 'natural' defect. Rather it is culture's demand that she separate herself from her own 'masculine' principle, in order to marry and gain access to the rewards culture grants to the 'real' woman – such things as wealth and social respectability and the possibility of children. In showing that Cathy dies of this separation, this being cut off from her partly masculine soul, Brontë thus undermines what is, perhaps, the most powerful of all binary oppositions: that between male and female. The female is partly 'male', she suggests; the male is partly 'female'. To divide the two has 'unnatural' results – the ghost haunts the moors, an apt metaphor for the separation of spirit from matter (*mater*). □

(p. 89)

The splitting of the female psyche referred to by Williams also figures in Elisabeth Bronfen's study of *Wuthering Heights* in *Over Her Dead Body: Femininity and the Aesthetic* (1992). Bronfen is mainly concerned with the strategies by which people represent death. In the course of her argument, however, she invokes Freud's diagnosis of the 'hysteric', which has been taken up by feminists such as Juliet Mitchell. For Freud, the hysteric was someone whose access to language was blocked, so that emotions registered themselves through 'symptoms'. For Mitchell, 'the woman novelist is necessarily the hysteric wanting to repudiate the symbolic definition of sexual difference under patriarchal law, unable to do so because without madness we are all unable to do so' (pp. 293–4). She goes on:

■ the choices for the woman within the novel, within fiction, are either to survive by making the hysteric's ambiguous choice into a femininity which doesn't work (marrying Edgar) or to go for oneness and unity, by suffering death (walking the moors as a ghost with Heathcliff). □

(p. 293)

For Bronfen, Catherine's 'hysteria' manifests itself as a simultaneous acceptance and refusal of the knowledge of her split state which is curiously repeated in her haunting of Heathcliff,

■ constantly oscillating between fading from his view and returning in his sensation and imagination . . . This uncanny preservation, the woman simultaneously *da* and *fort* . . . is what Heathcliff ultimately calls 'a strange way of killing'.[3] □

(p. 312)

Dreams

Because the unconscious is normally inaccessible to the conscious mind, therapists need to exploit the few ways there are of guessing at its contents. The main such route is via dreams, and one of Freud's earliest published works was *The Interpretation of Dreams* (1900). *Wuthering Heights* has proved a rich hunting-ground for dream-interpreters. As early as 1920 Edith Maud Fenton was using the dreams to distinguish *Wuthering Heights* from a conventional Gothic novel. Whereas dreams in the Gothic novel are 'definitely useful' – that is, they indicate solutions to problems – those in *Wuthering Heights*, Fenton argues, contain 'the revelation of personality, the vision of unsatisfied longings, the pathos of the unattainable in life' (pp. 107, 109–10).

Most studies of the dreams, however, do try to make them 'useful' in interpreting the novel. One branch of the 1950s debate about the narrative voices in *Wuthering Heights* (described in chapter two) concerned itself with Lockwood's dreams. Several critics try to identify Jabes Branderham's text. Ruth Adams (1958) argues that it is Genesis 4:24, which deals with the exile of Cain for the murder of his brother. Edgar F. Shannon (1959) disputes this and proposes Matthew 18:21–22:

■ Then came Peter to him, and said, Lord, how oft shall my brother sin against me, and I forgive him? till seven times?

Jesus said unto him, I say not unto thee, Until seven times: but, Until seventy times seven. □

Shannon is uninterested in what Freud calls the 'latent' (hidden) content of Lockwood's dreams; 'the sexual symbolism of his lacking a staff and the breaking of the window-membrane with attendant blood, pain and terror is obvious', but 'has no bearing on the central development of the novel' (p. 97 note). The 'manifest' content, on the other hand, points to Catherine's 'unpardonable sin' (p. 98) in marrying Edgar Linton (p. 99). Ronald E. Fine (1969) inclines toward the Cain reading because the ousting of Cain by his brother Abel can be seen as the matrix for all the situations where siblings – Hindley, Catherine, Heathcliff, Edgar and Isabella – have been unfairly repudiated.

William A. Madden's 1972 article, '*Wuthering Heights*: The Binding of Passion', argues, in effect, that Joseph is the 'villain' of *Wuthering Heights*.[4] Accepting Shannon's reading that Branderham's text is Matthew 18:21–22, Madden points out that all the participants in the dream – Joseph, Lockwood and Branderham, 'misunderstand the symbolic import' of Jesus's words when he says that we should pardon a brother's sin seventy times seven times,

■ interpreting them literally instead of as a command to practice unlimited forgiveness . . . Although the precise nature of the unforgivable sin has been debated, Emily Brontë makes it clear that for her the unforgivable sin consists in judging the human offenses of others as unforgivable. □

(p. 131)

Madden argues that the quality of 'unforgivingness' is particularly associated with Joseph and that he is active in turning Mr Earnshaw against each of his children (p. 135). In this context, Madden sees the second generation, especially the younger Catherine, as both strong and necessary to the story:

■ The story of the first generation indicates that rebellion against the radical perversion of spiritual values represented by Joseph is insufficient. Only when his malignity and its disruptive effects are confronted and subdued is peace restored. □

(p. 147)

Madden, moreover, does use Freudian analysis in his article. Freud's original hypothesis had been that all dreams represent a wish-fulfilment, but he noticed that where children or adults had been traumatised their dreams compulsively return to the source of neurosis in an effort to 'bind' the excess of emotion. This effort is usually unsuccessful, and the sufferers instead evade the problem by returning to a state prior to the trauma (p. 149). Madden argues that for Catherine and Heathcliff the trauma is their exclusion from the Earnshaw family presided over by Joseph, that their 'love' is 'rooted in their radical alienation' and is thus incapable of positive development (p. 150). In an extensive analysis of the younger Catherine's moral courage in confronting Heathcliff's oppression, Madden argues that she and Hareton succeed in 'binding' their emotion so that it is 'channeled into human wholeness and health through the transforming power of a love that both understands and forgives' (p. 154).

The Text

Most of the remaining extracts in this chapter are from studies deriving not from Freud himself, but rather from Jacques Lacan, whose theories have been particularly appealing to literary critics because of his focus on language. Where Philip Wion presents mother-loss as a pathological feature of *Wuthering Heights*, explicable by the fact that Emily Brontë's mother died when she was three, Lacan would argue that mother-loss is constitutive of the human condition. For Lacan, infants acquire language at the point where they realise that the mother's body is not exclusively theirs.

Language thus originates in loss, a sign of absence. Lacan would agree with Wion that the Catherine–Heathcliff relationship attempts to replicate the pre-linguistic relationship between mother and child, where there is no sense of separate existence and language is therefore not necessary, but would throw the emphasis of interpretation on to the (always inadequate) language in which the text attempts to recover, or gesture towards, that inaccessible blissful state. Lacanian psychoanalysis thus shares many of the features of Derridean deconstruction (discussed in the last section of chapter two), which also sees language as pointing towards an unreachable 'presence'.

One of the most influential discussions of *Wuthering Heights* in this theoretical context is in Leo Bersani's book, *A Future for Astyanax* (1976). The obscure-seeming title refers to the child Astyanax, the last member of the Trojan royal family, who in Euripides' play *The Trojan Women* is about to be sacrificed in order to end the Trojan war caused by Helen's abduction from Greece by the Trojan Paris. Bersani's discussion of *Wuthering Heights* is thus placed in a context of inter-dynastic desire, aggression and succession. Adopting the Freudian/Lacanian view that individual identity is always constructed within the family, Bersani reads the novel in terms of how difficult it is 'to locate and define human identity' (p. 197). Unlike those critics who see *Wuthering Heights* as having 'universal' significance, Bersani argues that '*Wuthering Heights* provides a familial solution to the problem of identity because it is imprisoned within the familial imagination of the problem itself' (p. 203).

Bersani argues that 'the frenzy of *Wuthering Heights* is the result of Heathcliff's sudden appearance in the middle of a family whose members know who they are, where they came from, what they belong to' (p. 205). Despite the usual opinion, Bersani insists that Catherine is not 'like' Heathcliff – she is sociable, manic; he is closed, silent – and thus 'it is through Catherine's relation to Heathcliff that Brontë dramatizes most powerfully her children's exhilarating and terrifying confusion about what and where the self is in and beyond the family' (p. 204). Heathcliff's function in the novel is partly as a dream of sibling recognition, but partly as an exploration of the results of the absence of a 'mirrored self'. Bersani here draws on two aspects of Lacanian theory – the mirror phase and the 'fort-da game'.

The 'mirror-phase' marks the first stage of separation between the mother and child. Until the child sees its reflection in a mirror, or recognises the shape of another child or even the mother herself as analogous with his own, s/he has no concept of separateness from the world which includes the mother. For Lacan, the mirror-phase is important because it precedes language and 'adult' identity, but remains in our consciousness as a primitive memory of a blissful 'Imaginary' (image-based and illusory) identity with an 'other' who both is and is not ourself. Throughout our adult life we continue to look for metaphorical 'mirrors' to confirm our sense of who we are. The 'fort-da game' derives from an anecdote by Freud, who watched his two-year-old grandson lowering a cotton-reel on a piece of string, marking its disappearance and reappearance with the simple words 'fort!' (gone) and 'da!' (here). For Lacan this demonstrates that language appears to fill the gap left by the absent object. Putting these two theories together, Bersani argues that the mirror is also

■ a spatial representation of an intuition that our being can never be adequately enclosed within any present formulation . . . of our being . . . Thus, although it is ourselves we see in the mirror, the experience can paradoxically be considered as a model for our imagination of being very different from ourselves. *Wuthering Heights* represents the danger of being haunted by alien versions of the self. □

(p. 208)

Bersani insists on the unsuitability of the 'mirrors' Catherine tries: 'Heathcliff is so radically the other that he is almost the beastly or even the inanimate' (p. 210), and as for 'nature', although it is 'usually spoken about . . . as a richly humanizing experience', Bersani maintains that '*Wuthering Heights* dramatizes the potential eeriness, the dehumanization, of a closeness to the land or to nature'.

■ Death is the most appropriate metaphor for that radical transference of the self to another which Emily Brontë dramatizes in Heathcliff and Catherine . . . The 'glorious world' is death, an escape from the boring immortality of familial self-reflections . . . [But] the fate of all fascination with the self as the other – the fate of a radical open-endedness of being – is a kind of restless immortality. □

(pp. 211–12)

Margaret Homans, in 'Repression and Sublimation of Nature in *Wuthering Heights*' (1978), the first of several essays on Emily Brontë's novel, takes up Bersani's point about the destructiveness of nature. Pointing out that nature is hardly ever directly represented in this novel which appears to be 'about' nature, Homans argues that Emily Brontë chooses indirect methods such as metaphor or anecdote as a mode of repressing its threatening aspects. In 'Dreaming of Children: Literalization in *Jane Eyre* and *Wuthering Heights*' (1983), Homans adopts a more specifically Lacanian approach to the figurative language of the text. Lacan's theory that language 'stands in' for the absent object means that language is, inevitably, 'figurative'; his word for the whole system of language is 'the Symbolic'. Nevertheless, because of the process which Derrida calls 'deferral', language also gestures towards a 'literal' meaning where the signifier would be identical with the signified. Language requires that we have a concept of the 'literal' even though it is in practice impossible.

■ The literal both makes possible and endangers the figurative structures of literature. That we might have access to some original and final ground of meaning is a necessary illusion that empowers acts of figuration: at the same time, literal meaning would hypothetically be fatal to any text it actually entered, collapsing it by making superfluous those very figures, and even all language acts. That fatality is always, but never more than, a threat, since literal meaning cannot be present in a text: it is always elsewhere. □

Homans goes on to point out the implications of the fact that, according to Lacan, language is a substitute for the loss of a *female* body.

■ The literal, always (regrettably or fortunately) somewhere beyond 'our' grasp, poses special problems for women readers and writers, because the literal is traditionally classified as feminine . . . The feminine, seen from the point of view of a masculine culture, is, like literal meaning, always elsewhere. This dualism of presence and absence, of subject and object, and of self and other, structures everything thinkable, yet women cannot participate in it as subjects as easily as can men because the feminine self is on the same side of that dualism with what is traditionally other. Women who do conceive of themselves as subjects – that is, present, thinking women rather than 'woman' – must continually guard against fulfilling those imposed definitions by being transformed back into objects. □

(p. 255)

What for Freud is a 'masculinity complex' is for feminists, therefore, a necessary strategy for survival, and this is particularly the case in the context of a Romantic identification of woman and nature.

■ The literal is historically associated with nature, and nature, especially in the Romantic period and later, becomes the chief form of the literal against which women stage this defense. Comprising the literal ground itself, an elusive nature ultimately grounds all referents, and wherever the mind is classified as masculine, nature is the feminized object of imaginative projects. Nature's voicelessness and object status are real, but these qualities are falsely transposed onto women by a process in which a metaphor becomes a matter of belief; and the wish not to be mis-seen as object or as the absent literal, and to have one's own voice, must therefore often be formulated as a resistance to being identified with nature. That identification is inscribed in masculine texts but it is also internalized by the women readers of those texts: disguised as nature, the literal is the ultimate object of desire, and to identify with that might seem to offer women their only access to power. That power is illusory, however, and to accept that identification would be to abdicate from consciousness, to cease writing and speaking and instead be written and spoken. This abdication, where human figures are concerned, is always imaged as death: if literal meaning would be fatal to a text, to become the literal would be to die . . . *Jane Eyre* and *Wuthering Heights* explore this feminine danger primarily through two kinds of literalization: the Gothic literalization of subjective states and the circumstances of childbearing, in which what was once internal acquires its own objective reality. Although any link between these two situations may at first seem quite improbable, in both the heroine is in danger of becoming identified with the object world on which her subjectivity is projected. In the two novels both these forms of literalization are associated with dire and ambiguous events, and both represent particularly feminine concerns. □

(pp. 257–8)

Dreaming of children, therefore, is a defense against literalisation:

■ To remain a child, for both heroines, would be to avoid the possibilities of self-duplication risked in adult womanhood, either through becoming a feminine object or through bearing children. Cathy's 'I'm sure I should be myself' means exclusively being her childhood self, and later in the same delirium she identifies death with the recollection of childhood, independent of nature. □

(p. 272)

■ Nelly's expanding account of Cathy's death . . . omits any mention of the birth and stresses Cathy's reversion to memories of childhood . . . Her tranquil childishness seems incompatible with childbirth, and perhaps that is the point: being a child is Cathy's way of 'being myself', an assertion of self that makes us forget, temporarily, about the real child. If the baby takes away her identity as Catherine, the description of her as a child can momentarily displace the baby. Since her wish to be a child again includes a rejection of any adult role, including motherhood, it seems quite unfair that her wish to be a child should be fulfilled by her becoming a mother, but that is what happens: dying as she gives birth, she is released to become the ghostly child who appears to Lockwood. There may not, furthermore, be much difference between the two children she produces as she dies. The child is the mother, not of the woman as in Wordsworth's paradigm for maturation, but of the child, and in this sense the real child and the childhood to which Cathy yearns to return are the same. Her death in childbirth is perhaps a way of expressing the dangers of such regressive wishes; the baby is a literalized form of the childishness Cathy seeks, and it is fatal to her. Instead of a myth of growth or development of the self, Cathy's history images a destructive cycle of repetition. □

(p. 276)

Homans's conclusion demonstrates the difference between psychoanalytic readings which focus on the text and those which analyse fictional characters. Although Catherine Earnshaw is a bleak prospect as a role model, the text in which she figures has a different impact:

■ The very brutality with which the novel passes over Cathy's death becomes the text's necessary salvation: by having her represent the feminine danger and the end of figuration, it reasserts its own figure-making powers. These powerful women writers' experiments with literalization probe the psychic and imaginative dangers that it represents, and move on unscathed. □

(p. 279)

In Margaret Homans's book, *Bearing the Word* (1986), she returns to this theme and comes to rather a different conclusion; this argument will be discussed in chapter five.

Marci M. Gordon presses further than Homans in her insistence on motherhood as a moment of 'splitting' for the female psyche. In 'Kristeva's Abject and Sublime in Brontë's *Wuthering Heights*' (1988), Gordon aims to set up 'a dialectic between Kristeva's *Powers of Horror* and Brontë's *Wuthering Heights*' (p. 44). The feminist theorist Julia Kristeva uses the idea of the 'abject' – that which we throw out or disown from the body as unclean or improper – to reconsider the traditional Victorian madonna/whore dichotomy. Gordon argues that because (as Homans argues) women experience childbirth as self-division, if they speak of their own experiences of motherhood, what has traditionally been seen as 'sublime' will slide into the realm of the 'abject':

■ Kristeva's *Powers of Horror* provides the basis for a re-coding of the dichotomous angel/whore representation of women in Victorian fiction into a contiguous representation of abjection and sublimity . . . In order for the abject, with its dangerous blurring of boundaries, to be seen as the sublime, a woman . . . must be prevented from speaking of herself or writing herself into 'being'. □

(pp. 44–5)

Gordon points out that Catherine's scenes of verbal excess – her mad and death scenes – are succeeded by scenes of passive calm which Nelly is able to represent as sublime. Catherine's maternity, which in Kristevan terms is

■ 'something *horrible* to see at the impossible doors of the invisible . . . incest turned inside out, flayed identity . . . scorching moment of hesitation (between inside and outside, ego and other, life and death), horror and beauty, sexuality and the blunt negation of the sexual' . . . can only be glorious, joyful, when it is sublimated to death through discourse. □
(pp. 46, 56)

One of the dangers of using psychoanalytic theory in literary criticism is that it can seem that only the 'modern' tools of analysis can reveal the meanings which were 'invisible' to the original writers or readers. One refreshing aspect of Jay Clayton's book, *Romantic Vision and the Novel* (1987), is that he allows Emily Brontë to have a different vision from the modern theorists with whom he compares her. Clayton agrees that *Wuthering Heights* is a novel which self-deconstructs, but he is also impressed by its refusal 'to relinquish the possibility [of] a realm of pure or unmediated desire' (p. 100). His focus is on what many readers feel to be quite central to the novel – its love story:

■ 'Nelly, I *am* Heathcliff.' (Ch. 9)

This sentence may be the most famous expression of love in the whole course of the English novel. Catherine and Heathcliff call to mind the most notable romantic pairs in myth and literature: Orpheus and Euridyce, Romeo and Juliet, Tristram and Iseult. [Earlier in Clayton's book] this passage was compared with the visionary conclusion to Shelley's 'Epipsychidion', where the poet fervently declares that he will be united with his lover in one being: 'We shall become the same, we shall be one/Spirit within two frames'. The similarities between the two utterances are both numerous and striking, but there are differences to be noticed as well. Shelley's moment of union with his lover will come sometime in the future: the poetry is prophetic; the consummation, still to be achieved. In *Wuthering Heights* Catherine and Heathcliff seem to have already achieved a complete fusion of beings. Their union exists in the present: 'He's more myself than I am', Catherine says. 'Whatever our souls are made of, his and mine are the same' (*WH* p. 80).

The lovers' union seems to exist in the present; but if we look more closely, we discover that in fact it occurred in the past, and only in the past, for even as Catherine proclaims her oneness with Heathcliff she and her lover have begun to be two. She confesses her passion for Heathcliff only after the two of them have been separated by her actions . . . □
(p. 81)

(And here Clayton acknowledges that Miller makes this point in *The Disappearance of God* (pp. 170–9), discussed above in chapter two.)

■ Catherine's declaration of love attempts to recover a lost state of being even as it claims that this lost unity will endure for ever . . . Catherine and Heathcliff's tragic tale depends upon their being separated. □

(p. 82)

Clayton combines this idea with the idea that language 'figures' the lost object of desire:

■ The imagery of this speech is its principal claim to fame . . . But . . . figurative language is itself a sign of the distance Catherine has come from a literal union with her lover. Metaphor, comparison, and hyperbole are tropes that balance one thing against another, measure similarity and difference, and exaggerate beyond all proportion, in a linguistic to-and-fro utterly removed from the undifferentiated realms of visionary union. The very words that bind the figures together – 'like' and 'resemble' and 'as' – reveal the pressure on the terms to spring apart. In place of the perfect silence of *is*, we receive the compensatory beauty of *as*.

If this paragraph from Chapter 9 does not record a moment of Romantic union, where should one turn for an instance of this kind of visionary experience? . . . If we move backward in time from Catherine's already-compromised declaration of love, looking for a place in the text that records an authentic moment of union, we can locate nothing but a gap, a hole in the narrative beyond which the topic of union becomes prominent. □

(p. 83)

■ The representational void is so great that William Wyler, making his movie of *Wuthering Heights*, felt required to fill it both with a place – Peniston Crags, where the lovers meet even after their death – and with an action, a sexual embrace.

If the place in the text where the lovers come together is no more than an absence, a significant silence, the figures for their love are all-pervasive. This substitution of trope for topos (place or site where a theme is presented) is one of the characteristic dis-placements involved in figurative language . . .

What to make of this absence hidden by a figurative presence? We would be wise to consider whether the novel is asking us to assume a deconstructive stance toward its own story. □

(p. 84)

■ Criticism, like all reading, is up against a blank wall, because there is no final resting place for the reader in his or her restless movement from figure to figure. The search is for a 'center', a 'transcendental signified', to use Derrida's term, that would fix and confirm a single meaning . . . Miller's critical vocabulary inscribes the problem of transcendence within the traditional categories of presence and absence, an inscription that Wordsworth would not have objected to but which Shelley . . . abhorred . . . But one wonders if Derrida and Miller have not too narrowly conceived the problem. □

(p. 85)

Now Clayton begins his modest dissent from deconstruction, since 'Emily Brontë, like Shelley, suggests the possibility of turning the indeterminacy of a text to other ends' (p. 86).

■ Let us return to the gap in *Wuthering Heights* that is marked by the figure of Heathcliff's name. This sentence will provide a concrete example of how the process of displacement in a text can possess an alien or non-human power. The name 'Heathcliff' represents an especially vivid case of the alienation inherent in figuration. The boy christened with this figure is dispossessed of his old identity. Not only is this name imposed from without, it belonged to someone else to begin with. Thus the boy loses his individuality and is assimilated to a position within a flexible but inescapable system, that of the family. As a single word, both Christian and surname, it seems even less related to his individual being than usual names, a label denoting his 'place' within the sliding system of kinship. As a position, this place can apparently be filled by any orphan or child. At this point, however, we come upon a paradox. Although the arbitrary imposition of a name dehumanizes him, it also brings him within the fold of the family. To have a role, a place in a system, reduces one's individuality yet makes one a partner in the transpersonal endeavor of civilization. Naming, then, civilizes Heathcliff but only at the cost of alienation.

Jacques Lacan can help us some of the way toward understanding this particular paradox. One of the most intriguing aspects of his psychoanalytic theory is that he sees language as alienating, yet regards alienation as a crucial part of our humanity. For Lacan, the thing that makes us human is our acquiescence in the otherness of words, particularly in our adjustment to the symbolic dimension of names: 'That a name, no matter how confused, designates a particular person – this is precisely what the passage to the human state consists in. If we must define that moment in which man becomes human, we would say that it is at that instant when, as minimally as you like, he enters into a symbolic relationship'.[5] What Lacan calls the Name-of-the-Father plays a crucial role in this acquiescence to otherness, for it is this name, beyond all others, that teaches us the 'Law', a concept that has complex meanings in Lacan's writing but which for our purposes can be defined as the awareness that one must submit to a place or position within a system larger than oneself. Names teach this lesson by instructing us that people possess roles or functions that are independent of their biological identities. Hence names reveal the role of roles, the otherness that can and must exist within the self to make one a member of a human community.

The imposition of a name on Heathcliff, by exaggerating the paradox involved in becoming human, reveals how ambivalent Emily Brontë feels about the entire process. Just as important, it discloses that the problem of the other cannot be contained by the thematics of external possession. Emily Brontë and Lacan, in their very different ways, both believe that otherness exists *within* texts, whether written or lived. Yet Lacan's version of psychoanalysis can only take us so far in our discussion of *Wuthering Heights*. Emily Brontë parts company with Lacan's conception of textuality at the same point where she diverges with modern theories about indeterminacy, and it is by no means certain which of the three visions of textuality is the most profound. Emily Brontë refuses to take either the realistic stance of Lacan or the skeptical posture of Miller toward the otherness of the text. For her, the 'unreasonable' element within the reason that makes us human is, both for good and for ill, wholly apocalyptic.

The degree to which Lacan and Emily Brontë differ can be measured by considering how the former would analyze Heathcliff's rebellion against the values of civilization. Few novels have dramatized the revolt against society as a rejection of the Law of the Father more vividly than *Wuthering Heights*. Heathcliff's hatred of Hindley represents a rebellion against a father figure who is, as a figure, twice removed from biological paternity, for Hindley is not even the kind image of a father, Mr Earnshaw, who originally adopts the orphan. Heathcliff's violent resistance to civilization might be seen as a resistance to the otherness of language when it becomes an arbitrary system or form of Law. The arbitrariness of this system is brilliantly underlined by the novel, for Heathcliff learns to turn all the forms of society – all its laws – against the 'rightful', which is to say the hereditary or biological, owners of Wuthering Heights.

So far, Emily Brontë and Lacan's analyses of the situation would seem to agree. But their stances toward this kind of rebellion differ entirely. Lacan views such a rejection of civilization from the 'realistic' perspective of psychoanalysis, which regards the undoing of psychic structures solely as a form of regression. In Lacan's terms, Heathcliff remains fixed in the stage of the 'Imaginary', a word that seems particularly apt when applied to a character who lives in a world haunted by the ghost of his lover. The term seems even more on the mark when we note that the Imaginary stage, in Lacan, is the locus of the individual's aggressive impulses, which are expressed primarily in terms of jealousy or rivalry, and that it tends to organize the world in terms of certain simple, bipolar categories, including master-slave and ownership-dispossession. For Emily Brontë, however, the attempt to 'locate' Heathcliff's attitude toward the other within an account of individual development misses the point. Psychoanalysis's realistic approach to such phenomena domesticates the potentially apocalyptic force of otherness. In a radical perspective, the other has no 'place' within the human at all; it is the trace of a power that points beyond the human entirely.

Emily Brontë gives this power a name so familiar . . . that it is difficult for us to recover the negative or antithetical way in which she uses it. The word she chooses is 'Imagination', a term whose superficial resemblance to Lacan's 'Imaginary' can be made to uncover their diametrically opposed meanings. In Lacan's term we are meant to hear the root of 'image' . . . In Emily Brontë's . . . Imagination becomes an unfocused or unmotivated form of desiring . . . Imagination might be defined as the will-to-power over representation . . . and it is the power of this desire that drives the text in its endless displacements from image to image, figure to figure. □

(pp. 88–90)

The venerable term 'imagination' now becomes the focus for an original argument about the relationship between (linguistic) representation and what we take to be 'reality'. Before Catherine's 'capture' by the Grange, 'words were hardly necessary' for her and Heathcliff, but once she enters a 'love story' with Edgar, sh demands words of a kind which are 'the very thing that makes narrative representation vivid and engrossing'. It is her difference from the Lintons which requires description, and which introduces a division both between her and Heathcliff and within herself (p. 92).

■ By showing us the evil that results from imitating another, the novel introduces the topic of representation as one of its themes . . . As Emily Brontë makes clear, imitation sets up a division within the very thing it means to organize as a single unit. Thus the reader learns to trust those modes of existence that do not depend upon the process of imitation . . . This suspicion of representation contributes to our sense of the visionary quality of Catherine and Heathcliff's union. We continue to believe in the visionary existence of their bond . . . precisely because the bond itself has never been represented. □

(p. 93)

Clayton's position, rather like that of Matthews (discussed in chapter two), is that 'representation' and 'vision' are mutually dependent:

■ Emily Brontë . . . understands . . . that the prophet depends upon the very limitations and values that she challenges. But *Wuthering Heights* . . . reveals that the proper institution (or renewal) of the social side of desire depends upon the existence of an asocial, apocalyptic vision of desire. Just as the prophet relies on the legislator, the legislator requires a prophet. In *Wuthering Heights* the two characters are comprised and united in one. □

(p. 102)

An interesting corroboration of Clayton's position appears in Crystal Downing's article 'Hieroglyphics (De)Constructed: Interpreting Brontë Fictions' (1991). Like Clayton, and like Heather Glen, whose Introduction to *Wuthering Heights* is discussed in chapter four, Downing argues that *Wuthering Heights* does offer a version of what Derrida would call the 'transcendental signified' – the ultimate term which would halt the chain of meaning. The fact that Downing's article appears in the theoretical journal *Literature Interpretation Theory* (*LIT*) suggests that deconstruction is becoming less inimical to such 'visionary' readings.

Further corroboration is offered by Stephen Vine. David Sonstroem, in his 1971 essay, '*Wuthering Heights* and the Limits of Vision', argued that Emily Brontë 'presents wuthering as basic to almost all human experience' (p. 61). Stephen Vine gives us a poststructuralist version of this argument in 'The Wuther of the Other in *Wuthering Heights*' (1994). Referring to Terry Eagleton, Gilbert and Gubar, Carol Jacobs, Anne Mellor, J. Hillis Miller and Julia Kristeva, Vine argues that Kristeva's concept of 'delirium' provides a model for the novel's gesturing towards what cannot be represented. He points out that oscillation or 'wuthering' is a feature of Catherine's psyche, and it is in this context that he introduces Kristeva's theory of delirium:

■ Julia Kristeva describes 'delirium' as that discourse in which knowledge is disturbed by desire: a discourse in which 'a presumed reality' is reconstituted less as truth than as wish, and where 'the paths of desire ensnarl the paths of knowledge' . . . Yet delirium holds: it asserts itself to the point of procuring for the subject 'both *jouissance* and stability'.[6] Thus . . . Cathy is 'held' by the names or narrative identities that comprise her history in the text even though she exceeds each of these identities in turn and, eventually, plunges into the abysmally delirious *jouissance* that undoes her stability in illness. □

(pp. 356–7)

The Lacanian term '*jouissance*' means 'bliss', particularly that associated with the pre-linguistic bliss of identity with the mother. Because *jouissance* is manifested in scenes which 'exceed' normal figuration, Vine argues that

■ the air that 'swarm[s] with Catherines' could be said to figure *Wuthering Heights* itself as a text that contains two characters called Catherine . . . and in which the first Catherine passes through plural incarnations . . . Cathy's 'delirium', then, enacts the delirium of *Wuthering Heights* as a text that uncannily repeats, deforms, and exhumes its own earlier incarnations . . . □

(p. 358)

It is through her 'delirium' that Catherine escapes the limiting identification with her (one) other:

■ if, in her relation to Heathcliff, Cathy literalizes the narcissistic object of Romantic quest (troping herself as the image of Heathcliff's self-hood), she finally exceeds that identification, and all others, in the theater of alterities that comprises her history . . . Like the mystical female prisoner in Emily Brontë's poem 'The Prisoner (A Fragment)', Cathy's subjectivity is constituted in an excess in which 'visions rise and change that kill me with desire'.[7] Whether it is marked as ecstasy, illness, or death, this exorbitant desire rises and changes in *Wuthering Heights* in a visionary delirium that, like the text itself, broaches the unsymbolized. □

(p. 359)

CHAPTER FOUR

Sources, Discourses, Disseminations

CHAPTER TWO of this book was concerned with overall strategies for reading the text of *Wuthering Heights*, and chapter three with various theories about its 'unconscious'. This chapter will be concerned with what we might call the 'genealogy' of the text: theories about where the text came from and how it is related to other texts.

Biography

Victorian critics, as we have seen in chapter one, thought that information about the author of *Wuthering Heights* would provide a clue to its meaning, and this conviction persisted well into the twentieth century. One of its more bizarre results is the energy which went into proving that someone other than Emily Brontë had written the novel.

J. Malham-Dembleby, in 1911, 'proves' that Charlotte Brontë wrote *Wuthering Heights*, reading it as a diary of her love life. Far more commentators, however, thought that Emily's brother Branwell had a hand in its composition. Some, like Flora Masson (1912), read the book as 'Emily Brontë's weird and powerful interpretation of her drug-sodden brother' (p. 74); others, like Alice Law (1923) argued that Branwell actually wrote the novel. This theory originated with the Keighley teacher William Deardon who in 1867 published an account of a meeting he had had with Branwell about 1842, in which Branwell read some scenes from what was recognisably *Wuthering Heights*. Deardon's article was reprinted in *Brontë Society Transactions* in 1927, seemingly in response to Alice Law's 1923 biography of Branwell. Apart from the evidence of the reading, Deardon puts stress on the fact that 'the novel in question never could have emanated from the pen of a young female' (p. 99), and Alice Law takes up this point even more strongly:

■ It is well-nigh incredulous [*sic*] that a book so marvellous in its strength, and in the dissection of the most morbid passions of diseased minds, could have been written by a young girl like Emily Brontë, who never saw much of the world, or knew much of mankind. □

(pp. 104–5)

Law's conclusions are based on a picture of Emily's character which was widely held during the interwar period. The diary papers, Law argues, show Emily to be 'one of the helpers of the world, a lifter of other people's burdens . . . And yet it is this bright and brave creature, hating every species of depression, who is to be credited with the creation of the dark, hopeless, tragic story unfolded in the gloomy pages of *Wuthering Heights*' (p. 121). The myth of Emily as selflessly devoting herself to Branwell is extravagantly expressed in J. A. MacKereth's long poem, 'Storm-Wrack' (1927), in which 'She with frail enfolding arm/Shields that torn Brother-soul from harm' (p. 27); it also provided the theme for Dan Totheroh's stage play, *Moor Born* (1934). Kathryn MacFarlane (1936) reverses the devotion, describing Emily's 'adoration of the one who did most for her, meteoric brother Branwell' (jacket blurb), and this mutual self-sacrifice reaches its apotheosis in the Warner Brothers film, *Devotion* (1946).[1] Juliet Barker, in her 1994 biography, writes:

■ it is curious that Emily should ever have gained the reputation of being the most sympathetic of the Brontës, particularly in her dealings with Branwell, as all the evidence points to the fact that she was so absorbed in herself and her literary creations that she had little time for the genuine suffering of her family. Her attitude at [times] seems to have been brusque to the point of heartlessness. □

(p. 455)

Another preoccupation of the interwar period was with finding a biographical origin for the love story in *Wuthering Heights*. Since the known facts of Emily's life do not produce an obvious lover, ingenuity was exercised in discovering one. Keighley Snowden (1928) argues that Emily was in love with her father's curate, William Weightman, and Alexander Woollcott that she was in love with absence – 'a woman wailing for her demon lover' (pp. 213–14). Virginia Moore (1936) is well known for her hypothesis that Emily's lover was the apparent addressee of one of her poems, 'Louis Parensell' – which later proved to be Moore's misreading of the manuscript title, 'Love's Farewell'. Moore's alternative hypothesis is, however, even more striking: it was 'a girl or young woman, not a man . . . whom she loved' (p. 193). Reading *Wuthering Heights* as an autobiographical allegory, Moore concludes that 'Emily . . . is, without a shadow of doubt, Heathcliff' (p. 327). Somerset Maugham (1948) thought that Emily 'was' both Catherine and Heathcliff, and that she had a lesbian attachment to her sister Anne. In 1968 Margaret Lane lists the speculations – Emily had by now had incestuous relationships with Anne, Branwell and her father Patrick; and conclusions could be drawn from the unexplained silence of some months which followed her sudden departure from Law Hill school . . . ! (pp. 190–1). As late as 1993 Derek Roper still found it necessary to argue against the idea that a 'real' original could be found for Emily's lover.

Phyllis Bentley, herself a writer, adds a sensible note to this ferment in 1947 by recalling that Henry James had compared the mind of the novelist to

■ a cauldron of broth simmering on a hot fire. Into this cauldron, as morsels, the novelist throws his real experiences, and when he requires a character, a landscape, an incident, of course he dips into the cauldron and draws one out. But meanwhile the real experience, acted upon by the heat of the fire and the other ingredients of the broth, has become saturated with the essential stuff of the novelist's mind, has experienced therefore a chemical change . . . By this rare alchemy, says James, it is recreated; it ceases to be a thing of fact and becomes a thing of truth. □

(p. 62)

Literature and Culture

■ Neither Emily nor Anne was learned; they had no thought of filling their pitchers at the well-spring of other minds; they always wrote from the impulse of nature, the dictates of intuition, and from such stores of observation as their limited experience had enabled them to amass. □

(*WH* p. 366)

The tradition thus begun by Charlotte Brontë in 1850 was reinforced by the 'humanist' critics of the twentieth century. May Sinclair, in 1912, wrote that *Wuthering Heights*

■ stands alone, absolutely self-begotten and self-born. It belongs to no school; it follows no tendency. You cannot put it into any category. It is not 'Realism', it is not 'Romance' . . . You will not find in it support for any creed or theory . . . You may call her what you will – Pagan, pantheist, transcendentalist, mystic and worshipper of earth, she slips from all your formulas. □

(pp. 223–4)

Lascelles Abercrombie in 1924 spoke of 'this English provincial girl, who had nothing to rely on but her own genius' (p. 197), and Lord David Cecil, in 1934, says confidently that 'Emily Brontë's mode of expression shows almost as little mark of outside influence as her view of life. Only in a few minor aspects does she ever recall other writers. The effect she makes would be the same, one feels, if she had never read a book at all' (pp. 169–70).

But it was during this same time that the first serious studies of the composition of the novel were made. Leicester Bradner's article, 'The Growth of *Wuthering Heights*' (1933) was one of the first to understand the relevance of Emily's own poems to *Wuthering Heights*, particularly those relating to Gondal, the imaginary country she and Anne had invented in childhood, but which continued to provide poetic subjects until her death. Although Gaskell knew about Gondal, the inaccessibility of the poems had prevented scholars from paying them much attention; the first complete edition was produced only in 1923.[2] Bradner provides a summary of

■ the elements in all of Emily's poetry which may throw light on the genesis of *Wuthering Heights*. First . . . the poems about a doomed child show that the child grows up into a character like Heathcliff and they also show, in one poem, a forecast of the childhood love of Heathcliff and Cathy. In the A. G. A. poems we have the theme of sin and exile combined with the laments of the surviving lover for the one who is dead. In the much more important Julius group appear two characters who must, in the complete story, have been highly developed and individualized. Julius and Rosina were apparently both proud and intractable, like Heathcliff and Cathy. Rosina, like Cathy, causes trouble by her ambition; Julius, like Heathcliff, is beset with sin and a tyrannical spirit. Then comes Julius' death, followed by long years of life for Rosina during which the memory of her lover is always poignantly with her. Here, as in the A. G. A. poems, it should be noticed that it is the woman who survives and mourns the man. Though Emily put something of herself into the lovers of both sexes, it is usually the woman into whose mouth she puts her finest poetry and through whose feelings she can best express her grief for a departed lover . . . by the creating of these personages of her imaginary world and by the building up of careers full of passionate intensity for them she was unconsciously preparing herself for the writing of *Wuthering Heights*. □

(p. 136)

Madeleine Hope Dodds had made tentative attempts to reconstruct the Gondal story as early as 1923 and 1926, returning in 1944 to argue that the country to which Heathcliff vanishes during his absence from *Wuthering Heights* is in fact Gondal. The critic whose name became permanently associated with the Gondal saga, however, is Fannie Ratchford, whose book, *The Brontës' Web of Childhood* (1941), provided the first sustained account of the Brontë juvenilia and made the Gondal story available for the first time to a large audience. In her section on *Wuthering Heights*, however, Ratchford is generally content to list possible parallels with the novel's characters and incidents, with no attempt to suggest an overall ethos. *The Brontës' Web of Childhood* was written before the publication of C. W. Hatfield's *Complete Poems of Emily Jane Brontë* (1941), which prompted Ratchford to attempt a narrative arrangement of the poems which she called *Gondal's Queen: A Novel in Verse by Emily Jane Brontë* (1955).

Phyllis Bentley, in 1944, renders the fascination (and dismay) of critics who discovered that

■ When Emily was 'brushing the carpet' or Anne sewing or Charlotte learning to iron or Emily and Anne walking home from Keighley, their minds were far away; outwardly demure, reserved, well-behaved, Christian, inwardly they were conquering kingdoms, assisting at Councils of State, wielding arrogant power or tenderest love, and planning the stories, essays and poems in which they recorded these experiences . . . But what a terrible expenditure of energy these dreamworlds involved! Would the Brontës have died so young if they had not so exhausted themselves? □

(pp. 26, 29)

It was, however, Mary Visick who, in 1958, elaborated Bradner's suggestions for broad thematic parallels between the poems and *Wuthering Heights*, arguing 'that the poems and the novel represent two workings . . . of what is in effect the same story' (p. xi). Visick's book, *The Genesis of 'Wuthering Heights'*, ends with an appendix of Gondal–*Wuthering Heights* correspondences, and the argument proceeds by detailed comparison which makes it difficult to extract; a significant example is her comparison between the poems, 'No coward soul is mine' and Catherine's 'I *am* Heathcliff' speech in Chapter 9; the poem includes the words:

■   . . . O God within my breast
Almighty ever-present Deity
Life, that in me hast rest
As I Undying Life, have power in Thee . . .
Though Earth and moon were gone
And suns and universes ceased to be
And thou wert left alone
Every Existence would exist in thee . . . □

If, Visick comments, we set these lines next to Catherine's speech in Chapter 9 from 'I cannot express it' to 'as my own being', then 'we see what *Wuthering Heights* is "about". Catherine betrays what amounts to a mystical vocation, for social position and romantic love' (pp. 8–9). Edward

Chitham, in *The Birth of Wuthering Heights* (1998), devotes a chapter to the most detailed analysis yet of the process of 'adapting Gondal', in particular corroborating Visick's argument by showing that 'No Coward Soul' was written within weeks of Chapter 9 of *Wuthering Heights*.

The availability of Emily's poems also prompted critics to look for other poetic sources for *Wuthering Heights*, especially among the English Romantic poets who were writing during Emily's youth. Among those who speak of Emily Brontë's debt to Shelley are Bradby (1930), Hewish (1969), Gérin (1971), Pinion (1975) and Chitham (1978). In his 1987 biography of Emily Brontë, Edward Chitham argues that Emily was effectively in love with the poet Shelley, although she knew him only through his poems, and he died when she was a child. Shelley's intense love poem, 'Epipsychidion', is particularly relevant. The link with 'Epipsychidion' rests on Shelley's statement of what is sometimes called its 'twin soul' theme (discussed by Jay Clayton in chapter three). The title, which seems to mean 'song for the soul outside the soul', matches closely Catherine Earnshaw's conviction that 'there is or should be an existence of yours beyond you'.

My own 1996 article, however, points out that Shelley's 'Epipsychidion' is at least as well known for its manifesto of free love as it is for this 'twin soul' theme. Lines 149–59 read:

■   I never was attached to that great sect,
     Whose doctrine is, that each one should select
     Out of the crowd a mistress or a friend,
     And all the rest, though fair and wise, commend
     To cold oblivion, though it is in the code
     Of modern morals, and the beaten road
     Which those poor souls with weary footsteps tread,
     Who travel to their home among the dead
     By the broad highway of the world, and so
     With one chained friend, perhaps a jealous foe,
     The dreariest and the longest journey go. □

My argument, following from this, is that Catherine never intended to relinquish Heathcliff after her marriage to Edgar, and that what destroys her is their implacable hostility to one another, fuelled by ancient traditions of masculine rivalry going back to medieval tournaments:

■ **In her last meeting with Heathcliff she claims that 'you and Edgar have broken my heart, Heathcliff! And you both come to bewail the deed to me, as if you were the people to be pitied!' (*WH* p. 158). This speech can only be explained if we accept that while Catherine still relates to both her lovers, Edgar and Heathcliff have broken her heart** by defining love as exclusive.

Catherine's haunting of Heathcliff must now be read as her (unacknowledged) appeal against his failures of generosity. There is, after all, something in the haunting which the usual readings of the novel fail to explain. If the ghost of Catherine wails to be let in, and Heathcliff begs her to return, what is it that keeps them apart? It has seemed that the long-drawn-out separation could only be attributed to Catherine's wilfulness: 'By God! she's relentless', Heathcliff exclaims in his last speech (*WH* p. 334). But her apparent relentlessness may be only an effect of his own implacable obsession with revenge, which effectively shuts her out of his consciousness, even though she seems to be its motivation. □

(pp. 531–2)

■ The ending of the novel is notoriously ambiguous; Catherine and Heathcliff's ghostly 'walking' seems incompatible with Lockwood's final sentences about 'the sleepers in that quiet earth'. It is worth remembering, however, that the restless ghosts of 'Heathcliff and a woman' are seen by the 'country folks' – people who . . . would understand the prosecution of a grudge and appreciate Heathcliff's final possession of his 'woman' (*WH* p. 336). Moreover, it has been assumed that Lockwood in the churchyard describes these same two lovers. But Lockwood describes *three* headstones, and we know that Catherine, in the centre, wears a locket in which Heathcliff's hair is twisted together with Edgar's (*WH* p. 168). We may put what emphasis we will on the fact that this peaceful co-existence follows death, but the fact remains that 'the sleepers in that quiet earth' are not two but three. □

(p. 533)

As early as 1855 Matthew Arnold had recognised Emily Brontë's affinity with Byron; in 'Haworth Churchyard' he writes:

■ How shall I sing her? whose soul
Knew no fellow for might,
Passion, vehemence, grief,
Daring, since Byron died. □

James A. MacKereth, quoting these lines in 1929, comments that 'Emily Brontë plumbed depths and soared to heights that Byron could not dream of' (p. 176); but later critics have more soberly argued that Byron did influence Emily. Margiad Evans (1948), Rebecca West (1954), Ann Lapraik Livermore (1962), Winifred Gérin (1972), Judi Osborn (1990) and F. B. Pinion (1995) deal with different aspects of the Byronic inheritance. Dorothy Cooper (1952), Allan R. Brick (1959), Charles I. Patterson (1972),

Peter Widdowson (1972) and T. E. Apter (1976) are among those who have commented on other Romantic elements in Emily Brontë's work.

In chapter five we shall see that various political readings depend on the argument that *Wuthering Heights* is not 'influenced by' but instead reacts against, various 'canonical' texts. The most prominent of such arguments is that by Gilbert and Gubar (1979), who argue that *Wuthering Heights* is a feminist revision of Milton's *Paradise Lost*. Gilbert and Gubar are themselves arguing against Harold Bloom's theoretical book, *The Anxiety of Influence* (1973), which, they say, offers an exclusively masculine model of literary influence (Gilbert and Gubar p. 47). In his 'Introduction' to a 1987 collection of essays on *Wuthering Heights*, Bloom takes the opportunity to reply to Gilbert and Gubar:

■ I find it difficult . . . to accept Gilbert and Gubar's reading in which *Wuthering Heights* becomes a Romantic feminist critique of *Paradise Lost*, akin to Mary Shelley's *Frankenstein*. Emily Brontë is no more interested in refuting Milton than in sustaining him. What Gilbert and Gubar uncover in *Wuthering Heights* that is antithetical to *Paradise Lost* comes directly from Byron's *Manfred*, which certainly *is* a Romantic critique of *Paradise Lost*. *Wuthering Heights* is *Manfred* converted to prose romance, and Heathcliff is more like Manfred, Lara, and Byron himself than is Charlotte Brontë's Rochester.

Byronic incest – the crime of Manfred and Astarte – is no crime for Emily Brontë . . . so that *Wuthering Heights* becomes a critique of *Manfred*, though hardly from a conventional feminist perspective. The furious energy that is loosed in *Wuthering Heights* is precisely Gnostic; its aim is to get back to the original Abyss, before the creation-fall . . . which is neither sane nor possible, and which does not support any doctrine of liberation whatsoever.[3] □

(pp. 5, 7)

Irene Taylor, in her book, *Holy Ghosts: The Male Muses of Emily and Charlotte Brontë* (1990), also argues that Emily's work is best read in the context of the Romantic poets. Central to her account of the creative development of the Brontë sisters is the proposition that each of them 'created a male muse, a Holy Ghost – one that was partly, but only partly, the gender-reversed female muse of their male Romantic predecessors' (p. vii). This reading requires her to read Catherine and Heathcliff as 'not so much friends or lovers as they are male and female elements of a single being, fictional embodiments of the female artist and her muse' (p. 74). Although J. Hillis Miller, in *Fiction and Repetition* (p. 61), argues that 'the reader is nowhere given access to the generative unity from which the pair [is] derived', Taylor replies that 'that "origin" is not lost in Emily's poetry', which 'renders with great poetic richness the treasured content of memory, the maternal "Being" that is the object of her faith, and even the holy "Breath" that returns her to its presence' (pp. 74–5). Like Visick, she argues that

■ Emily's poetry provided most of what we need in order to understand the novel's metaphysical substructure: chiefly the idea of a woman's masculine element (the female artist's male muse) and her longing to reclaim him. The character Heathcliff is a diminished, human form of the divine spirit messenger who embodied the artist's creative energies and swept her back to her origins in the mother-world. □

(p. 77)

Ultimately, however, Taylor's reading of the novel is biographical: 'in this novel Emily depicts a struggle of her own, the competition within herself between the values of "ambition" and "fidelity"' (p. 91). 'Only love of the muse, of her own energies projected as a male messenger from the mother-world, could take her to her heaven' (p. 95), so that 'in permitting Charlotte to persuade her to join her sisters in the publication of their poems, Emily had in effect fallen into marriage with Edgar' (p. 97).

In contrast to Irene Taylor, who sees Emily Brontë as a female poet with a male muse, Anne K. Mellor insists on the masculine characteristics of Emily as a person and of her alignment with the Romantic poets. She also links the story of Catherine and Heathcliff with that of Byron's Manfred and his sister Astarte, and with Shelley's 'Epipsychidion' (p. 195). In the second generation story, however, 'by offering an alternative . . . to . . . erotic passion, Brontë registers her femaleness . . . her need to imagine *what is the best possible* for women who wish to survive, to bear children, to become mothers' (p. 205). She

■ remained a female in her enduring consciousness that the *body* determines one's options: to die – and thus enable the ultimate triumph of the body, the reabsorption of the self into nature – or to live and be socially constructed as a woman – a daughter, sister, wife or mother – and hence a dependent on patriarchal power. □

(p. 208)

Not all commentators saw poetry as the prime source of *Wuthering Heights*. Lew Girdler (1956) takes up comparisons made by several late Victorian critics to argue that Shakespeare was an important influence, identifying allusions in *Wuthering Heights* to *Twelfth Night*, *King Lear*, *The Taming of the Shrew* and *Hamlet*, but suggesting an overall similarity of character, plot, structure and theme.

Stevie Davies (1998), following an article by Robert K. Wallace, makes a persuasive case for Emily Brontë's musical sensibility. While she was in Brussels, Emily would have had the opportunity to hear symphonic works by Beethoven and Berlioz, and on her return she acquired an extensive anthology of orchestral music transcribed for piano, which she performed herself. Davies writes that the practice of transcription 'seems to me hauntingly appropriate to the symphonic compass of Emily Brontë's novel: a sense of cosmic reverberation confined in little space' (p.43). Arguing that *Wuthering Heights* is 'a musician's novel' (p.44), she goes on to analyse its '"score"' (p.47).

Grace Elsie Harrison, writing in 1948, provided the first extended analysis of Emily's religious background in *The Clue to the Brontës*; the 'clue' was the Wesleyan Methodism in which Patrick and Maria Brontë had both been brought up. Although Harrison's book is, in detail, inaccurate in the light of modern information, her demonstration that Haworth was at the very centre of eighteenth-century 'visionary' Methodism paved the way for many interesting links between this extravagant form of religion and the wilder aspects of *Wuthering Heights*. Ruth Adams (1958) is the first of a line of critics in *Nineteenth-Century Fiction*, including Edgar Shannon, Ronald Fine and William Madden, who were to investigate the Biblical text referred to in the Rev. Branderham's sermons. My own 1978 paper, 'The Brontës and Death', considers the Wesleyan inheritance in terms of Gramsci's theories of the intelligentsia, and argues that the Brontës' Methodism, outdated in the predominantly evangelical atmosphere of the 1840s, located them as 'traditional' rather than 'organic' or fully-integrated intellectuals. They were thus not radical or 'emergent' in Gramsci's terms, but not complicit with contemporary capitalist society, either. Expressions of quasi-religious 'transcendence' such as a longing for death could thus function as social resistance for speakers who had no access to revolutionary action.

In chapter five, I discuss the argument made in 1987 by the Marxist critic David Musselwhite, who points to the essays set as stylistic models for the Brontë sisters by M. Heger, their Belgian tutor, which obliged Emily to spend concentrated time reading and writing accounts of two notable revolutionary leaders, Mirabeau and Cromwell. The Belgian essays are thoroughly discussed by Sue Lonoff in her 1996 edition.

A more obvious source for *Wuthering Heights*, however, is the novelistic tradition. Wilbur Cross, in 1899, argues that 'the long vista of the purely Gothic romance, at whose entrance stands the blood-stained castle of Otranto, is closed by a storm and passion beaten house on the Yorkshire moors' (pp.166–7). Mary Ward (1900), Robin Gilmour (1983), Rose Lovell-Smith (1994) and F.B. Pinion (1996) are among those who make links between *Wuthering Heights* and the writing of Sir Walter Scott. Leicester Bradner, who began the serious consideration of the Gondal poems in 1933 (above), suggests for the first time the stories carried by *Blackwood's Magazine*, including the anonymous tale, *The Bridegroom of*

Barna, which has several similarities with *Wuthering Heights* including a scene where a bereaved man embraces the corpse of his dead lover. Bradner carefully reconstructs the sequence of Emily Brontë's reading, working on the new pattern of criticism established by John Livingston Lowes's *The Road to Xanadu* (1927), which reconstructed the literary origins of Coleridge's 'Kubla Khan'. Possible sources for the novel are later summarised by Jacques Blondel (1955), John Hewish (1969), Walter L. Reed (1974), Edward Chitham (1987) and Juliet Barker (1994).

Gilbert and Peggy Cross, in a somewhat exasperated article in 1970, patiently review all these possibilities (and others) and conclude that 'a source study should always be considered as a limited piece of criticism' (p. 415). Of Hoffmann's *Das Majorat*, they find it 'distressing . . . that a virtually unexamined theory can gain such a wide currency. Certainly there may be a link . . . but that adds nothing to our appreciation of *Wuthering Heights*'. Reminding us that 'a novel such as *Wuthering Heights* is the result of a very complex process', they entitle their article, 'Farewell to Hoffmann?'.

The problem with many source studies is that they look for correspondences at the level of plot or character. Edward Chitham, who in 1998 discusses 'the birth of *Wuthering Heights*' from a variety of angles, is concerned to discuss what shaped Emily's thought processes as well as her information, and it is from this point of view that he discusses his original discovery that Emily Brontë was competent to approach complex Latin texts with a sharp and inventive understanding of the processes of translation. Stevie Davies also approaches the question of 'What Emily Knew' in an expansive mode. In her 1998 book, Davies argues that the metaphors of affinity and dissolution in *Wuthering Heights* suggest that Emily knew Humphry Davy's *Elements of Chemical Philosophy* (1812), which her father owned (p. 71), and in *Emily Brontë: Heretic* (1994) she argues that Emily knew and was consciously influenced by German Romanticism not via poetry and novels but directly through philosophical essays and English review articles in *Blackwood's Magazine* (p. 50). In her latest book (1998) she summarises these influences:

■ through the 1820s–1840s, de Quincey, Carlyle and Emerson worked to popularize its avant-garde ideas: dualist and dynamic idealist philosophy (Schelling and Schlegel); emphasis on the infinity of the 'world within', the night-world and the 'love-death' (Novalis); the pathology of 'split personality' (G. H. Schubert), with its electrifying effect on Hoffmann; the distinction between conscious and unconscious minds; the concept of 'Romantic irony'; the recreation of folk poetry and the *Märchen*, or folktale, as significant literary forms. These concepts would confirm Emily Brontë's binary mental world, at the stressful conjunction of idealism and realism. □

(pp. 48–9)

Davies concludes that:

■ As a work of **Romantic rebellion**, *Wuthering Heights* takes **Promethean** issue with human limitation, whilst earthing its thunder and lightning in substantial realism and bracing it in a system of attraction and repulsion, with its roots in science. □

(p. 76)

Myth

An 'influence' on *Wuthering Heights* which had been noted from the beginning was that of the landscape, and after the institution of the Brontë Society in 1893, the Haworth-based *Brontë Society Transactions* in particular carried a number of articles about the relationship between the novel and its geographical setting. These include Halliwell Sutcliffe (1903), T. W. Hanson (1924), Hilda Marsden (1957 and 1991), Paul Simpson-Housley *et al.* (1989) and Christopher Heywood (1993). Swinburne, writing in 1883, elevated the landscape to mythic proportions, claiming that Catherine's mad scenes, which surpass even Ophelia's,

■ could never have been written by any one to whom the motherhood of earth was less than the brotherhood of man – to whom the anguish, the intolerable and mortal yearning, of insatiate and insuppressible homesickness, was less than the bitterest of all other sufferings endurable or conceivable in youth. □

(p. 441)

James A. MacKereth, a Yorkshireman writing in 1929, borrows Brontëan similes to make his point:

■ A townsman inside the walls of his own making, who has forgotten the great skies, the grand spaces littered still with the rock-ruins of old chaos, or coated with the primal heath, can no more know a genius born of these than a mouse can know an eagle, or a tadpole the 'Great White Whale'. To know a Heathcliff, or a Captain Ahab, we must . . . clothe ourselves with the elements primordial and elemental. □

(p. 179)

If *Wuthering Heights* has this intimate relation to the landscape, it follows that its expression should derive from 'earthy' sources. G. D. Klingopulos, in 1946–47, sees in the novel 'a level of experience which does not often come into the world of letters. It is a quality of suffering: it has anonymity. It is not complete. Perhaps some ballads represent it in English . . . It is found amongst genuine peasants and is a great strength' (p. 285).

Q.D. Leavis (1969), Katherine Ankenbrandt (1969), Terence McCarthy (1979), Sara E. Selby (1988) and Michael Grosvenor Myer (1988) have discussed the extent to which *Wuthering Heights* is indebted to actual ballads such as Scott's 'The Mother Beneath the Earth', the song sung by Nelly Dean in Chapter 9. Edward Chitham (1986) has written of *The Brontës' Irish Background*, which included oral ballads, and in 1987 also, he points out that 'Emily's grandfather was a ballad-singer and a story-teller'; the tales of Angria were in effect practice in ballad-making (p. 188). 'The fabric of' *Wuthering Heights* itself, he insists, 'is oral' (p. 199).

Sheila Smith (1992) uses the traditional ballads in the novel to reach the same conclusion as Jay Clayton (discussed in chapter three, above) about the imagination, but in the context of political readings. (Terry Eagleton's essay to which she refers is discussed in chapter five.)

■ In *Wuthering Heights* imagination, in the supernatural manifestations, *is* insight, as against the cloudy perceptions of reason and orthodox morality. [Emily Brontë's] version of reality challenges the materialistic, class-ridden structure of the society of 1847, as Arnold Kettle and Terry Eagleton have suggested. But as Q.D. Leavis maintains that the allusions to fairy-tales in the novel are a sign of immaturity, so Eagleton argues that the supernatural is a weakness in the book, that Emily Brontë makes a 'metaphysical' challenge to society, but can do this 'only by refracting it through the distorting lens of existing social relations, while simultaneously, at a 'deeper' level, isolating that challenge in a realm eternally divorced from the actual'. But, as I have tried to show, the novel's power lies in Emily Brontë's perception of the supernatural as an essential dimension of the actual, and this theme, central in ballad and folk-tale, is expressed by techniques which can be related to those of ballad and folk-tale. She uses the supernatural in her narrative to give direct, dramatic, and objective expression to the strength of sexual passion, as so many of the ballads do. It was this directness which so shocked Emily Brontë's first readers [but also what led Swinburne to call *Wuthering Heights*] a poem . . . For 'poem' read 'ballad'. □

(pp. 516–17)

Elliott B. Gose, Jr (1966) sees Emily Brontë's novel as based on at least four mythic patterns,

■ stemming from the fairy tale, . . . religion and the Bible, . . . traditional elements of nature, . . . [and the] process of initiation . . . All are based on a parallel opposition and reveal the same theme – the difficulty experienced by the psyche in its attempts to realize itself under the pressures of its surroundings. □

(p. 2)

The 'parallel oppositions' are to do with fire: 'the fire from the hearth we have seen to be associated with weak, childish characters . . . The fire from within is associated with those who have learned to be self-sufficient' (pp. 9–10). Nelly, however, represents the positive associations of the hearth, and her 'fruitfulness' (she is often seen carrying apples and oranges) 'has connections with the patterns of initiation, the Bible, and fairy tales' (p. 15). Catherine and Hareton, then, have a chance of re-capturing, under the guidance of Nelly Dean, the 'enchantment, heaven, nourishment' which 'all the children in the novel have sought . . . in front of the fire' (p. 19).

Stevie Davies, in the first of four books on Emily Brontë (1983), argues that *Wuthering Heights* is based on a myth of rebirth and return. Q. D. Leavis (1969) has a whole appendix concerning the tradition about the pigeon feathers in Catherine's 'mad' scene in Chapter 12, and William H. Scheuerle (1975) has also commented on it, but Davies relates this haunting scene to the myth of Cupid and Psyche, where Psyche has to sort a huge pile of seeds. In both cases,

■ pointless 'baby-work' leads, as in all great structuring myths, to rediscovery, reunion and return in a changed form to an earliest truth with which we are finally able to deal.

The legend of Psyche is an allegory of the soul's expulsion, quest and reunion with the beloved. *Wuthering Heights* . . . is an original myth of loss, exile, rebirth and return. It has the self-contained and opaque quality of all myth. It imagines the human soul as being female, seeking a lost male counterpart. □

The search is not, Davies argues, incestuous or sexual but 'metaphysical and "human" in the largest sense' (p. 97). Analysing the feather scene in detail, she goes on,

■ Someone has made this pillow, the paranoid's 'they' . . . [Catherine] takes what 'they' have fabricated to pieces and restructures it; traces the finished (dead) product back to its living sources . . . The task, like Psyche's, is not in any way viable unless the riddle can be solved, the code broken, which explains the system in which we all grow. □

(pp. 99–100)

The birds who lie behind the feathers are both symbolic and real, and the symbols are local and general; just as the story about the nest of lapwings who die when their mother is prevented from feeding them figures the exposed orphans in the novel, so 'the world is a system for orphaning the young . . . killing mothers; undoing twins' (p. 103). Davies relates this 'symbolism' to the structure of the novel:

■ At the very centre of the whole novel, Catherine suffers, dies and gives birth. If we take a radius from that point, we encompass the whole novel, so that the structure is a perfect circle. Like the great myths of antiquity, *Wuthering Heights* presents us not only with a story of rebirth but also with a myth of return. The narrative at once presses forward and doubles back to its source. □

The 'Hareton' of the beginning leads to the 'Hareton' of the end. The novel is full of repetitions and recapitulations: it is 'not so much about individuals as about humanity . . . in the person of the female', offering 'a female vision of genesis . . . the child as mother of the woman' (pp. 103–5).

In this system, Heathcliff is the 'cuckoo in the nest' who upsets the symmetry and harmony, but beneath Catherine's death and Heathcliff's loss 'is revealed a buried principle of a benign though pagan shaping-out of a destiny that is ultimately fruitful and kind' (p. 109). Maintaining the bird-imagery of her argument, Davies instances the ring ousels – known as good and co-operative parents – who build a nest next to the bereaved Heathcliff. Heathcliff is ultimately 'an instrument of regeneration and of harmonious balance between eternal oppositions' (p. 111). His blood on the tree is like a pagan rebirth ritual; as he grieves among larches on the night of Catherine's death, so the child born on that night 'grew like a larch', as if, Davies argues, he 'has given up some of his life to her' (p. 113).

In startling opposition to Davies's beautifully consoling reading of the novel is Georges Bataille's essay in *The Literature of Evil* (1957):

■ the moral significance of the revolutionary nature of [Emily Brontë's imagination] is the revolt of Evil against Good. Formally it is irrational. What does the kingdom of childhood, which Heathcliff demoniacally refuses to give up, signify if not the *impossible* and ultimate death? . . . Heathcliff . . . represents a very basic state – that of the child in revolt against the world of Good. □

(pp. 154–5)

Catherine, however,

■ is absolutely moral . . . so moral that she dies of not being able to detach herself from the man she loved when she was a child . . . Evil, therefore . . . is not only the dream of the wicked: it is to some extent the dream of Good . . . *Wuthering Heights* has a certain affinity with Greek tragedy . . . The tragic author agreed with the law . . . but he based all emotional impact on communicating the sympathy which he felt for the transgressor . . . The lesson of *Wuthering Heights*, of Greek tragedy and, ultimately, of all religions, is that there is an instinctive tendency towards divine intoxication which the rational world . . . cannot bear.

This tendency is the opposite of Good. Good is based on common interest which entails consideration of the future. Divine intoxication, to which the instincts of childhood are so closely related, is entirely in the present. In the education of children preference for the present moment is the common definition of Evil. □

(pp. 156–7)

■ The road to the kingdom of childhood . . . is thus regained *in the horror of atonement*. The purity of love is regained in its ultimate truth which . . . is that of death. Death and the instant of divine intoxication merge when they both oppose the intentions of good, which are based on rational calculation. □

(p. 158)

Patricia Dreschel Tobin makes a similar point in a less dramatic way in '*Wuthering Heights*: Myth and History, Repetition and Alliance' (1978). Referring to a point made by both Dorothy Van Ghent and by Wade Thompson, Tobin argues that in *Wuthering Heights*, 'the adults of the first generation are the children, and the children of the second generation are the adults'. Tobin sees Catherine and Heathcliff as representing mythical, not historical man: 'Because we cannot trace the descent of the historical from the mythic . . . we sanctify the two lovers at the very moment we expel them from the story time' (pp. 39–40).

Nancy Armstrong (1992) puts the question of time in the context of industrialisation: 'the new sense of time produced a rupture in ordinary life between one setting, where the body belonged to "society", and another, where it belonged to oneself – an irreparable rupture, that is, between social and subjective life' (p. 434). Armstrong points out, however, that the 1840s were precisely the time when 'folklore' was being collected and classified; 'folklore', then, is not the 'mythic' voice of non-social being, but one of the ways in which people were being organised to 'keep time' .

Dialogue

Reading through the abbreviated accounts of the 'source studies' in this chapter may give the impression that *Wuthering Heights* is a cacophony of literary allusion, but Robert Kiely could write in 1972 that

■ It is part of the distinction of *Wuthering Heights* that it has no 'literary' aura about it . . . Emily Brontë does not go out of her way to call attention to the fact that what she is presenting has been written down and must necessarily be comparable to other things which have been written down. □

(pp. 233–4)

The nature of the 'influence' of previous writing is difficult to define, especially given the variety of identified possibilities and the 'non-literary' quality which Kiely describes. Critics agree that the 'influences' merge: '*Wuthering Heights* is like dream *and* like life *and* like history *and* like other works of literature precisely because Brontë rejects the exclusiveness of these categories. They continually inform and define one another' (p.236). An over-insistence on 'plurality' or 'all-inclusiveness' of influences, however, leads to a position analogous to the humanist's 'harmonising' of interpretations, discussed in chapter two.

One fruitful response to this difficulty is via Mikhail Bakhtin's theory of 'dialogism'. Bakhtin, writing in Russia in the 1920s, saw literary texts as constructed from different 'discourses' in dialogue with one another. Where formalists see works of art as self-contained unities, Bakhtin insists that meaning always depends on context because language itself is 'dialogic' – uttered in response to a previous utterance and expecting a subsequent reply. Peter K. Garrett uses Bakhtinian ideas to analyse *Wuthering Heights* in *The Victorian Multi-Plot Novel* (1980). Rehearsing all the structural forms of 'doubleness' in the novel, Garrett concludes that traditional attempts to harmonise differences are misguided, whereas

■ To consider *Wuthering Heights* and other Victorian multi-plot novels as dialogical forms requires us to follow the movement in which meaning is continually produced and effaced. To read them in this way is not to claim mastery of their complexity or to unmask their latent contradictions but to continue the process of setting one perspective against another in which the novels themselves are already engaged, a process which the conventions neither of narrative nor of critical argumentation ever bring to more than a provisional conclusion. □

(pp. 20–21)

Heather Glen, in her 'Introduction' to the 1988 Routledge edition of *Wuthering Heights*, offers some thoughtful comments on this problem. She begins by posing the contradiction between those readings of the novel which find in it 'universal' meanings, and those which find 'local' or particular meanings. The 'universal' readings have, as we saw in chapter two, persisted throughout the novel's history, despite apparently opposing critical movements such as formalism, poststructuralism and, as we shall see in chapter five, various political readings which place the novel in particular contexts of class, race and gender. Glen concludes that the novel itself 'demands' such 'universal' readings:

■ There is, then, a sustained and central emphasis in *Wuthering Heights* on that which is most resistant to socio-historical transformation: on the unchanging laws of the natural world; on those facts of human experience – individual separateness and death, the primary need for a relation beyond the self – which seem most fundamental and most enduring. It is clearly this emphasis which has led even avowedly historicist critics to speak of this novel in essentialist and universalist terms. And it appears to be this which has caused generations of readers in widely differing times and places to find in it a peculiarly direct articulation of concerns which they too most intimately share. The novel has thus come to seem, like its subject-matter, in some peculiar way outside history, speaking timelessly from and to a universal shared dimension of human experience.

Yet it is precisely a work such as this, which has seemed so readily and continuingly accessible, that most requires that leap of the historical imagination which can recognize it as other, foreign, shaped by and responsive to historical and cultural experiences rather different from those of its multifarious readers . . . And it is precisely that aspect of the work which has led to the view that it is concerned with a common, transhistorical human condition which most requires historical understanding. For it is only by seeing this in its historical specificity that we can cease to assimilate it to our own unexamined categories: only thus will we be able to move beyond the revelation that the novel affirms and speaks for what everyone already knows – 'spiritual essence', 'a necessary experience of what it is to be human', 'life as such' – and begin to discern its precise and distinctive import, that in it which might enlarge or unsettle, rather than confirm, what 'we' take for granted.

But how can we make such a leap of the historical imagination? . . . It is through the language in which it is framed that *Wuthering Heights* most intimately reveals its implication in and engagement with history. And it is by examining its language that we can begin to understand more clearly the nature of that engagement. ◻

(pp. 12–14)

Glen illustrates her argument by referring to one of the essays Emily Brontë wrote at school in Belgium. It is called 'The Butterfly', and presents 'all creation' as 'equally insane', since 'every creature must be the relentless instrument of death to others, or himself cease to live' (Glen p. 16). The argument is concerned with 'timeless' topics, yet it clearly derives from the Darwinian anxieties of Emily Brontë's own time. The same can be said of *Wuthering Heights*:

■ Emily Brontë is indeed concerned with that in human experience which seems to be universal and unchanging. But it appears in her novel less in unproblematic, unmediated form than through the prism of a whole constellation of quite specific early Victorian discourses, each of which carries its own distinct and distinctive resonances, implications, and senses of possibility within it. The disjunctions between these different discourses are not, as in 'The Butterfly', awkwardly apparent; they coexist with and contradict one another in often quite unobtrusive ways. Yet the tense, ambiguous interplay between the different mentalities they embody is central to the novel.

To isolate and separate these discourses, which in *Wuthering Heights* are interwoven and combined and juxtaposed in many different ways, is inevitably a rather schematic exercise. None is a simple or monolithic language; each has many different early-nineteenth-century inflections; each is in the novel far more richly and concretely represented, in its social manifestations and implications, than are those philosophical views of 'nature' which are entertained in 'The Butterfly'. To describe even one in a way that did justice to all its contemporary multi-facetedness would take a good deal more than the space of this essay. Yet merely to be aware of their presence – to recognize that the language of *Wuthering Heights* is not timeless and unitary, but historically shaped and multi-dimensional – is to begin to see something of the distinctive way in which Emily Brontë is exploring those 'universal' and 'eternal' human truths which she is all too often seen as unproblematically affirming. □

(pp. 17–18)

As examples of separable 'discourses', Glen instances three:

■ Each of these discourses – of Methodism, of romanticism, of a long-established rural way of life – embodies a culturally and historically specific set of responses to the apparently universal and unchanging human experiences of living within a non-human world, of love, and of death. Each is differently, and centrally, preoccupied with the clash between subjective aspirations and desires and the fact of an objective reality: an experience equally pressing for the believer imprisoned in a sinful world, for the speculative intellectual faced with individual mortality, for men and women farming an unresponsive landscape. Such languages might, and did, in practice interconnect with one another; they might in different combinations enter into the mental universe of a single individual (Tabitha Aykroyd, teller of old Haworth tales, was also a 'joined Methodist'). Certainly, in *Wuthering Heights* they intertwine in complex ways: they cannot be neatly separated, or simply attributed to different characters. (Nelly Dean, for example, seems to move between all three.) Yet, equally, they cannot be seen as blending, unproblematically, into a harmoniously univocal vision. Indeed, much of the disturbing life of the novel comes from the tensions and the contradictions between them.

For each embodies a mentality which in quite crucial respects conflicts with that which is assumed by the others. □

(p. 28)

To emphasise the peculiarity of *Wuthering Heights* in this respect, Glen compares the novel with those of another, contemporary, woman writer: 'Mrs Gaskell too, writes of love, of death, of nature'. In her work, however, these tropes offer resolution or escape from social problems;

■ similar tropes may be found in most Victorian social-realist novels. But in *Wuthering Heights* that which is here seen through the prism of an unexamined ideology becomes radically, centrally problematic. Nature, love, and death are present not as offering resolution of or liberation from socio-historical conflict, but as bearing subtly or sharply conflicting socio-historical meanings. And the tensions and contradictions between those meanings pose a wholly different set of questions to the world of mid-Victorian England than does Mrs Gaskell's social protest.

Emily Brontë does not turn away from the 'historical' to deal with the 'universal'. Rather, her concern with the 'universal' – as revealed in her complex reworking of those mid-Victorian discourses through which it was most powerfully mediated – is far more intimately, intelligently historical than that of her contemporaries. It is as we become alert to this that we can begin to see that what she offers is not just a vague affirmation of the primacy of the elemental in human experience, but a searching interrogation of what it might mean. In taking this seriously, as the central subject of her novel, we may arrive at a clearer understanding, not merely of the particular and searching question towards which it is pointing, but also of the continuing challenge those questions present to the terms of our own thinking – of the ways in which, to borrow the words of her sister Charlotte, Emily Brontë's imagination may be 'in advance' of ours in travelling its 'different road'. □

(pp. 31–2)

Michael Macovski's 1987 essay deals with the ways in which the discourses of the novel offer themselves for interpretation. Macovski argues that the novel itself 'foregrounds the act of interpretation', not only by the device of 'a framed succession of interpreters' but also by framing 'the two climactic exchanges in which Heathcliff and Catherine respectively describe their preternatural union to Nelly . . . within the context of sustained audition' (pp. 364–5). Referring to the lengthy debate, discussed in chapter two, about the 'limits of vision' created in *Wuthering Heights* by its 'unreliable narrators', Macovski 'ultimately reject[s] the notion that

Brontë leaves us only with circumscribed vision and misinterpretation', arguing instead 'that the novel continually keeps the possibility of interpretation open *by sustaining a rhetorical process of understanding*, by enacting a series of hermeneutic forms' (p. 368).

Macovski identifies in the novel a series of 'narrative exposures' corresponding to the forms of confession (as theorised by Michel Foucault), psychoanalytic transference (as identified by Freud and Lacan) and dialogue (in the Bakhtinian sense discussed above, in relation to Peter Garrett). All of these situations, involving a speaker and a listener, are also processes of 'self-creation' (p. 368), so that 'self-affirmation in *Wuthering Heights* is literally the articulation of the self to the other' (note 15). It follows, he goes on, quoting Bakhtin, that '"the most important acts constituting self-consciousness are determined by a relationship towards another consciousness"', so that (quoting Emily Brontë), 'dialogue with the "existence . . . beyond" enacts the ego' (p. 375). The 'other' of dialogue 'can also manifest itself collectively as . . . "society"' (p. 376), Macovski argues, so that 'Bakhtin's discussions of the dialogic consciousness of self thus serve to clarify Brontë's concepts of existence and social intercourse' (p. 377).

John P. Farrell (1989) takes up Macovski's point about the social aspects of dialogue, arguing that successive social discourses do not altogether supersede one another but persist in a kind of muted dialogue.[4] 'The text as palimpsest is a key term for order in the novel', Farrell argues. A 'palimpsest' occurs literally when one manuscript is written over the top of another, like Catherine's diary or Heathcliff's calendar, but metaphorically 'we can see this phenomenon in many ways' – for instance in seeing the facial characteristics or patterns of behaviour of one person imprinted on another. What Farrell calls the 'lamination of texts' can also be seen at the level of the plot, where the second generation is 'superimposed upon the first'.

■ *Wuthering Heights* is thus calculated to make all our reading multiple by presenting us with a pleating of texts . . . The novel's symbolic code of doors, locks, windows, keys, and gates has as its primary reference not so much anything beyond the text as the text itself that we are trying to unlock and penetrate. □

(pp. 174–5)

An example of this is when Catherine talks to Heathcliff 'through the boards' (*WH* p. 59). In analysing these related phenomena, Farrell also appeals to Bakhtin, for whom

■ discourse forms itself as a drama of voices. Sedimented or layered, it is volatile in its unity and tinctured by the concrete sociohistorical context in which expression must occur. . . .

Catherine's poetic discourse, Joseph's unintelligible muttering, Lockwood's superior tone, Heathcliff's verbal violence, Nelly's homiletic rhetoric, and the talk of all the other characters constitute distinctive accents of identity. Everyone is speaking in dialect. At the same time, the interplay of these accents and idioms forms the 'dialogical hetero-glossia' that Bakhtin sees as the primary script of the social world. □

(p. 176)

It is here that Farrell arrives at the theme of his essay, which is entitled, 'Reading the Text of Community in *Wuthering Heights*'. Citing 'the vignette of Joseph with his Bible and his dirty bank-notes', he argues that one of these texts offers

■ a perfected social order, one of them a contaminated social order . . . Brontë makes a distinctively Victorian effort to distinguish between the text of society and the text of community . . . this point . . . supplies, in part, the contemporary intellectual and ideological context from which *Wuthering Heights* has so often been pointlessly severed. □

(p. 177)

Farrell posits as relevant to *Wuthering Heights* the contrasted social orders represented by *Gemeinschaft* and *Gesellschaft*: 'an individual . . . belongs to community or *Gemeinschaft* presumptively. In society or *Gesellschaft*, relations between people are engineered by contract, formal conventions of behavior, and remote institutional forces' (pp. 178–9).

Farrell extends this contrast to cover what is sometimes easily referred to as 'the community of readers'. We must not, Farrell argues, neglect 'the cultural and social identity' of readers, since '*Wuthering Heights* is itself concerned precisely with the problem that readers, as well as texts, are polyphonic'. In general, 'narrative discourse may address three quite different figures . . . a character in the novel . . . the implied reader . . . and the actual reader' (pp. 180–1). In *Wuthering Heights*, the

■ astonishing discrimination of idiolects . . . layering of time . . . [and] patterned repetitions of plot . . . attribute to the implied reader an attentiveness, cooperativeness, and skill in performance that is both temperamentally and politically beyond Lockwood's scope. If the text finally consigns its Lockwoodian reader to the world of cash-nexus, it regards its performing reader as one capable of communal nexus. □

(p. 184)

Farrell also interestingly extends his reading to cover the (inaccessible) 'real' reader who, he argues, is analogous to the (inaccessible) 'truth' of the novel:

■ Our experience as performing readers is . . . fraught. We can *almost* see Catherine and Heathcliff, and yet we *cannot*. We are compelled to remain within the decorum of the novelistic text, and though we may desire to get to essences, our performance depends on dialogism . . . we can only locate the transcendent identities of Catherine and Heathcliff by analogy with the charmed point on the horizon of consciousness at which we locate the 'real reader' in ourselves. For the 'real reader' is the hypostatized self behind our performance, the self that is, mysteriously, separate from the world of signs and deeply schooled in the same lush desires that make Catherine and Heathcliff both magnificent in our eyes and quite beyond our ken. □

(pp. 191–2)

Farrell then turns his attention to the ending of the novel:

■ the novel maintains its heteroglossia and refuses to be reduced to a unitary statement . . . Lockwood's rhetorically ambivalent epitaph . . . supplies what Bakhtin would reject as a 'finalizing frame of reality'.[5] Brontë's dialogic text typically moves against finalizing frames. *Wuthering Heights* has three other endings that are all superimposed over Lockwood's safely elegiac disposal of the dead. In the first of these endings, Catherine and Heathcliff are emancipated from the novelistic text and assimilated to the moors and to the folklore of the country people. They are situated in a spoken discourse that the novel has always respected as a medium where echoes of the ineffable self may be heard. This self is legendary. Cathy and Hareton, in reverse direction, return from a ramble on the moors to the house where they will await their marriage and begin their restoration of the social environment . . . They alone volunteer for the 'dialogic *concordance* of unmerged twos . . . '[6] The third ending occurs when Lockwood drops his desacralizing coin into Nelly's hand. He re-objectifies Nelly and materializes the act of story-telling . . . he has returned to the *Gesellschaft* that owns him.

These are the conclusions of the novel's entwined stories, each depending on a distinct language of identity that Brontë's text has addressed to the striated self of its reader. But we, of course, don't hear these endings as separable languages. The work of the whole novel has been to cross boundaries, to recognize, as Bakhtin insists we do, the simultaneous discourses that operate in all our enterprises. The language of community cannot unfold except in relation to the language of society and the language of the self. □

(pp. 199–200)

Farrell's dialogic reading does, however, offer an explanation for the 'metaphysical' aura of the novel:

■ Like Hareton and Cathy, the narrator and implied reader volunteer for the dialogic concordance of unmerged twos . . . but, ultimately, our desire is for the unfathomable figure who has created not only our partner but the allegory itself. *Wuthering Heights* is expressly written to leave not a trace of this figure in the text. There is no biographical author peering at us around the corner of the narrative discourse . . . Emily Brontë is, at best, a specter. She is the partner of the 'real reader', a being who has no being as far as the text is concerned . . .

Nevertheless, we hypothesize an Emily Brontë somewhere behind the narrator Ellis Bell. This 'Emily' is a project of the reader's self-intuition, a corresponding partner for the self beyond roles and beyond text that centers the Romantic concept of personal identity . . . The burden of the real reader's hermeneutics is always to declare, 'I *am* Emily'. □

(p. 201–2)

Farrell now turns to the second generation, pointing out that

■ any critical attempt to legitimize Cathy and Hareton usually entails the unconvincing notion that they achieve thematic victory over Catherine and Heathcliff. But the contest of values in *Wuthering Heights* is not between these two pairs of lovers. The contest is between the unnameable and the narratable, the self as sovereign and the self as social. And there is no question of victory. Brontë is not trying to exclude, but to include, to preserve all the variations and levels of identity that come into play whenever the social act of authoring – or reading – a text takes place.

. . . As Bakhtin reminds us, the 'I-for-myself' is inexpressible. '"I" can realize itself verbally only on the basis of "we"'[7] . . . If we see Cathy and Hareton as 'diluted' second generation characters, we are only responding to the generational structure of personal identity. The inexpressible 'I' seems to parent an expressible social self just as the actual author or actual reader parents a performing self capable of establishing bonds, constituting significance, achieving 'communion'. In other words, the dilution of the second generation is also the foregrounding of a social text . . . The role of Cathy and Hareton, then, is not to serve as thematic representatives of a new social ideology, but to reflect the adequacy of novelistic discourse to the discovery of communal identity . . . The marriage of Cathy and Hareton instances but does not nearly measure what the novel has to reveal. The actual measure is the magnificent power with which Brontë converts novelistic discourse into a model for reading the text of community as it remains stubbornly legible within the competing and hostile social texts of her time. □

(pp. 203–4)

Dissemination

So far this chapter on the 'genealogy' of *Wuthering Heights* has focused on its origins – the variously theorised experience, reading or social discourses which contributed to its production. Texts, however, have progeny as well as progenitors, and although *Wuthering Heights* was slow to capture the public imagination, the twentieth century has seen a still-increasing number of derivatives of the novel, whether versions cast in a different medium, such as stage or film, or new literary productions which rework the original material.

Q. D. Leavis, in her ground-breaking book, *Fiction and the Reading Public* (1932), could still say that '*Wuthering Heights* is not and never has been a popular novel (except in the sense that it is now an accepted classic and so on the shelves of the educated)'. Comparing Emily's novel with the phenomenal popular success of *Jane Eyre*, she explains:

■ *Wuthering Heights* is not an instrument of wish-fulfilment. It proceeds from a stronger mind, a sensibility that has triumphed over starvation and is not at its mercy. The cries of hunger and desire that ring through this book do not distress by a personal overtone, the reader is not made to feel embarrassed by the proximity of the author's face. The emotion exhibited in *Wuthering Heights*, unlike the emotion exhibited in *Jane Eyre*, has a frame round it . . .

But it is the Charlotte Brontës, not the Emilies, who have provided the popular fiction of the last hundred years . . . □

(p. 238)

As if in corroboration, Walter Cunliffe's 1950 article on 'The Brontës in Other People's Books' does not record any influence or allusion from *Wuthering Heights* among his examples. Even as an 'accepted classic', moreover, *Wuthering Heights* meets problems of categorisation. F. R. Leavis explains the absence of *Wuthering Heights* from his book, *The Great Tradition* (1962), by saying that it forms part of no major tradition, before or after its publication; indeed, 'that astonishing work seems to me a kind of sport' (p. 38).

From 1920 onwards, however, when the first silent film of *Wuthering Heights* was made, the novel tempted reproducers. George Bluestone, in his book, *Novels into Film* (1957), particularly discusses the 1939 film by William Wyler, which, he claimed, had transformed the novel into 'the story of the stable boy and the lady'. Geoffrey Wagner in *The Novel and the Cinema* (1975) takes up the same argument: 'each new film version of *Wuthering Heights* inherits this idea that it is a great love story. In fact, it has nothing to do with what the cinema-going public of the Thirties called sex. It is England's one outstanding ontological fiction' (p. 235). John

Harrington (1981) contests this judgement, using a technical analysis of camera-angles, lighting, sound and motifs to argue that 'the images of [Wyler's] film suggest . . . the difficulty of resolving the forces of nature and society' (p. 81).

Philip Cox (1992) places the film in history by arguing that it was perceived as part of American culture as opposed to the English novel, so that the cool reception of the film in England repeats on a cultural level the political friction between Britain and America at the outbreak of war in 1939. Robert Lawson-Peebles (1996) gives a great deal more detail about the context of the film in the outbreak of war, and argues that it was produced in an atmosphere where 'films that have nothing to do with the European war' were being 'loaded with lies and ideas' calculated to induce America to side with Britain (p. 3). Like Harrington, Lawson-Peebles thinks that Bluestone underestimates the film, suggesting that 'the film replaces the novel's demonism with a darkness that is of this world'.

Lawson-Peebles detects specifically American themes in the film, with Mr Earnshaw telling his children that 'he is ashamed of them' for not accepting the immigrant Heathcliff (p. 6), and Penistone Crag becoming 'a New World, an imaginative, sacred, protected, and egalitarian space removed from the oldworldly decadence of the two houses' (p. 7). In contrast to a 1939 review of the film, suggesting that it 'pretends, for a moment, that there is no crisis in the world', Lawson-Peebles

■ has tried to show, on the contrary, that it is an engaged text which maps American ideology onto the Yorkshire moors. The film suggests that some central American virtues may be found in England, if only in one protected utopian space . . . It is dark because those virtues are seen to be marginalized; and its darkness reveals that it is a text for 1939, concerned to relate the ordinary experience of growth and love to contemporary issues of egalitarianism and class structure. □

(p. 9)

My own 1992 essay, 'Reading Across Media: the case of *Wuthering Heights*', also deals with Wyler's film but places it in the context of David Cecil's 1934 essay, Clare Leighton's 1931 illustrations, and John Davison's 1937 stage play. My argument agrees with Wagner in assuming that Wyler replaces the 'ontological' preoccupations of the novel – its questions about the ultimate nature of things – with the more manageable social dream of a classless society, but adds that he does it by creating gender inequality between Catherine and Heathcliff, where none exists in the book. The major instrument in this filmic shift of emphasis is the scene, invented by Wyler, where Catherine incites Heathcliff to act out a tournament in which she is the prize.

■ The tournament scene in the film ends with Heathcliff, in his role as triumphant knight, raising Catherine from her role as his 'slave' to be 'the Princess Catherine of Yorkshire'. The class issue is thus neatly solved, in fantasy; she is allowed to be a princess, but only because he has raised her to that status; her gender status, on the other hand, is established as inferior to his. The visual image with which this scene ends, with Heathcliff looking out from Penistone Crag over the distant landscape and claiming his sovereignty over it, thus includes the gender-construction of his sovereignty over Catherine. The later image of the adult Catherine and Heathcliff on Penistone Crag . . . might seem congruent with Cecil's 'Romantic' reading of the lovers as 'elemental forces', unrelated to 'societies and codes of conduct', if we view it as an isolated still. Implicit in the film image, however, for the viewer who has already seen the knight-and-lady scene, is Catherine's subjugation by virtue of her sex to Heathcliff's dominance by virtue of his. What has happened is that the Catherine-and-Heathcliff pair are allowed to appear to transcend class differences at the cost of accepting gender-difference as an essential part of the film's 'epic truth'. Viewers who believed themselves to be part of the 'classless society' of the 1930s could identify sympathetically with the victims of the less enlightened days of costume drama, when stable-boys could not marry ladies, but the mythic status of the pair of lovers includes gender-differences which have been naturalized as 'eternal truths', with a status which Kristeva calls, precisely, 'metaphysical'. □

(p. 189)

There are, of course, other accounts of this and other stage, film and other versions of *Wuthering Heights*. The distinguished American critic, U. C. Knoepflmacher (1989), discusses Buñuel's film *Abysmos de Pasión*, together with the sketches and oil paintings from *Wuthering Heights* by the French artist Balthus, and Henri-Pierre Roché's novel *Jules et Jim*, filmed by François Truffaut. The most extensive source of both primary and secondary information about derivatives and commentaries on them is, however, my own book, *Brontë Transformations* (1996), which includes a comprehensive chronological list of derivatives in all media, including illustrations, parodies and incidental references as well as operatic, musical, stage, film and television adaptations and later fictional reworkings of the text, from the date of publication to 1995. The book also offers analysis and commentary which attempts to place popular and esoteric, imaginative and intellectual versions of the text together in a historical context, including a later version of the 1992 essay quoted above. Since that essay dealt with the Wyler film and other texts of the interwar period, I shall represent my book by an extract dealing with *Changing Heaven* (1990), a novel by the Canadian writer Jane Urquhart.

Changing Heaven has two interlocking stories: one concerns the ghosts of Emily Brontë and of Arianna Ether, a lady balloonist who was wrecked on Haworth Moor at the turn of the century, and the other a modern academic, Anne, who is writing about *Wuthering Heights*. The novel shows how obsessive, mirroring love is eventually replaced by dialogue and story-telling. Emily the story-teller is shown as having 'made' the landscape of *Wuthering Heights* ('The rocks were particularly difficult') and also 'Mr Capital H' ('practically unkillable') (pp. 179–80). She understands very well how the mechanisms of obsession work ('Absence was essential, after childhood . . . a permanent state of unfulfilled desire' (p. 84)), but also knows that the desired 'other' is a self-created illusion, a response to social pressures. My comment is to point to the similarities between Urquhart's witty dialogue and the argument of John T. Matthews's deconstructive essay (discussed in chapter two):

■ Matthews's argument is that it is impossible to detach this ideal love from the society which appears to prevent it because 'Catherine and Heathcliff's love is the ghost of the prohibitions that structure society'. Not only is it impossible to realize a love which is a 'hallucination' born of desire, it is also impossible to escape from this desire, because 'the oppressions of society not only compromise our present, they condition the dreams of its reversal'. This is not such a pessimistic position as it may sound, for two reasons. One is that if desires and prohibitions, as Matthews claims, 'incessantly dissolve' into one another (p. 54), there is no way of assigning primacy to either. Our dreams may be shaped by 'the oppressions of society', but this is a reciprocal interaction, in which the discourse of dreams can 'shape forms of consciousness and unconsciousness' which in turn can motivate 'transformation of our existing systems of power'.[8] Secondly, therefore, 'the oppressions of society' are not themselves immutable. The rhetoric of our desires, the intensity with which we tell ourselves stories of tragic love, is a social force which erodes the prohibitions that structure tragedy, just as weather, as it 'wuthers' round obstructive crags, makes new shapes of 'obdurate' landscape. Society, like landscape, changes slowly, but our weathered crags no longer have quite the contours seen by Emily Brontë. As we read old stories, we half recognise the landscape of past prohibitions, but our pleasure comes from moving with the narrative as it wuthers through to its appropriate heaven. □

(p. 252)

Political Readings: Marxism, Postcolonialism, Feminism

Marxism

V.S. PRITCHETT's 1946 article on *Wuthering Heights* was palpably influenced by history; Heathcliff, he writes, is the 'slum orphan . . . So utterly crushed, he will crush utterly if he arises . . . He would – indeed he does – run a concentration camp' (p.453). The following year, in 1947, David Wilson made the first consistent attempt to read *Wuthering Heights* in terms of class oppression and struggle. Dissociating himself from the 'moorland recluse' theory of the novel's origins, Wilson proposes 'to picture Emily Brontë in a new light: in the light of West Riding social history' (p.94). He begins with a detailed history of Haworth and its region, pointing out the freedom of its independent yeomen in medieval times from both the feudal system and from the Roman church. He quotes 'Thoresby, the Leeds Presbyterian topographer' as saying,

■ 'Hence a spirit of equality and republican independence becomes universal, acknowledging no superiors and practising no civilities; a sour and sturdy humour, defiance in every voice and fierceness in every countenance, a people as savage as they were thievish. In rank somewhat above there is wealth perpetually increasing but without tendency to civilisation, so that a man whose estate would enable him to keep a coach will drive his own cart and is not to be distinguished in gait or dialect from a labourer.' □

The picture is readily recognisable from *Wuthering Heights*. Wilson continues by describing how mechanised industry devastated local hand-loom weavers and gives detailed evidence that 'these social storms were far too near for the sisters to have lived the quiet secluded lives that have been pictured' (p.96) – a view which has recently been confirmed by Juliet Barker's biography.

Wilson relates one of Emily's poems to the 'turmoil and riot' of the Plug Riots of 1843 in which desperate workers tried to destroy the steam boilers which were reducing them to starvation (p. 105).

■ Why ask to know what date, what clime?
  There dwelt our own humanity,
  Power-worshippers from earliest time,
  Foot-kissers of triumphant crime
  Crushers of helpless misery,
  Crushing down Justice, honouring Wrong:
  If that be feeble, this be strong.[1] □

The poem is now thought to have been written in 1846 and revised in 1848, but Stevie Davies, in her 1994 book, *Emily Brontë: Heretic*, supports the kind of reading Wilson is making:

■ It is possible that, having visited Manchester in August 1846, Emily had had her eyes opened to the evils of industrialisation. It was the decade of Chartism, Mrs Gaskell's novels of working-class life, and Friedrich Engels had by the date of Emily Brontë's brief visit been working in Manchester amongst the slum-dwellers, and written his *Condition of the Working Classes in England in 1844.* □

In contrast with those critics who see Gondal in 1846 as 'palling', Davies argues:

■ Gondal was not palling, it was changing, shifting into a new alignment with history . . . Gondal no longer offered sanctuary and fresh air: it was filthy with bloodshed and rank with human cruelty. A new concern with the relationship between the oppressor and the oppressed emerged . . . At last she brings into the play-space of the Gondal world the perceptions analysed in 'The Butterfly' concerning a universe constructed upon 'a principle of destruction' and the corruption of human nature. □

(pp. 240–1)

Although Edward Chitham does not agree with this reading, his 1998 book corroborates it, showing in detail how the drafting and redrafting of 'Why ask to know' was interspersed with the drafting and redrafting of *Wuthering Heights* during 1846 and 1847 (pp. 147–52).

Linking the 1848 redrafting of the poem with the 'year of revolutions' in Europe, Davies argues that 'Emily Brontë by 1848 was on her way to becoming a war-poet and a poet of class-war' (pp. 245–6). David Musselwhite, in his 1987 essay (discussed below), also points out that

Emily read Guizot's essay on Cromwell during her stay in Brussels, and argues that this and other revolutionary writings were direct influences, not only on her essays, such as 'The Butterfly', but also on *Wuthering Heights*. These arguments corroborate David Wilson's much earlier essay, which reads *Wuthering Heights* in terms of 'class-war':

■ Whether Emily Brontë was fully conscious of it or not, we can see in the character of Heathcliff a true representation of the working men of her time, after enduring suffering and degradation at the hands of their 'betters', turning to defiance and destruction and to the violent movement for the People's Charter. □

(p. 110)

Wilson points out that Heathcliff is hardly a conventional hero:

■ Yet it is a measure of Emily's art that ... she ... shows Heathcliff not only as hateful, cruel, and destructive; she shows also how he became so. She must have seen the same process going on behind the pale and haggard faces that met her eyes in the village streets, faces often squalid and subdued, but sometimes caught by waves of sullen hatred and defiance. □

(p. 111)

In the context of class division, 'the most vital and courageous minds do cross that gulf', and if, like Catherine, they are tempted to opt for luxury, 'the flavour turns bitter in the mouth' (p. 112).

■ That this view of Heathcliff as representing the rebellious working men, and of Catherine as that part of the educated class which feels compelled to identify itself with their cause, was not unconscious in Emily Brontë is suggested by the passage on the return of Heathcliff. The question arises as to how he is to be received. '"No", she added, after a while, "I cannot sit in the kitchen. Set two tables here, Ellen: one for your master and Miss Isabella, being gentry; the other for Heathcliff and myself, being of the lower orders"'.

In Catherine Earnshaw we see the figure of Emily Brontë herself, a mind divided like that of Hamlet: unable to reconcile the path before her with her reason and her understanding. □

(p. 113)

In conclusion, Wilson notes that his aim has been to bring Emily Brontë 'out of that mystic never-never land of the moors and heath in which she has so exclusively been placed, and to plant her firmly among the lives of our forebears, where she belongs' (p. 114).

Arnold Kettle's essay on *Wuthering Heights*, in his 1951 *Introduction to the English Novel,* is in the same tradition as Wilson's but reached a much wider audience. Like Wilson, Kettle is irritated by the mystical aura surrounding Emily Brontë, even taking up Wilson's phrase about 'never-never land':

■ Because so much nonsense has been written and spoken about the Brontës and because Emily in particular has been so often presented to us as a ghost-like figure surrounded entirely by endless moorland, cut off from anything so banal as human society, not of her time but of eternity, it is necessary to emphasize at the outset the local quality of the book.

Wuthering Heights is about England in 1847. The people it reveals live not in a never-never land but in Yorkshire. Heathcliff was born not in the pages of Byron, but in a Liverpool slum. The language of Nelly, Joseph and Hareton is the language of Yorkshire people. The story of *Wuthering Heights* is concerned not with love in the abstract but with the passions of living people, with property-ownerships, the attraction of social comforts, the arrangement of marriages, the importance of education, the validity of religion, the relations of rich and poor.

There is nothing vague about this novel; the mists in it are the mists of the Yorkshire moors; if we speak of it as having an elemental quality it is because the very elements, the great forces of nature are evoked, which change so slowly that in the span of a human life they seem unchanging. But in this evocation there is nothing sloppy or uncontrolled. On the contrary the realization is intensely concrete: we seem to smell the kitchen of Wuthering Heights, to feel the force of the wind across the moors, to sense the very changes of the seasons. Such concreteness is achieved not by mistiness but by precision. □

(p. 139)

The affinity between Catherine and Heathcliff, Kettle argues, 'is forged in rebellion' which is 'concrete and unromantic' – and he quotes from '"An awful Sunday"' to '"await his advent"', in Chapter 3.

■ Against this degradation Catherine and Heathcliff rebel, hurling their pious books into the dog-kennel. And in their revolt they discover their deep and passionate need of each other. He, the outcast slummy, turns to the lively, spirited, fearless girl who alone offers him human understanding and comradeship. And she, born into the world of Wuthering Heights, senses that to achieve a full humanity, to be true to herself as a human being, she must associate herself totally with him in his rebellion against the tyranny of the Earnshaws and all that tyranny involves.

It is this rebellion that immediately, in this early section of the

book, wins over our sympathy to Heathcliff . . . And it is from his association in rebellion with Catherine that the particular quality of their
relationship arises. It is the reason why each feels that a betrayal of
what binds them together is in some obscure and mysterious way a
betrayal of everything, of all that is most valuable in life and death.

Yet Catherine betrays Heathcliff and marries Edgar Linton, kidding
herself that she can keep them both, and then discovering that in deny-
ing Heathcliff she has chosen death. The conflict here is, quite
explicitly, a social one. Thrushcross Grange, embodying as it does the
prettier, more comfortable side of bourgeois life, seduces Catherine.
She begins to despise Heathcliff's lack of 'culture' . . .

. . . from the moment of Heathcliff's reappearance Catherine's
attempts to reconcile herself to Thrushcross Grange are doomed. In
their relationship now there is no tenderness, they trample on each
other's nerves, madly try to destroy each other; but, once Heathcliff is
near, Catherine can maintain no illusions about the Lintons. The two
are united only in their contempt for the values of Thrushcross Grange
. . . When Nelly tells Heathcliff that Catherine is going mad, his
comment is:

'"You talk of her mind being unsettled . . ."' □

and Kettle continues to quote from Chapter 14 as far as '"shallow cares!"'.

■ The moral passion here is so intense, so deeply imbedded in the
rhythm and imagery of the prose, that it is easy to be swept along without grasping its full and extraordinary significance. Heathcliff at this
point has just perpetrated the first of his callous and ghastly acts of
revenge, his marriage to Isabella. It is an act so morally repulsive that it
is almost inconceivable that we should be able now to take seriously
his attack on Edgar Linton, who has, after all, by conventional,
respectable standards, done nobody any harm. And yet we *do* take the
attack seriously because . . . Emily Brontë convinces us that what
Heathcliff stands for is morally superior to what the Lintons stand for
. . . The words 'duty' and 'humanity', 'pity' and 'charity' have precisely
the kind of force Blake gives such words in his poetry. □

(pp. 143–7)

■ The astonishing achievement of this part of the book is that, despite
our protests about probability (protests which, incidentally, a good
deal of twentieth-century history makes a little complacent), despite
everything he does and is, we continue to sympathize with Heathcliff –
not, obviously, to admire him or defend him, but to give him our
inmost sympathy, to continue in an obscure way to identify ourselves
with him *against* the other characters. □

Heathcliff keeps our sympathy because his revenge

■ is not at bottom merely neurotic. It has a moral force. For what Heathcliff does is to use against his enemies with complete ruthlessness their own weapons, to turn on them (stripped of their romantic veils) their own standards, to beat them at their own game. The weapons he uses against the Earnshaws and Lintons are their own weapons of money and arranged marriages. He gets power over them by the classic methods of the ruling class, expropriation and property deals. He buys out Hindley and reduces him to drunken impotency, he marries Isabella and then organizes the marriage of his son to Catherine Linton, so that the entire property of the two families shall be controlled by himself. He systematically degrades Hareton Earnshaw to servility and illiteracy. 'I want the triumph of seeing *my* descendant fairly lord of *their* estates! My child hiring their children to till their father's lands for wages' (Ch. 20). (This is a novel, which, some critics will tell you, has nothing to do with anything as humdrum as society or life as it is actually lived.) □

(pp. 149–51)

Kettle now analyses the last section of the novel:

■ Heathcliff, watching the love of Cathy and Hareton grow, comes to understand something of the failure of his own revenge . . . From the moment that Cathy and Hareton are drawn together as rebels the change begins. For now for the first time Heathcliff is confronted not with those who accept the values of Wuthering Heights and Thrushcross Grange but with those who share, however remotely, his own wild endeavours to hold his right. □

(pp. 151–2)

■ Just as Catherine had to face the full moral horror of her betrayal of their love, he must face the full horror of his betrayal too . . .
It is this re-achievement of manhood by Heathcliff . . . which, together with the developing relationship of Cathy and Hareton and the sense of the continuity of life in nature, gives to the last pages of *Wuthering Heights* a sense of positive and unsentimental hope . . . Life will go on and others will rebel against the oppressors. □

(p. 153)

■ *Wuthering Heights* then is an expression in the imaginative terms of art of the stresses and tensions and conflicts, personal and spiritual, of nineteenth-century capitalist society . . . the men and women of *Wuthering Heights* are not the prisoners of nature; they live in the world and strive to change it, sometimes successfully, always painfully, with almost infinite difficulty and error.

This unending struggle, of which the struggle to advance from class society to the higher humanity of a classless world is but an episode, is conveyed to us in *Wuthering Heights* precisely because the novel is conceived in actual, concrete, particular terms, because the quality of oppression revealed in the novel is not abstract but concrete, not vague but particular. And that is why Emily Brontë's novel is at the same time a statement about the life she knew, the life of Victorian England, and a statement about life as such. □

(p.155)

Although Kettle's essay clearly reveals his Marxist orientation, he does not make it explicit in his terminology. The first avowedly Marxist study of the Brontës was Terry Eagleton's important book, *Myths of Power* (1976). Where Wilson and Kettle implicitly rely on Marx's own concept of literary representation as being part of the cultural 'superstructure' which relates directly to the economic 'base' of society, Eagleton locates himself within a structuralist development of Marxist theory which allows more autonomy to cultural formations. Because such Marxists see ideology – the general system of beliefs within a culture – as what makes people choose to 'work by themselves' within the class structure, they are particularly interested in the contradictions which arise at boundaries between classes and other social groups, which reveal ideology as such, and not as 'nature'.

For Eagleton, the fascination of Heathcliff is that he appears to have no place in society; he thus throws into question all kinds of ideological assumptions and also highlights Catherine's less obvious rootlessness.

■ Catherine, who does not expect to inherit, responds spontaneously to Heathcliff's presence; and because this antagonises Hindley she becomes after Earnshaw's death a spiritual orphan as Heathcliff is a literal one. Both are allowed to run wild; both become the 'outside' of the domestic structure. Because his birth is unknown, Heathcliff is a purely atomised individual, free of generational ties in a novel where genealogical relations are of crucial thematic and structural importance; and it is because he is an internal *émigré* within the Heights that he can lay claim to a relationship of direct personal equality with Catherine who, as the daughter of the family, is the least economically integral member. Heathcliff offers Catherine a friendship which opens fresh possibilities of freedom within the internal system of the Heights; in a situation where social determinants are insistent, freedom can mean only a relative independence of given blood-ties, of the settled, evolving, predictable structures of kinship. Whereas in Charlotte's fiction the severing or

141

lapsing of such relations frees you for progress up the class-system, the freedom which Cathy achieves with Heathcliff takes her down that system, into consorting with a 'gypsy'. Yet 'down' is also 'outside', just as gypsy signifies 'lower class' but also asocial vagrant, classless natural life-form. As the eternal rocks beneath the woods, Heathcliff is both lowly and natural, enjoying the partial freedom from social pressures appropriate to those at the bottom of the class-structure. In loving Heathcliff, Catherine is taken outside the family and society into an opposing realm which can be adequately imaged only as 'Nature'.

The loving equality between Catherine and Heathcliff stands, then, as a paradigm of human possibilities which reach beyond, and might ideally unlock, the tightly dominative system of the Heights. Yet at the same time Heathcliff's mere presence fiercely intensifies that system's harshness, twisting all the Earnshaw relationships into bitter antagonism. He unwittingly sharpens a violence endemic to the Heights – a violence which springs both from the hard exigencies imposed by its struggle with the land, and from its social exclusiveness as a self-consciously ancient, respectable family. The violence which Heathcliff unwittingly triggers is turned against him: he is cast out by Hindley, culturally deprived, reduced to the status of farm-labourer. What Hindley does, in fact, is to invert the potential freedom symbolised by Heathcliff into a parody of itself, into the non-freedom of neglect. Heathcliff is robbed of liberty in two antithetical ways: exploited as a servant on the one hand, allowed to run wild on the other; and this contradiction is appropriate to childhood, which is a time of relative freedom from convention and yet, paradoxically, a phase of authoritarian repression. In this sense there is freedom for Heathcliff neither within society nor outside it; his two conditions are inverted mirror-images of one another. It is a contradiction which encapsulates a crucial truth about bourgeois society. If there is no genuine liberty on its 'inside' – Heathcliff is oppressed by work and the familial structure – neither is there more than a caricature of liberty on the 'outside', since the release of running wild is merely a function of cultural impoverishment. The friendship of Heathcliff and Cathy crystallises under the pressures of economic and cultural violence, so that the freedom it seems to signify ('half-savage and hardy, and free') is always the other face of oppression, always exists in its shadow. With Heathcliff and Catherine, as in Charlotte's fiction, bitter social reality breeds Romantic escapism; but whereas Charlotte's novels try to trim the balance between them, *Wuthering Heights* shows a more dialectical interrelation at work. Romantic intensity is locked in combat with society, but cannot wholly transcend it; your freedom is bred and deformed in the shadow of your oppression, just as, in the adult Heathcliff, oppression is the logical consequence of the exploiter's 'freedom'.

Just as Hindley withdraws culture from Heathcliff as a mode of domination, so Heathcliff acquires culture as a weapon. He amasses a certain amount of cultural capital in his two years' absence[2] in order to shackle others more effectively, buying up the expensive commodity of gentility in order punitively to re-enter the society from which he was punitively expelled. This is liberty of a kind, in contrast with his previous condition; but the novel is insistent on its ultimately illusory nature. In oppressing others the exploiter imprisons himself; the adult Heathcliff's systematic tormenting is fed by his victims' pain but also drains him of blood, impels and possesses him as an external force. His alienation from Catherine estranges him from himself to the point where his brutalities become tediously perfunctory gestures, the mechanical motions of a man who is already withdrawing himself from his own body. Heathcliff moves from being Hindley's victim to becoming, like Catherine, his own executioner.

Throughout *Wuthering Heights*, labour and culture, bondage and freedom, Nature and artifice appear at once as each other's dialectical negations and as subtly matched, mutually reflective. Culture – gentility – is the opposite of labour for young Heathcliff and Hareton; but it is also a crucial economic weapon, as well as a product of work itself. The delicate spiritless Lintons in their crimson-carpeted drawing-room are radically severed from the labour which sustains them; gentility grows from the production of others, detaches itself from that work (as the Grange is separate from the Heights), and then comes to dominate the labour on which it is parasitic. In doing so, it becomes a form of self-bondage; if work is servitude, so in a subtler sense is civilisation. To some extent, these polarities are held together in the yeoman-farming structure of the Heights. Here labour and culture, freedom and necessity, Nature and society are roughly complementary. The Earnshaws are gentlemen yet they work the land; they enjoy the freedom of being their own masters, but that freedom moves within the tough discipline of labour; and because the social unit of the Heights – the family – is both 'natural' (biological) and an economic system, it acts to some degree as a mediation between Nature and artifice, naturalising property relations and socialising blood-ties. Relationships in this isolated world are turbulently face-to-face, but they are also impersonally mediated through a working relation with Nature. This is not to share Mrs Q. D. Leavis's view of the Heights as 'a wholesome primitive and natural unit of a healthy society'; there does not, for instance, seem much that is wholesome about Joseph. Joseph incarnates a grimness inherent in conditions of economic exigency, where relationships must be tightly ordered and are easily warped into violence. One of *Wuthering Heights'* more notable achievements is ruthlessly to demystify the Victorian notion of the family as a pious, pacific space within social conflict. Even so, the Heights does pin together contradictions which the entry of Heathcliff will break open. Heathcliff disturbs the Heights because he is simply superfluous: he has no defined place within its biological and economic system. (He may well be Catherine's illegitimate half-brother, just as he may well have passed his two-year absence in Tunbridge Wells.) The superfluity he embodies is that of a sheerly human demand for recognition; but since there is no space for such surplus within the terse economy of the Heights, it proves destructive rather than creative in effect, straining and overloading already taut relationships. Heathcliff catalyses an aggression intrinsic to Heights society; that sound blow Hindley hands out to Catherine on the evening of Heathcliff's first appearance is slight but significant evidence against the case that conflict starts only with Heathcliff's arrival. □

(pp.103–6)

■ Nature and culture, then, are locked in a complex relation of antagonism and affinity: the Romantic fantasies of Heathcliff and Catherine, and the Romantic Linton drawing-room with its gold-bordered ceiling and shimmering chandelier, both bear the scars of the material conditions which produced them – scars visibly inscribed on Cathy's ankle. Yet to leave the matter there would be to draw a purely formal parallel. For what distinguishes the two forms of Romance is Heathcliff: his intense communion with Catherine is an uncompromising rejection of the Linton world. □

(p.107)

Three years before Eagleton's *Myths of Power*, in 1973, the Marxist critic Raymond Williams had published a thoughtful account of *Wuthering Heights* in his book, *The Country and the City*, explaining the relationship between Catherine and Heathcliff in terms less of oppression than of alienation:

■ It is class and property that divide Heathcliff and Cathy . . . but it is not in social alteration that the human solution is at any point consciously conceived. What is created and held to is a kind of human intensity and connection which is the ground of continuing life . . . The tragic separation between human intensity and any available social settlement is accepted from the beginning in the whole design and idiom of the novel. The complication of the plot is then sustained by a single feeling, which is the act of transcendence. □

(p.176)

This concept of transcendence as a response to alienation from social possibilities is also important in Eagleton's reading:

■ The relationship of Heathcliff and Catherine, however, produces a third term. It really is a personal relationship, yet seems also to transcend the personal into some region beyond it. Indeed, there is a sense in which the unity the couple briefly achieve is narrowed and degutted by being described as 'personal'. In so far as 'personal' suggests the liberal humanism of Edgar, with his concern (crudely despised by Heathcliff) for pity, charity and humanity, the word is clearly inapplicable to the fierce mutual tearings of Catherine and Heathcliff. Yet it is inadequate to the positive as well as the destructive aspects of their love. Their relationship is, we say, 'ontological' or 'metaphysical' because it opens out into the more-than-personal, enacts a style of being which is more than just the property of two individuals, which suggests in its impersonality something beyond a merely Romantic-individualist response to social oppression. Their relationship articulates a depth inexpressible in routine social practice, transcendent of available social languages. Its impersonality suggests both a savage depersonalising and a paradigmatic significance; and in neither sense is the relationship wholly within their conscious control. What Heathcliff offers Cathy is a non- or pre-social relationship, as the only authentic form of living in a world of exploitation and inequality, a world where one must refuse to measure oneself by the criteria of the class-structure and so must appear inevitably subversive. Whereas in Charlotte's novels the love-relationship takes you into society, in *Wuthering Heights* it drives you out of it. The love between Heathcliff and Catherine is an intuitive intimacy raised to cosmic status, by-passing the mediation of the 'social'; and this, indeed, is both its strength and its limit. Its non-sociality is on the one hand a revolutionary refusal of the given language of social roles and values; and if the relationship is to remain unabsorbed by society it must therefore appear as natural rather than social, since Nature is the 'outside' of society. On the other hand, the novel cannot realise the meaning of that revolutionary refusal in social terms; the most it can do is to universalise that meaning by intimating the mysteriously impersonal energies from which the relationship springs. □

(pp.107–8)

There follows a more detailed examination of Heathcliff, who in class terms 'is, indeed, contradiction incarnate – both progressive and outmoded, at once caricature of and traditionalist protest against the agrarian capitalist forces of Thrushcross Grange' (pp.112–13).

■ The contradiction of the *novel*, however, is that Heathcliff cannot represent at once an absolute metaphysical refusal of an inhuman society and a class which is intrinsically part of it. Heathcliff is both metaphysical hero, spiritually marooned from all material concern in his obsessional love for Catherine, and a skilful exploiter who cannily expropriates the wealth of others. It is a limit of the novel's 'possible consciousness' that its absolute metaphysical protest can be socially articulated only in such terms – that its 'outside' is in this sense an 'inside'. The industrial bourgeoisie is outside the farming world of both Earnshaws and Lintons; but it is no longer a *revolutionary* class, and so provides no sufficient social correlative for what Heathcliff 'metaphysically' represents. He can thus be presented only as a conflictive unity of spiritual rejection and social integration; and this, indeed, is his personal tragedy. □

(p.116)

In conclusion, Eagleton returns to the vexed question of 'local' and 'universal' meanings. It is interesting that Eagleton's original argument predates J. Hillis Miller's deconstructive reading in *Fiction and Repetition* (1982), which explains the yearning for a 'meaning beyond' in terms of Derrida's concept of language as an endless chain of meaning which never comes to rest in a final term. Eagleton's explanation has some similarities with this, but shows the need for and appearance of universality as socially produced.

■ *Wuthering Heights* has been alternately read as a social and a metaphysical novel – as a work rooted in a particular time and place, or as a novel preoccupied with the eternal grounds rather than the shifting conditions of human relationship. That critical conflict mirrors a crucial thematic dislocation in the novel itself. The social and metaphysical are indeed ripped rudely apart in the book: existences only feebly incarnate essences, the discourse of ethics makes little creative contact with that of ontology. So much is apparent in Heathcliff's scathing dismissal of Edgar Linton's compassion and moral concern: 'and that insipid, paltry, creature attending her from *duty* and *humanity*! From *pity* and *charity*! He might as well plant an oak in a flower-pot, and expect it to thrive, as imagine he can restore her to vigour in the soil of his shallow cares!' The novel's dialectical vision proves Heathcliff both right and wrong. There *is* something insipid about Linton, but his concern for Catherine is not in the least shallow; if his pity and charity are less fertile than Heathcliff's passion, they are also less destructive. But if ethical and ontological idioms fails to mesh, if social existence negates rather than realises spiritual essence, this is itself a profoundly social fact. The novel projects a condition in which the available social languages are too warped and constrictive to be the bearers of love, freedom and equality; and it follows that in such a condition those values can be sustained only in the realms of myth and metaphysics. It is a function of the metaphysical to preserve those possibilities which a society cancels, to act as its reservoir of unrealised value. This is the history of Heathcliff and Catherine – the history of a wedge driven between the actual and the possible which, by estranging the ideal from concrete existence, twists that existence into violence and despair. The actual is denatured to a mere husk of the ideal, the empty shell of some tormentingly inaccessible truth. It is an index of the dialectical vision of *Wuthering Heights* that it shows at once the terror and the necessity of that denaturing, as it shows both the splendour and the impotence of the ideal. □

(pp. 120–1)

In the same year as *Myths of Power*, David Musselwhite published an essay on *Wuthering Heights* in the Marxist literary journal, *Red Letters*, based on Althusser's theory of ideology, elaborated in response to Pierre Macherey's *Theory of Literary Production* (1966). Macherey, in analysing the role of ideology in the production of literature, argues that a literary text will have a conscious project aligned with the dominant ideology, and thus concealing the conditions of its own production. (The word 'production' is used deliberately to suggest labour rather than inspiration.) A Machereyan critic will, therefore, tend to ignore the 'obvious' meaning of the text (such as the love story between Catherine and Heathcliff) and look in the margins and gaps of the narrative for clues to the 'real conditions' of its existence. Musselwhite thus looks at the normative voices of Lockwood and Nelly and also at the pervasive imagery of books and literature, all of which work hard to render acceptable – as a love story – what could have been threatening as a tale of rebellion and insubordination. The 'marginal' features of the narration constitute what Musselwhite calls the 'unacceptable text' of *Wuthering Heights*, which exposes the very mechanisms by which bourgeois culture comes to terms with its problems.[3]

Ten years later, Musselwhite returns with a plural title and a fascinating thesis. In '*Wuthering Heights*: The Unacceptable Texts', he points out that while Emily was in Brussels she had to read, as a stylistic exercise, essays by Hugo, Bossuet, Guizot, Carlyle and de la Vigne. Musselwhite points out that this exercise required Emily Brontë to focus on two revolutionary leaders – Cromwell and Mirabeau – and claims that 'Heathcliff is a complete digest of [the] accounts of Cromwell' written by Bossuet, Guizot and Carlyle (p. 104). Hugo's essay on Mirabeau, 'a man of no beginnings and no ends' who 'may be seen to be dying on purpose' (p. 99), is also clearly relevant. These, then, are the 'unacceptable texts' embedded in *Wuthering Heights*. The reason why they have not before been perceived must partly lie with Charlotte, who wished to maintain the myth of Emily's untutored innocence and involuntary creation.

■ To have recognized that Heathcliff owed his very existence to [Mirabeau and Cromwell] would have entailed the bringing into the full light of consciousness that spectre that at precisely that moment (1847–8) was haunting all Europe, the spectre not so much of 'communism' as that of revolution itself. □

(p.105)

Musselwhite, however, maintains that *Wuthering Heights* itself, with its ideologically-motivated system of narration, 'prevents us from reading' these 'passionate chronicles of revolution' (p.108), and disguises Heathcliff's 'revolutionary provenance'. He thus concludes with the 'heretical statement' that 'I don't think *Wuthering Heights* is a "great" novel' (p.107).

One of the theorists invoked by Musselwhite is Fredric Jameson, whose book, *The Political Unconscious*, appeared in 1981. As the title suggests, Jameson's aim was to co-ordinate Marxist analysis of class struggle with a psychoanalytic analysis of how texts process the movements of history. His methodology derives partly from techniques of narrative analysis developed by structuralists such as Vladimir Propp, and in particular he argues that Heathcliff is best read not as a protagonist in the story, but as what Propp calls the 'donor' – the figure who appears in folk-tales as the 'magical agent or helper' of the protagonist(s) (p.120). Jameson marries this structuralist analysis to Marxism in order to argue that

■ Heathcliff is the locus of *history* in this romance: his mysterious fortune marks him as a protocapitalist, in some other place, absent from the narrative, which then recodes the new economic energies as sexual passion. The aging of Heathcliff then constitutes the narrative mechanism whereby the alien dynamism of capitalism is reconciled with the immemorial (and cyclical) time of the agricultural life of a country squiredom. □

(p.128)

Four years later, in 1985, this hint was taken up on a large scale by James Kavanagh, in his book, *Emily Brontë*:

■ From the standpoint of an early nineteenth-century rural, parsonist ideology, *Wuthering Heights* might be seen as offering the dream of a social family in which the destabilizing, 'demonically' masculine, capitalist energies are either/both exiled or/and assigned a dominated position within rural petty-aristocratic structures. But *Wuthering Heights* also offers an extraordinary, anticipatory image of the fraught relationship between, and preferred but precarious separation of, two social spheres – the sphere of social production, in which economically valuable goods and services are produced, and the sphere of social reproduction, in which the relations of production are reproduced through the ideological formation of social subjects – as well as of the family's crucial role within the latter. For the family in *Wuthering Heights* is certainly a significant institution ideologically as well as economically – indeed, it is a site of both economic and ideological *production*. The family in this text is what Althusserian theory would call an 'ideological apparatus' – that is, a social mechanism for producing appropriate class subjects, who are prepared to assume their place in the system of social relations that supports a given mode of production. □

(p. 88)

■ But the membrane that separates the sphere of social reproduction from the sphere of social production, the ideological factory from the commodity factory, is always too permeable. The male and female subjects that migrate across it continually tend to bring the disruptive need for dynamic individual growth into the family, and the disruptive need for collective support into the market-place. In fact, this strict separation can only represent the impossible Anglo-capitalist dream of ideological, flowing from familial, stability, and part of *Wuthering Heights*'s peculiar power derives from its reluctance to imagine any stable, 'compromise' resolution that would deny the integrity and tenacity of the psycho-sexual and socio-ideological tensions that constitute the novel. The final sense of precariousness that the text projects – the sense that all of this can happen again, that the energies which Heathcliff unleashed are doomed repeatedly to intervene in, and transform, the everyday family world – is a recognition both of the inevitable, unforeseeable return of repressed phallic desire within the Oedipal family, and of the constant cycle of disruption and renewal that capitalism – not the elements – imposes on the social family. □

(pp. 95–6)

Like Kavanagh, Nancy Armstrong (1982) takes as her starting point Fredric Jameson's notion of Heathcliff as 'the locus of history' in *Wuthering Heights*. Unlike Kavanagh, however, Armstrong uses Foucauldian discourse theory to discuss Heathcliff's progress from the *genre* of Romanticism to that of Realism. Like Farrell, whose essay, 'Reading the Text of Community' was discussed in chapter four, Armstrong sees the major shift in *Wuthering Heights* as from individual to community consciousness. An article which oddly corroborates both Jameson and Armstrong is Richard Nemesvari's 'Strange Attractors on the Yorkshire Moors: Chaos Theory and *Wuthering Heights*' (1997). Nemesvari follows previous critics in seeing Heathcliff as the 'small alteration' which the 'system' represented by the two houses is unable to absorb. Whereas Eagleton sees Heathcliff's intervention as negative, however, Nemesvari, like Jameson, sees him as a catalyst in 'a society which absolutely requires new energy and information' (p. 17). Using the technical language of chaos theory, he argues that 'Heathcliff . . . comes to act as the strange attractor around which this newly chaotic system organizes itself' (pp. 17–18).

■ Brontë, unlike later Victorian commentators such as Matthew Arnold, perceives chaos as a force for social diversity and regeneration, and thus as an empirical, historically representable quality. Thus it is too simplistic to see Heathcliff as the barrier which must be overcome in order to achieve the story's successful resolution. Rather he is the influence which *generates* that resolution. □

(p. 20)

Postcolonialism

George Washington Peck, writing in America in 1848, notes that Catherine's announcement that she and Heathcliff 'are going to rebel' (*WH* p. 18) 'must have been written . . . in the very year of the Declaration of American Independence' (*CH* p. 237). Criticism of *Wuthering Heights* has, however, been slow to place the novel in the context of Britain's imperialist past, and I have found no criticism of *Wuthering Heights* which shows this awareness before 1987, when Christopher Heywood published an important study demonstrating from empirical evidence that colonies of black slaves were used to work Yorkshire farms in the eighteenth century. Two years later he reminds us that the Angrian stories of the Brontë childhood were set specifically in West Africa, and that African slavery is a continuing theme in the juvenilia. This general indebtedness of the Brontës to African locations and themes is investigated very thoughtfully in Firdous Azim's 1993 book, *The Colonial Rise of the Novel*, which, although it does not deal with *Wuthering Heights*, is a valuable source of contextualising information.

Startlingly different is an essay by the American radical feminist Andrea Dworkin, which also appeared in 1987. Originally part of her book, *Letters from a War Zone*, the essay was partially reprinted in the British *Observer* newspaper as 'A Chauvinist Monster'. The Monster is Heathcliff, and his 'chauvinism' is both gender- and race-related. Heathcliff's obscure origin makes it possible, as we have seen, for him to be adopted as an exemplary victim of the class war; the description of his appearance, however, allows him to be seen as of foreign, even black, origin. Mr Earnshaw describes the child as 'dark almost as if it came from the devil', speaking 'some gibberish that nobody could understand'

(*WH* pp. 34–5). The elder Lintons describe him as 'a gypsy' and as 'a little Lascar, or an American or Spanish castaway' (*WH* p. 48). A 'Lascar' is a derogatory term for an (East) Indian, especially a seaman, while the 'American' or 'Spanish' might, as more recent scholars have suggested, refer to slaves from the North or South American colonies.

Although Dworkin's argument is mainly gender-based, the racial element is thoroughly integrated with it. She argues that Emily Brontë 'anticipated contemporary sexual politics by more than a century', showing that while 'the great love is in sameness, not difference',

■ this true love is destroyed by the divisive imperatives of a racist hierarchy that values white, fair, rich and despises dark, poor . . . *Wuthering Heights*, perhaps uniquely, shows an interlocking chain of men socialised to hate and to cause pain through abusing power . . . [Heathcliff's] self-consciousness, rooted in race, is necessarily political, foreshadowing Fanon's 'The Wretched of the Earth' . . . Emily Brontë wrote a psychological and physical profile of the power dynamics of the English ruling class, gender male: how boys, treated sadistically, learn to take refuge in a numb, orthodox dominance. □

(p. 35)

Nailing her colours to the mast, she concludes, 'I want us to read [Emily Brontë] when we read Fanon and Millett; when we think about race and gender and revolution' (p. 36).

A different approach again can be found in Nancy Armstrong's 1992 essay, 'Imperialist Nostalgia in *Wuthering Heights*', which deals with the 'colonisation' of the British regions by the centre, using the devices of investigative anthropology – the collection and photography of folklore, dialect and costume. These processes are echoed, Armstrong argues, by the novel's own 'textualizing procedures', in which the 'central' story is seen only through the 'framing' devices of a consciously superior, investigative southerner (p. 448).

Elsie Michie, in 'From Simianized Irish to Oriental Despots: Heathcliff, Rochester, and Racial Difference' (1992), argues that Heathcliff's racial ambiguity is exploited in the novel according to his status as victim or exploiter. While he is poor and oppressed, references to his blackness and links with the east also suggest 'contemporary stereotypes of the Irish' (p. 129), while after his success, these references give way to 'the figure of the oriental despot' (p. 134).

Terry Eagleton, in 1995, speculates that Heathcliff might have been one of the starving Irish children shown in 1845 in *The Illustrated London News* – or he 'may be a gypsy, or . . . a Creole, or any kind of alien. It is hard to know how black he is' (p. 3). Like Armstrong, Eagleton argues that current Romanticisation of the English landscape repressed knowledge of the countryside as the site of labour and of history. Ireland, as a rural and unknown place,

■ comes to figure as the monstrous unconscious of the metropolitan society, the secret materialist history of endemically idealist England . . . Nature, for English pastoral ideology, is plenitude and bountiful resource. In Irish culture and Brontë's novel . . . it also figures as harsh, niggardly, mean-spirited, and so as peasant rather than aristocrat. □

(pp. 8–9, 17)

Eagleton now chooses to read Heathcliff as an allegory of Irish history:

■ Heathcliff starts out as an image of the famished Irish immigrant, becomes a landless labourer . . . and ends up as a symbol of the constitutional nationalism of the Irish parliamentary party . . . oppressor and oppressed in one body, condensing in his own person the various stages of the Irish revolution. □

(p. 19)

In the same year (1995) Maja-Lisa Von Sneidern returns to the question of slavery in her densely-documented article on 'Wuthering Heights and the Liverpool Slave Trade'. She points out that Mr Earnshaw's journey to Liverpool coincided with the 1771 'Mansfield Judgment' which effectively outlawed slavery on British soil. By Victorian times, the notion of Britain as champion of liberty which underlay this judgment had been built into the ideology of racial superiority which, paradoxically, underpinned the continuing slave trade which was vital to British economic superiority. Von Sneidern reads Wuthering Heights as the site in which this complex situation is explored.

Von Sneidern maintains that 'Heathcliff's racial otherness cannot be a matter of dispute'. If not 'a regular black' (WH p. 56), he is at least an irregular black, a mongrel, a source of great anxiety for the mid-nineteenth-century Victorian' (p. 172). Corroborating Heywood's evidence about Yorkshire slavery, she goes on to point out that Brontë 'locates her plantation colony not on the margins of the empire . . . but in the heart of Yorkshire. In the novel the Heights, corrupted by the introduction of the racially other, is the place where the figures of a system of bondage work out their relationships' (p. 174). Perhaps the most interesting part of Von Sneidern's argument is her explanation of Heathcliff's particular horror as lying in his reversal of 'normal' racial relationships:

■ Discovering Isabella's infatuation with him, Heathcliff stares at her 'as one might do at a strange repulsive animal, a centipede from the

Indies, for instance, which curiosity leads one to examine in spite of the aversion it raises' (*WH* p. 105). The colonizing gaze has been reversed. □

(pp. 180–1)

The novel investigates, but does not resolve, these issues. At the end, 'the plantation site' – Wuthering Heights – 'is abandoned . . . to become a crumbling reminder that, given the opportunity, all are capable of infinite brutality and falling victim to the addictive pleasure of possessing another human being' (p. 188).

The 'reverse gaze' argument had already been made in a feminist context by Karen Chase (1989) and Beth Newman (1990), discussed later in this chapter, and in a postcolonial context it is elaborated in Susan Meyer's 1996 book, *Imperialism at Home: Race and Victorian Women's Fiction*. Beginning from Heathcliff's doubtful racial origin, Meyer argues:

■ In *Wuthering Heights*, Emily Brontë makes an extended critique of British imperialism. She does so in part by exploring what would happen if the suppressed power of the 'savage' outsiders were unleashed. Brontë relentlessly explores the nature of forces external to, subordinated to, marginalized by, or excluded from the British social order. And like her sister Charlotte, Emily Brontë invokes the metaphorical link between white women and people of nonwhite races as she explores energies of resistance to the existing social structure. In *Wuthering Heights* these energies have a universal resonance – they suggest the external, untamable energies that forever threaten the cozy domestic internal. But the novel also gives them a local specificity, associating them with nineteenth-century social issues of topical significance.

Critics such as David Wilson, Arnold Kettle, and Terry Eagleton have accounted for the threatening power of *Wuthering Heights* by reading Heathcliff as a representative of the discontented working class of the 'hungry forties', rising in rebellion against an oppressive society and learning himself to wield the oppressive tools of capitalism . . . But the novel is most powerfully concerned, I would argue, not with economic injustice within the domestic class system, but with the economic injustice imposed by British imperialism on the 'dark races' of the world. To read Heathcliff simply as a working man within a domestic context does not sufficiently account for the novel's threatening power. Read as a discontented worker, Heathcliff does not behave in a particularly dangerous manner. He does not form alliances with other workers (Nelly, Joseph, or Michael, for example), as the middle class most feared discontented labourers would. Instead, Heathcliff simply makes an individual rise, enacting, although in a vengeful form, the individualistic rags-to-riches plot, a plot that in fact reinforces the values of capitalism. Such a reading thus fails to explain what remains menacingly resonant in the novel. Considered in the interpretive context of imperialist history, however, Heathcliff suddenly looks, as it were, collective – accruing associations with India, China, Africa and the West Indies. Reading the novel in this context, one also linked with the discontents of gender, helps to explain its potently disruptive and threatening energy. □

(pp.100–102)

Meyer's main argument is that Heathcliff – the oppressed alien – starts off in the novel as a metaphoric vehicle for the oppression of women – Catherine in particular –

■ but as the novel goes on, Heathcliff increasingly escapes the bounds of metaphor . . . Emily Brontë gleefully unleashes Heathcliff's energies of social resistance, and that resistance takes the form of the worst nightmare of the imperialist power: reverse colonization. As Heathcliff takes this revenge on an oppressive British society, however, he himself becomes a subjugator of women. □

(pp. 107, 112)

Nelly's apparently fanciful Chinese/Indian genealogy for Heathcliff also suggests a different colonial relationship from the starving slaves of Liverpool. The Chinese empire was in the 1840s successfully resisting British colonisation, so that when Nelly says that the Emperor of China would be

■ able to buy up the two houses with 'one week's income', she hints at a possible relationship between the Chinese and the British empire in which the British might not find themselves so easily triumphant . . . In restoring to Heathcliff a history, Nelly suggests to the nineteenth-century British reader a way in which dark-skinned people like Heathcliff might be able to take revenge for the subjugation they have suffered at British hands. □

(p. 114)

Meyer also links Heathcliff's three years' absence to her theme:

■ Heathcliff's absence, as a calculation of dates in the novel reveals, takes place between 1780 and 1783, the last three years of the American Revolutionary War. By suggesting that Heathcliff has been in the American army in the years he was away, Brontë associates him with the archetypal war of successful colonial rebellion, one in which England was even at one point in fear of invasion. □

(p.115)

Heathcliff then actualises these threats by buying up the two houses, creating 'a world in which physical force and economic power – coming from a mysterious external source – take the place of law or local standards of morality. His actions hideously mimic the ugly brutality of British imperialism' (p.116). Working through the ghostly aspects of the novel and its window imagery, Meyer argues that 'Heathcliff represents the return of the colonial repressed' (p.119).

Feminism

In a mainly approving review of *Wuthering Heights* written in 1857, Emile Montégut paraphrases Catherine's famous speech about Heathcliff: 'He is so *much me*, she says, he is more myself than I am; he is the thunder and I am only the lightning' (*CH* p.378). Montégut probably never even noticed that he had assimilated this dramatically radical speech to the norm of gender hierarchy. The early reviewers, as Nicola Thompson (1996) has shown, were confused and upset by Emily Brontë's failure or refusal to conform to what was expected of the 'lady novelist'. But it was not only men who were confused by *Wuthering Heights*. Unlike *Jane Eyre*, *Wuthering Heights* is not recognisably 'about' the 'woman question'. Catherine Earnshaw is too wayward to be a female role model, and her fate is not to be emulated. It took a long time for *Wuthering Heights* to be read as a positive text for women.

Virginia Woolf's 1916 essay (discussed in chapter two) does much to establish the stature of *Wuthering Heights*, but it is not noticeably feminist. As I wrote in a survey of 'Feminist Criticism of *Wuthering Heights*' (1992),

■ Fifty years go by before we find the real groundwork for later feminist studies of *Wuthering Heights* in Inga-Stina Ewbank's book *Their Proper Sphere: The Brontë Sisters as Early Victorian Female Novelists* (1966). As its subtitle insists, this is a book which works by contextualisation, a book in the spirit of Virginia Woolf's later perception that 'intellectual freedom depends upon material things . . . and women have always been poor'.[4] Moving freely from text to biography and from novel to poems, it lays the foundations for both author-based and text-based criticism. Q.D. Leavis's influential 'Fresh Approach to *Wuthering Heights*' (1969) [discussed in chapter two], assumes some of this context, but is mostly notable for its assertion of the heroine's centrality . . .

Q.D. Leavis's essay appeared too late to be included in either Lettis and Morris's *A Wuthering Heights Handbook* (1961) or Miriam Allott's

Casebook (1970). Neither of these widely disseminated anthologies of criticism included, therefore, any feminist perspective, and Carol Ohmann, in her 1971 essay, 'Emily Brontë in the Hands of Male Critics', demonstrates a pervasive misogyny in criticism of *Wuthering Heights* up to that date. □

(pp. 147–8)

If Inga-Stina Ewbank's chapter can be described as 'images of women' criticism, Carol Ohmann's essay falls into the category called 'feminist critique' – a feminist critic's effort to set the record straight by correcting earlier biases. The 1960s also, however, saw more positive approaches to *Wuthering Heights* depending on psychoanalysis. Juliet Mitchell's 1966 essay and Helen Moglen's study of 1971 (discussed in chapter three) both see the novel as focused on women's psychological development, and following a smooth line from the first to the second generation; this positive reading of the second generation is characteristic of many feminist readings – for instance Patricia Spacks's (1976). Carolyn Heilbrun, in *Toward a Recognition of Androgyny* (1973), makes another point that has become widely accepted among feminist critics – that the separation of Catherine and Heathcliff involves gender-polarisation:

■ Catherine and Heathcliff, whose love represents the ultimate, apparently undefined, androgynous ideal, betray that love, or are betrayed by the world into deserting it . . . Catherine . . . betrayed their love because she was seduced by the offers the world makes to women to renounce their selves: adornment, 'respect', protection, elegance, and the separation, except in giving birth, from the hardness of life. □

(p. 80)

■ Heathcliff has followed the conventional pattern of his sex, into violence, brutality, and the feverish acquisition of wealth as Cathy had followed the conventional pattern of her sex into weakness, passivity, and luxury. They sank into their 'proper sexual roles'. □

(p. 82)

If 'the world' will only accept fully socialised adults, *Wuthering Heights* can be read as a refusal of these 'proper sexual roles'. It is in this context that Ellen Moers (1976) points to the regressive nature of Catherine and Heathcliff's love:

■ The puzzles of *Wuthering Heights* may best be resolved if the novel is read as a statement of a very serious kind about a girl's childhood and the adult woman's tragic yearning to return to it. Catherine's impossible love for Heathcliff becomes comprehensible as a pre-adolescent (but not pre-sexual) love modeled after the sister-brother relationship. The gratuitous cruelties of the novel thus are justified as realistic attributes of the nursery world – and as frankly joyous memories of childhood eroticism. □

(p. 106)

My 1992 survey of 'Feminist Criticism' continues:

■ This psychoanalytic tendency in criticism of the 1970s was balanced in 1976 when Terry Eagleton published his important Marxist study of the Brontës [discussed above] . . . Eagleton, despite his impeccably materialist analysis of ideology, still tends to take Heathcliff as the novel's central character, and he was famously taken to task for his lack of feminist perspective by the Marxist-Feminist Literature Collective in 1977. It is, however, indicative of the uncertain position of *Wuthering Heights* in the developing feminist consciousness that the Collective chose *Jane Eyre* and *Shirley*, not *Wuthering Heights*, to represent 'Women's Writing' of 1848. Similarly, Jenni Calder's *Women and Marriage in the Victorian Novel* (1976) gives *Wuthering Heights* only the merest mention while Elaine Showalter, in a book dedicated to 'establishing a more . . . accurate and systematic literary history for women writers', also deals with Charlotte but not Emily Brontë. It is as if feminist critics of this early phase are establishing their own 'great tradition', which is different from F. R. Leavis's, but which still tends to see *Wuthering Heights*, as he did, as 'a kind of a sport'.[5]

All this changes decisively in 1979 with Sandra Gilbert's and Susan Gubar's *The Madwoman in the Attic*. Although its title derives, once more, from Charlotte rather than Emily, *The Madwoman* is an inclusive text. Whereas Showalter's *A Literature of Their Own* had attempted to define a *female* literary tradition, Gilbert and Gubar are concerned with the position of women writers as they relate, inevitably, to the male mainstream. In particular they take issue with the American critic Harold Bloom, who, in *The Anxiety of Influence*, explains literary history as 'the crucial warfare of fathers and sons', a process in which younger writers struggle to resist the influence of their elders. Gilbert and Gubar point out that a woman writer in this context suffers 'an even more primary "anxiety of authorship" – a radical fear that she cannot create . . . not fight a male precursor on "his" terms and win' (pp. 47–9). Identifying Milton's *Paradise Lost* as a culturally definitive 'story of woman's secondness' (p. 191), *The Madwoman in the Attic* analyses *Wuthering Heights* as a series of strategies for negotiating 'Milton's bogey'.

Firstly, Gilbert and Gubar argue, 'the story of *Wuthering Heights* is built around a central fall', so that the novel is in part 'a *Bildungsroman* about a girl's passage from "innocence" to "experience"' (pp. 253–4).

'This fall', however, 'is not a fall *into* hell. It is a fall *from* "hell" into "heaven"' (p.255). Gilbert and Gubar employ an eclectic mixture of formal, structuralist, Marxist and psychoanalytic arguments to demonstrate that 'Emily Brontë thought in polarities' (p.273), whether the Miltonic 'hell and heaven' or Claude Lévi-Strauss's anthropological 'raw and cooked'. Heaven, the 'cooked', is associated with patriarchy, represented in *Wuthering Heights* by Edgar Linton. 'In Freudian terms he would . . . be described as her superego, the internalized guardian of morality and culture, with Heathcliff, his opposite, functioning as her childish and dangerous id' (p.281). □

(pp.148–9)

This summary of Gilbert and Gubar's methodology demonstrates well the eclectic nature of much feminist criticism. It is not by chance that this section on feminism comes after everything else in this book – it is because feminists have appropriated for their purposes just about all other possible approaches, so that there are humanist feminists (like Virginia Woolf), sociological (Ewbank) and psychoanalytic (Mitchell) feminists, and feminists using structuralism, deconstruction, discourse theory, Marxism, postcolonial theory and various combinations of all these. Gilbert and Gubar themselves incorporate not only the feminist perceptions of, say, Heilbrun and Moers, but also the structuralist anthropology of Lévi-Strauss and the historicist and psychoanalytic approaches of J. Hillis Miller and Leo Bersani (discussed in chapters two and three). Beginning from Lévi-Strauss, they argue that:

■ If we identify with Lockwood, civilized man at his most genteelly 'cooked' and literary, we cannot fail to begin Brontë's novel by deciding that hell is a household very like Wuthering Heights. Lockwood himself, as if wittily predicting the reversal of values that is to be the story's central concern, at first calls the place 'a perfect misanthropist's heaven' (Ch. 1). But then what is the traditional Miltonic or Dantesque hell if not a misanthropist's heaven, a site that substitutes hate for love, violence for peace, death for life, and in consequence the material for the spiritual, disorder for order? Certainly Wuthering Heights rings all these changes on Lockwood's first two visits. □

(p.260)

They then proceed to identify the 'mythic' story underlying *Wuthering Heights* in terms which bring gender issues into prominence:

■ Why is Wuthering Heights so Miltonically hellish? And what happened to Catherine Earnshaw? Why has she become a demonic, storm-driven ghost? The 'real' etiological story of *Wuthering Heights* begins, as Lockwood learns from his 'human fixture' Nelly Dean, with a random weakening of the fabric of ordinary human society.[6] Once upon a time, somewhere in what mythically speaking qualifies as pre-history or what Eliade calls 'illo tempore', there is/was a primordial family, the Earnshaws, who trace their lineage back at least as far as the paradigmatic Renaissance inscription '1500 Hareton Earnshaw' over their 'principal doorway'. And one fine summer morning toward the end of the eighteenth century, the 'old master' of the house decides to take a walking tour of sixty miles to Liverpool (Ch. 4) . . . 'What shall I bring you?' the old master asks, like the fisherman to whom the flounder gave three wishes. And the children reply, as convention dictates, by requesting their heart's desires. In other words, they reveal their true selves, just as a father contemplating his own ultimate absence from their lives might have hoped they would.

Strangely enough, however, only the servant Nelly's heart's desire is sensible and conventional: she asks for (or, rather, accepts the promise of) a pocketful of apples and pears. Hindley, on the other hand, the son who is destined to be next master of the household, does not ask for a particularly masterful gift. His wish, indeed, seems frivolous in the context of the harsh world of the Heights. He asks for a fiddle, betraying both a secret, soft-hearted desire for culture and an almost decadent lack of virile purpose. Stranger still is Catherine's wish for a whip. 'She could ride any horse in the stable', says Nelly, but in the fairy-tale context of this narrative that realistic explanation hardly seems to suffice, for, symbolically, the small Catherine's longing for a whip seems like a powerless younger daughter's yearning for power.

Of course, as we might expect from our experience of fairy tales, at least one of the children receives the desired boon. Catherine gets her whip. She gets it figuratively – in the form of a 'gypsy brat' – rather than literally, but nevertheless 'it' (both whip and brat) functions just as she must have unconsciously have hoped it would, smashing her rival-brother's fiddle and making a desirable third among the children in the family so as to insulate her from the pressure of her brother's domination . . . ☐

Gilbert and Gubar now progress from the mythic to the psychoanalytic:

■ Having received her deeply desired whip, Catherine now achieves, as Hillis Miller (*God* pp. 155–211) and Leo Bersani have noticed, an extraordinary fullness of being. The phrase may seem pretentiously metaphysical (certainly critics like Q.D. Leavis (p. 321) have objected to such phrases on those grounds) but in discussing the early paradise from which Catherine and Heathcliff eventually fall we are trying to describe elusive psychic states, just as we would in discussing

Wordsworth's visionary childhood, Frankenstein's youth before he 'learned' that he was (the creator of) a monster, or even the prelapsarian sexuality of Milton's Adam and Eve. And so, like Freud who was driven to grope among such words as *oceanic* when he tried to explain the heaven that lies about us in our infancy, we are obliged to use the paradoxical and metaphorical language of mysticism: phrases like *wholeness, fullness of being,* and *androgyny* come inevitably to mind.[7] All three, as we shall see, apply to Catherine, or more precisely to Catherine-Heathcliff, . . . because as Catherine's whip he is (and she herself recognizes this) an alternative self or double for her, a complementary addition to her being who fleshes out all her lacks the way a bandage might staunch a wound. Thus in her union with him she becomes, like Manfred in his union with his sister Astarte, a perfect androgyne. As devoid of sexual awareness as Adam and Eve were in the prelapsarian garden, she sleeps with her whip, her other half, every night in the primordial fashion of the countryside . . . And if Heathcliff's is the body that does her will – strong, dark, proud, and a native speaker of 'gibberish' rather than English – she herself is an 'unfeminine' instance of transcendently vital spirit. For she is never docile, never submissive, never ladylike. On the contrary, her joy – and the Coleridgean word is not too strong – is in what Milton's Eve is never allowed: a tongue 'always going – singing, laughing, and plaguing everybody who would not do the same' and 'ready words: turning Joseph's religious curses into ridicule . . . and doing just what her father hated most' (Ch. 5). ☐

(pp. 263–5)

After six years 'in the earthly paradise of childhood', Catherine begins her 'fall' when Hindley becomes her effective step-father (p. 267).

■ Why do parents begin to seem like step-parents when their children reach puberty? The ubiquitousness of step-parents in fairy tales dealing with the crises of adolescence suggests that the phenomenon is both deepseated and widespread. One explanation – and the one that surely accounts for Catherine Earnshaw's experience – is that when the child gets old enough to become conscious of her parents as sexual beings they really do begin to seem like fiercer, perhaps even (as in the case of Hindley and Frances) younger versions of their 'original' selves. Certainly they begin to be more threatening (that is, more 'peevish' and 'tyrannical') if only because the child's own sexual awakening disturbs them almost as much as their sexuality, now truly comprehended, bothers the child. Thus the crucial passage from Catherine's diary which Lockwood reads even before Nelly begins her narration is concerned not just with Joseph's pious oppression but with the cause of those puritanical onslaughts, the fact that she and Heathcliff must shiver in the garret because 'Hindley and his wife [are basking] down-stairs before a comfortable fire . . . kissing and talking nonsense by the hour – foolish palaver we should be ashamed of'. Catherine's defen-siveness is clear. She (and Heathcliff) are troubled by the billing and cooing of her 'step-parents' because she understands, perhaps for the first time, the sexual nature of what a minute later she calls Hindley's 'paradise on earth' and – worse – understands its relevance to her. □

(pp. 269–70)

■ Realistically speaking, Catherine and Heathcliff have been driven in the direction of Thrushcross Grange by their own desire to escape not only the pietistic tortures Joseph inflicts but also, more urgently, just that sexual awareness irritatingly imposed by Hindley's romantic paradise. Neither sexuality nor its consequences can be evaded, how-ever, and the farther the children run the closer they come to the very fate they secretly wish to avoid. Racing 'from the top of the Heights to the park without stopping', they plunge from the periphery of Hindley's paradise (which was transforming their heaven into a hell) to the boundaries of a place that at first seems authentically heavenly, a place full of light and softness and color, a 'splendid place carpeted with crimson . . . and [with] a pure white ceiling bordered by gold, a shower of glass-drops hanging in silver chains from the centre, and shimmering with little soft tapers' (Ch. 6). Looking in the window, the outcasts speculate that if they were inside such a room 'we should have thought ourselves in heaven!' From the outside, at least, the Lintons' elegant haven appears paradisaical. But once the children have experi-enced its Urizenic interior, they know that in their terms this heaven is hell.[8] □

(pp. 271–2)

■ It has often been argued that Catherine's anxiety and uncertainty about her own identity represents a moral failing, a fatal flaw in her character which leads to her inability to choose between Edgar and Heathcliff. Heathcliff's reproachful 'Why did you betray your own heart, Cathy?' (Ch. 15) represents a Blakeian form of this moral criticism, a contemptuous suggestion that 'those who restrain desire do so because theirs is weak enough to be restrained.'[9] The more vulgar and common-sensical attack of the Leavisites, on the other hand – the censorious notion that 'maturity' means being strong enough to choose not to have your cake and eat it too – represents what Mark Kinkead-Weekes calls 'the view from the Grange' (p. 86). To talk of morality in connection with Catherine's fall – and specifically in connection with her self-deceptive decision to marry Edgar – seems pointless, however, for morality only becomes a relevant term where there are meaningful choices. □

The argument now embraces a materialist perspective, placing the question of individual choice in the context of economic and social possibilities:

■ As we have seen, Catherine has no meaningful choices. Driven from Wuthering Heights to Thrushcross Grange by her brother's marriage, seized by Thrushcross Grange and held fast in the jaws of reason, education, decorum, she cannot do otherwise than as she does, must marry Edgar because there is no one else for her to marry and a lady must marry. Indeed, her self-justifying description of her love for Edgar – 'I love the ground under his feet, and the air over his head, and everything he touches, and every word he says' (Ch. 9) – is a bitter parody of a genteel romantic declaration which shows how effective her education has been in indoctrinating her with the literary romanticism deemed suitable for young ladies, the swooning 'femininity' that identifies all energies with the charisma of fathers/lovers/husbands. Her concomitant explanation that it would 'degrade' her to marry Heathcliff is an equally inevitable product of her education, for her fall into ladyhood has been accompanied by Heathcliff's reduction to an equivalent position of female powerlessness, and Catherine has learned, correctly, that if it is degrading to be a woman it is even more degrading to be *like* a woman. Just as Milton's Eve, therefore, being already fallen, had no meaningful choice despite Milton's best efforts to prove otherwise, so Catherine has no real choice. Given the patriarchal nature of culture, women must fall – that is, they are already fallen because doomed to fall. □

(pp. 276–7)

■ Catherine Earnshaw Linton's decline follows Catherine Earnshaw's fall. Slow at first, it is eventually as rapid, sickening, and deadly as the course of Brontë's own consumption was to be. And the long slide toward death of the body begins with what appears to be an irreversible death of the soul – with Catherine's fatalistic acceptance of Edgar's offer and her consequent self-imprisonment in the role of 'Mrs Linton, the lady of Thrushcross Grange'. □

(p. 278)

■ But Heathcliff's mysterious reappearance six months after her wedding intensifies rather than cures her symptoms. For his return does not in any way suggest a healing of the wound of femaleness that was inflicted at puberty. Instead, it signals the beginning of 'madness', a sort of feverish infection of the wound. Catherine's marriage to Edgar has now inexorably locked her into a social system that denies her autonomy, and thus, as psychic symbolism, Heathcliff's return represents the return of her true self's desires without the rebirth of her former powers. And desire without power, as Freud and Blake both knew, inevitably engender disease. □

(pp. 279–80)

■ Edgar's victory once again recapitulates that earlier victory of Thrushcross Grange over Wuthering Heights which also meant the victory of a Urizenic 'heaven' over a delightful and energetic 'hell'. At the same time, it seals Catherine's doom, locking her into her downward spiral of self-starvation. □

(p. 282)

Gilbert and Gubar now pay attention to the realities of the female body – another approach which was to prove fruitful for later feminists:

■ Critics never comment on this point, but the truth is that Catherine is pregnant during both the kitchen scene and the mad scene, and her death occurs at the time of (and ostensibly because of) her 'confinement'. In the light of this, her anorexia, her madness, and her masochism become even more fearsomely meaningful. Certainly, for instance, the distorted body that the anorexic imagines for herself is analogous to the distorted body that the pregnant woman really must confront. □

(p. 285)

■ Birth is, after all, the ultimate fragmentation the self can undergo, just as 'confinement' is, for women, the ultimate pun on imprisonment. As if in recognition of this, Catherine's attempt to escape maternity does, if only unconsciously, subvert Milton. For Milton's Eve 'knew not eating Death'. But Brontë's does. In her refusal to be enslaved to the species, her refusal to be 'mother of human race' [*sic*], she closes her mouth on emptiness as, in Plath's words, 'on a communion tablet'. It is no use, of course. She breaks apart into two Catherines – the old, mad, dead Catherine fathered by Wuthering Heights, and the new, more docile and acceptable Catherine fathered by Thrushcross Grange. □

(pp. 286–7)

Now Gilbert and Gubar offer a specifically feminist version of the genealogical readings of the novel we have seen in essays by Frank Kermode and others (chapter two):

■ Joseph's important remark about the restoration of the lawful master and the ancient stock, together with the dates – 1801/1802 – which surround Nelly's tale of a pseudo-mythic past, confirm the idea that *Wuthering Heights* is somehow etiological. More, the famous care with which Brontë worked out the details surrounding both the novel's dates and the Earnshaw-Linton lineage suggests she herself was quite conscious that she was constructing a story of origins and renewals. Having arrived at the novel's conclusion, we can now go back to its beginning, and try to summarize the basic story *Wuthering Heights* tells. Though this may not be the book's only story, it is surely a crucial one. As the names on the windowsill indicate, *Wuthering Heights* begins and ends with Catherine and her various avatars. More specifically, it studies the evolution of Catherine Earnshaw into Catherine Heathcliff and Catherine Linton, and then her return through Catherine Linton II and Catherine Heathcliff II to her 'proper' role as Catherine Earnshaw II. More generally, what this evolution and de-evolution conveys is the following parodic, anti-Miltonic myth:

There was an Original Mother (Catherine), a daughter of nature whose motto might be 'Thou, Nature, art my goddess; to thy law/My services are bound'.[10] But this girl fell into a decline, at least in part through eating the poisonous cooked food of culture. She fragmented herself into mad or dead selves on the one hand (Catherine, Heathcliff) and into lesser, gentler/genteeler selves on the other (Catherine II, Hareton). The fierce primordial selves disappeared into nature, the perversely hellish heaven which was their home. The more teachable and docile selves learned to read and write, and moved into the fallen cultured world of parlors and parsonages, the Miltonic heaven, which, from the Original Mother's point of view, is really hell. Their passage from nature to culture was facilitated by a series of teachers, preachers, nurses, cooks, and model ladies or patriarchs (Nelly, Joseph, Frances, the Lintons), most of whom gradually disappear by the end of the story, since these lesser creations have been so well instructed that they are themselves able to become teachers or models for other generations. Indeed, so model are they that they can be identified with the founders of ancestral houses (Hareton Earnshaw, 1500) and with the original mother redefined as the patriarch's wife (Catherine Linton Heathcliff Earnshaw). □

(pp. 302–3)

Like many other feminists, including Margaret Homans, Gilbert and Gubar point to the double effect of the novel's ending; the marriage of the younger characters effecting a reintegration into society which is nevertheless undercut by the memory of the older pair. However,

■ the random weakening of Wuthering Heights' walls with which Brontë's novel began – symbolized by old Earnshaw's discovery of Heathcliff at Liverpool – suggests that patriarchal culture is always only precariously holding off the rebellious forces of nature. Who, after all, can say with certainty that the restored line of Hareton Earnshaw 1802 will not someday be just as vulnerable to the onslaughts of the goddess's illegitimate children as the line of Hareton Earnshaw 1500 was to Heathcliff's intrusion? And who is to say that the carving of Hareton Earnshaw 1500 was not similarly preceded by still another war between nature and culture? The fact that everyone has the same name leads inevitably to speculations like this, as though the drama itself, like its actors, simply represented a single episode in a sort of mythic infinite regress. In addition, the fact that the little shepherd boy still sees 'Heathcliff and a woman' wandering the moor hints that the powerfully disruptive possibilities they represent may some day be reincarnated at Wuthering Heights.

Emily Brontë would consider such reincarnation a consummation devoutly to be wished. □

(p. 305)

Gilbert and Gubar's feminist myth-making is inspiring, and the 1980s saw an explosion of feminist studies of *Wuthering Heights* from a wide variety of perspectives. Where Gilbert and Gubar focus on the 'central' story, Margaret Homans, in her 1986 book, includes the 'frame' narratives in order to argue, more soberly, that within a predominantly masculine culture, the woman writer can hardly avoid simply *Bearing the Word* for patriarchy. In chapter three, I gave an extensive extract from Homans's 1983 essay, 'Dreaming of Children', which explains her linking of women with 'literal' rather than 'figurative' language, a position which derives from her idiosyncratic combination of Lacanian and Chodorowian theory. *Bearing the Word* uses the same theoretical framework but argues that, in the stories of the two Catherines, Emily Brontë has created

■ two contrasting myths of her own possible relation to language . . . The first Cathy's story is about a girl's refusal to enter something very like the Lacanian symbolic order, while the second Cathy's story revises her mother's, by having the girl accept her entry into the father's law. These two stories chart differing possibilities for the woman writer. □

(p. 68)

Recapitulating her theory of 'literal' language, Homans reminds us that 'it is through nature that texts in our dominant literary tradition articulate both the female and the literal in language' (p. 68). For Lacan (as for Derrida) each of these elusive referents represents the (unattainable) final term in a chain of meaning and thus the death of consciousness, so that 'just as, erotically, Lockwood never wants to come to the end of a series of substitutes, one woman for another, linguistically he never wants to refer in a determinate way to nature' (p. 69). As for Nelly, although she is a woman,

■ as a servant . . . she must identify her interests with those of her male employer and of the patrilineal family . . . Lockwood and Nelly believe that literal nature entering the realm of textuality would be as fatal to their vulnerable narratives as the snowstorm nearly was to Lockwood's life. Both narrators distance actual nature . . . by turning it into a source of figurative language. □

(p. 70)

Within this framework, Homans returns to the often-noticed fact that although *Wuthering Heights* seems to be 'about' nature, there are no 'set-piece' descriptions such as we find in Hardy. (This fact is thrown into relief by, for instance, Bernard Herrmann's opera, which begins with a quite improbable conversation between Catherine and Heathcliff on the beauties of nature.)[11] Although Catherine 'avoids writing nature . . . out of love for it' (pp. 72–3), this is not a practicable stance for a writer:

■ the problem is that a novel could never be written following Cathy's principles of writing . . . Brontë must transform herself from wild girl to male writer if for a woman to write is for her interests to become merged, like those of a female servant, with the interests of andro-centric culture. And yet . . . because Cathy will never grow up to become Lockwood, . . . Brontë's voice, and her motives for not repre-senting nature, may be divided between those of Cathy and those of Nelly and Lockwood. □

(p. 73)

■ This conflict, between the desire to be within the law and to remain outside it, is mediated in the novel's second, revisionary story of female development and language use, that of the second Cathy, who negoti-ates the passage from lawless childhood to adulthood within the symbolic order far more successfully than her mother does. □

(p. 74)

The younger Catherine's impulse to put her feelings into words comes with her recognition that the bluebell will die; 'reading nature thus begins with loss' (p. 75). Homans argues that Heathcliff, the orphan of no known origin, has a similar relation to language. Referring to Freud's anecdote of his grandson's 'fort-da game' (described in relation to Bersani in chapter three) she argues that Heathcliff's starvation of the young lapwings (Chapter 12) 'is a symbolic repetition of what he had himself experienced as a child . . . A ghoulish avatar of Freud's grandson, . . . Heathcliff reiterates and thus symbolically controls his own painful loss'. The compensatory power granted by language thus separates him from Catherine:

■ Instead of being identified with the brute forces of literal nature, as we would expect from Cathy's identification with him as a child, Heathcliff turns out to be for Cathy, as he is later for Cathy's daughter, a proponent of the Law of the Father. □

(p. 79)

Homans's depressing conclusion draws on what Nancy Chodorow calls *The Reproduction of Mothering* – the process whereby mothers are doomed by gender-polarisation to reproduce daughters who will in their turn serve the needs of patriarchal capitalism. Of the elder Catherine, Homans writes:

■ Because she has never fully abandoned her allegiance to the mother, never fully entered the father's law, she equates motherhood with a return to childhood . . . Cathy's history represents an extremely literal version of what Chodorow would call a daughter's reproduction of her own childhood, and this return through maternity to childhood collides with the devaluation of such a cycle within the symbolic order . . . And so precisely what she might have expected to give her power and life deprives her of it, since to be a mother in the culture in which she lives is to be the excluded term.

This, then, is what it means for the second Cathy to succeed to the first. The first Cathy, with her refusal to grow up into the symbolic, her allegiance to the mother and nature, and her vision of Nelly as powerful mother, is replaced, with her author's ambivalent reluctance, by the second Cathy, whose entry into the novel as an heir causes her to see Nelly as a vulnerable mother and predicts her greater acceptance of the Law of the Father . . . The very brutality with which the novel passes over Cathy's death is necessary to the text's self-preservation. □

(pp. 82–3)

Homans's glimmer of hope seems oddly to require us, like earlier 'humanist' readings, to jettison much of the text:

■ Brontë thus identifies her project with Lockwood's, with the son's, and with that of Nelly as the female servant of patriliny, repressing literal nature in favor of figuration. But through her heroine, we glimpse a different view, a different allegiance, through which the oppressive writing of nature, and of the mother, would be foregone. □

(p. 83)

In my 1992 'Feminist Criticism' article, I argue that Stevie Davies

■ provides a really startling contrast to both Gilbert and Gubar and Homans in her two books on Emily Brontë (1983 and 1988). Whereas it has almost become feminist orthodoxy to see nineteenth-century women writers as excluded and repressed by masculine culture, Davies argues that Emily Brontë was a 'free woman'. □

(p. 150)

I go on to quote Davies's second (1988) book, where she refers to Protestant theology and to Emily Brontë's own poetry in order to argue that

■ Uniquely among mythopoeic works of fiction *Wuthering Heights* raises the mother-principle (projected as the earth, the traditional *terra mater*) to the status of deity, presenting it as the focal object of human aspiration and the final end of Emily Brontë's language of desire. □

(Davies p. 25)

Like Juliet Mitchell (discussed in chapter three), Davies sees the novel as preoccupied with childhood and the family, and like Gilbert and Gubar she acknowledges its story as 'stages of the fall'. Unlike them, however, she reads the novel as an iconoclastic protest against the (father) God who has orphaned his children (p. 60).

■ Emily Brontë's work commands a unique view of childhood within our literature by exposing a language which hoarded verbatim the values, joys and pains of that state which, if not prelapsarian, presented the fall as an evolutionary sequence of stages of schism . . . The stages of the fall – birth, weaning into consciousness, mother-loss, father-loss, sibling-love and -rivalry, adolescence, marriage, parturition, the final split into a dead self (Catherine I) and its daughter-self – are encountered at every stage with protest by the novel's characters and as a riddle by the narrative voices. Most especially, the value of the adult culture that led to the meeting of author and reader is questioned, most memorably in the voice of Catherine in her final breakdown: '"What in the name of all that feels, has he to do with *books*, when I am dying?"' □

(*WH* p. 122) (Davies pp. 44–5)

In Chapter 1 of her book, Davies offers a detailed analysis of the 'childishness' of the novel's speech, taking for instance Catherine's deathbed scene after her plea to Heathcliff, 'Do come to me' (*WH* p. 160):

■ Language from this point syllables itself in Catherine's mouth as the pure and unmixed child-speech of extreme desire. It speaks in sentences of two or three words only; it has one point to make, and one only, whose expression it obsessively doubles: '"Let me alone. Let me alone . . . If I've done wrong, I'm dying for it. It is enough! You left me too; but I won't upbraid you! I forgive you. Forgive me!"' (*WH* p. 161) *Alone/ alone; forgive/Forgive:* the language makes its point by purely echoic devices. It commands; asserts; begs, within the cursory limit of an existence which has (literally) not breath enough left to afford the waste of one word. One final stream of words completes the process whereby the language of naked childhood emotion becomes the soul's last resort in the struggle 'never to be parted': . . . '"No!" she shrieked. "Oh, don't, don't go. It is the last time! Edgar will not hurt us. Heathcliff, I shall die! I shall die!"' (*WH* p. 162). Catherine proclaims the end of the world, in a detaining volley of negatives: her last word in the novel is *die,* her final articulate terror is that of separation from Heathcliff. □

(pp. 55–6)

Passing to Heathcliff after Catherine's death, Davies quotes his desperate plea:

■ '"Be with me always – take any form – drive me mad! only *do* not leave me in this abyss, where I cannot find you! Oh God! it is unutterable! I *cannot* live without my life! I *cannot* live without my soul!"
He dashed his head against the knotted trunk.' □

(*WH* p. 167)

Her analysis combines textual precision with a theoretical alertness which is, however, never advertised in her work:

■ Signs, as Hillis Miller has said, in *Wuthering Heights* codify absence, vacancy, no thing (*Repetition* p. 67). Heathcliff's 'abyss' derives from the *prima materia* from which the Creator-Spirit of Genesis divulged form and meaning, through Milton's 'wild abyss,/The womb of nature and perhaps her grave' (*PL* II 910–11), the abortive 'vast vacuity' (I 932). Hence he is left stranded in a no-man's-land at once prior to and subsequent to time and space. It is an uncreated world beyond any words, which his language seeks to transform into plenitude by conjuring Catherine to declare her whereabouts. What he resists is her evacuation from reality. He does not resist, rather welcomes, his own pain as a testament to the possibility of her immanence, invoking her to haunt him. The great double assertion which consummates his rage of loss: '"I *cannot* . . . I *cannot*"' demonstrates the stern literality with which Emily Brontë had contemplated the resources of language: compelling it to stand or fall by the buried metaphors which informed it. The conventional equation of another person with one's own 'life' and 'soul' is accorded by the novel's literalists the status of congruence with human actuality. But in confronting its own self-consistency, this unifying language of mutual identity breaks upon the invincible contradiction offered to it by exterior reality: the loss of Catherine. Hence the passionate repeated negatives – *cannot, cannot* – and the resort of the speaker to an act of expression outside the circumference of words: 'He dashed his head . . . howled, not like a man'. The language of human culture is abject before the confounding 'abyss' of hollowness in the universe to which [Heathcliff] is committed. Heathcliff has prayed directly into the abyss and will repeat his prayer 'till my tongue stiffens', that this vast vacuity should yield up a semblance of the desired beloved. The perception that the prayer is unanswerable by the voiceless world beyond the ego is the signal for his human voice to respond by adjusting its form to the formlessness of the Abyss: to collapse into howls for what cannot be found, as the child howls for its mother in the night, *infans*, languageless. Heathcliff nowhere more profoundly than in this passage of degenerating grief incarnates a central theme of the novel – the orphaning of God's child as a cast-off in the universe. □

(pp. 58–60)

In compensation for the 'disappearance of God', however, Davies sees 'mother nature' in a much more positive light than Homans, incorporating some of the 'mythic' material discussed in chapter four. The novel, she says,

■ locates an alternative area of the divine to that of the Father-God. Deep in its own experience of lack, absence and loss, the psyche in *Wuthering Heights* perceives a spiritual home identifiable with the mother. A void in the communal life of the characters, (the first generation of mothers, Catherine and Frances, die in or just after childbirth) is wistfully transferred, and thence to some degree filled, to a new location in the created and suffering universe itself. Beneath the action of the novel, readers are impressed by their intuition of the attending and waiting presence of the moor, despite the seldom-noted fact that it is barely described in physical terms during the crucial first half of the novel. It receives, endorses and forgives; or rather, endorses the fact that there is nothing to forgive. It is the realm of silence and retreat, a playground for children; the mythic ground of action. Beyond the human focus of desire (Catherine's love for Heathcliff) is implied the larger object of desire (Catherine's love for the heath). On the psychological level, the children's refusal of control in *Wuthering Heights* is also a mute demand for the embrace that gathers the child in to himself, providing the limit to his ire and destructiveness. The voices exhibit the combined relish and terror of the uncontrolled idiom that distorts the face of childhood into that of a monster, magnifying its angers into a demonic threat to existence itself. The means of such embrace (the mother) is almost wholly absent from the text, though its children rage and wail loudly enough to wake the dead. Nelly, rocking on her knee the motherless Hareton, hums a snatch of a ballad from Scott: 'It was far in the night, and the bairnies grat,/The mither beneath the mools heard that' (*WH* p.76). In the song, as I have shown elsewhere (1983, pp.156–7), the natural mother awakens in her grave at the keening of her orphaned children tortured by their stepmother. Her corpse trespasses across the barrier of mortality, impelled by the fiat of their grief, to remedy their situation. The motherless author of *Wuthering Heights* releases the voices of her characters as a universal cry of need. The novel records both the potency of that need and its absolute failure to register or to obtain the satisfaction of a reply. Yet each time we reread, this fearful hope is freshly aroused, and the novel with profound artfulness never denies that either the dead may walk with us or we sleep with them, in the fullest reunion. □

(pp.63–4)

Davies's close attention to the language of the novel allows her to make an unusually positive case for the novel:

■ Emily Brontë's novel does, on the face of it, appear to argue against the accepted meaningful events of human life, being born, growing up, and for the desirability of death. The tenor is sombre. But the tonality of the novel's voices is quite otherwise: it is joyous. Its language, from the wicked ironies of the narrative voice to the dream speech of its lyricism, is pure *jeu d'esprit*. The act of writing appears as the unique means of immortalising and authorising the energies of childhood, whereby words (a sign in themselves of loss, since they occur in a child's development after the initially wordless eye-contact with the mother has been forfeited) are liberated from their original conditions to be inscribed in the form of a homeopathic – not palliative – remedy for the very conditions they record. □

(pp.89–90)

From this position of relative strength, Davies rewrites what Gilbert and Gubar perceive as 'Milton's bogey':

■ In the Scriptures, redemption is worked for man by the mediatorial Son of the Father. In Emily Brontë's heretical reversal of paternal traditions, it is achieved by reincorporation within the daughter of the mother. *Wuthering Heights* is remarkable for the uxoriousness of its male protagonists: Heathcliff's passion for Catherine is paralleled by Linton's, Hindley's for Francis, Hareton's for the second Catherine. The thwarting of these primal allegiances – a love which worships its idolised object as a version of God – represents the exile from Paradise. Hence, what is sin in Milton is virtue in Emily Brontë. The principle of likeness between male and female in the matrix of familial bonding is perhaps the supremely anti-Miltonic stance held by *Wuthering Heights*. □

(p. 116)

Davies is thus able to argue against the dramatic contrast which most critics see between the two houses:

■ Ultimately, Catherine's grave centralises those of Linton and Heathcliff: the warring tribes of Seth and Cain concur at either side of the self to whom each refers, exemplifying to eternity the same virtue: fidelity. The 'feminine' Linton and the 'masculine' Heathcliff are equally exemplary in this virtue, like fraternal twins, light and shadowy.

Hence, Emily Brontë's joyous literary feud with Milton is conducted not just through the Church-hating, God-daring passion of Catherine and Heathcliff, but – more straightforwardly, through the God-fearing Edgar Linton's preference for the religion of human love over the religion of his fathers. □

(p. 118)

What Davies was in 1994 to call Emily Brontë's heresy thus consists in 'the displacement of heaven made by *Wuthering Heights* from the supernatural to the natural, the Father's transcendence to the mother's immanence' (p. 119).

Gilbert and Gubar, Homans and Davies are all concerned to give what we might call a global reading of the text. There are a number of feminists, however, who focus on particular aspects of the narrative technique. Charlotte Goodman and Syndy McMillen Conger, both writing in 1983, argue respectively that *Wuthering Heights* revises the traditional *Bildungsroman* form and the traditional Gothic plot. Naomi Jacobs, in 'Gender and Layered Narrative in *Wuthering Heights* and *The Tenant of Wildfell Hall*' (1986), gives a legal-social dimension to the question of the narrative frame, suggesting, unlike Homans, that the process of exposing the real constraints of women's lives represents at least a partial loosening of those constraints. Jacobs points out that

■ in both *Wuthering Heights* and *The Tenant of Wildfell Hall*, we approach a horrific private reality only after passing through and then discarding the perceptual structures of a narrator – significantly, a male narrator – who represents the public world that makes possible and tacitly approves the excesses behind the closed doors of these pre-Victorian homes. □

(p. 204)

■ Each of these books depicts an unpleasant and often violent domestic reality completely at odds with the Victorian ideal of the home as a refuge from the harshly competitive outside world. And each shows that those with social power inflict violence on the powerless, including children, women, and landless men. □

(p. 205)

Jacobs then proceeds to document the prevalence of nineteenth-century wife-abuse and the reluctance of reviewers to accept its existence – a context which reveals the Brontë sisters as writing what was regarded as 'unwritable' in contemporary terms. Jacobs argues that 'the narrative structure of both these novels represents an authorial strategy for dealing with the unacceptability of the subject matter' (p. 206); 'the outer reality is male and the inner reality is largely female', mimicking the legal concept of the 'femme couverte' – the 'covered woman' whose interests were supposed to be included in those of a male guardian, and whose abuse was thus 'hidden' from the public gaze. Jacobs agrees with Conger that *Wuthering Heights* revises the Gothic norm:

■ the evil hidden at the centre of these pseudo-gothic narratives is not supernatural or even particularly diabolical; it is mundane, vulgar, and grounded in the legal and economic structures of the time and the effects of these structures on the consciousness of both those in power (the 'covering' narrators) and those without power (the 'covered' narrators). □

(p. 207)

Like Homans, Jacobs accepts that

■ we return to the world of normality, as Hareton and Cathy will return to Thrushcross Grange and some version of the domestic bliss that was the Victorian ideal. But we have seen an under-world or other-world that is still latent in the structures of the comfortable reality. □

(p. 217)

Jacobs's article reminds us of the importance of the material, social, aspect of *Wuthering Heights* as it relates to women, and Carol Senf's article,

'Emily Brontë's Version of Feminist History' (1985), also uses this perspective to claim that Emily Brontë incorporates feminist history into her
novel, moving from a past characterised by the masculine violence of
Lockwood, Heathcliff and Hindley to a future where gentleness and co-
operation, virtues normally associated with women, can be expected to
modify patriarchal behaviours (p. 205).

Lyn Pykett's 1989 book on *Emily Brontë* draws together the insights of
these critics – in particular the revision of Gothic and the sense of historical
progress represented by the sequence of generations and genres. Her
Chapter 5 focuses on the generic instability of *Wuthering Heights.*

■ *Wuthering Heights* has proved impossible to categorise, and continues
to confront its reader with a sometimes alarming sense of disorienta-
tion, a feeling of finding themselves in 'really different novels'.[12] The
novel begins in fictional territory which is reasonably familiar to readers of the eighteenth- and nineteenth-century Domestic novel: a date
(1801), the genteel narrator's ironic description of a social visit, the
careful description of the domestic interior at the Heights, and the
beginnings of an investigation of a code of manners and a particular
way of life. However, even in the opening chapter the codes and conventions of polite fiction do not seem adequate either to comprehend or
represent life at the Heights. For example, Lockwood's description
focuses on the *absence* of the *expected* 'glitter of saucepans and tin
cullenders on the walls' (Penguin p. 47) and the presence of 'villainous
old guns, and a couple of horse pistols'. Certainly, by the second and
third chapters, the genteel narrator and the reader find their generic
and social expectations increasingly at odds with the literary genre and
social world into which the narrative has moved. The appearance of
Catherine's ghost, and Heathcliff's passionate response, take the novel
into the literary genre of Gothic and the forms of the fantastic which
provide much of its extraordinary power. □

(pp. 74–5)

■ Embedded within this Gothic framework, however, is a second
narrative, which seems to move progressively in the direction of
Victorian Domestic Realism. The second half of the novel's double plot
– the second generation story of Linton Heathcliff, Hareton Earnshaw
and Catherine Linton – appears to move from Gothic beginnings, in
which a monstrous Hareton implicitly collaborates in the abduction of
Catherine, her forced marriage to Linton and her effective imprisonment at the Heights, to the conventional closure of a dominant form of the
Victorian Domestic novel, in which the hero (Hareton) and heroine
(Catherine) overcome the obstacles of an obstructive society and with-
draw into a private realm of domesticity, where social, co-operative

values are renewed within the bosom of the family. In this case the pattern of closure is completed by the planned removal of Hareton and Catherine from the Heights to Thrushcross Grange.

Gothic is usually taken to be the dominant genre of the first generation plot of *Wuthering Heights*, and is associated with its Romanticism, its mystical, fantastic and supernatural elements, and its portrayal of wild nature. In the eighteenth and nineteenth centuries Gothic was a genre particularly identified with women writers, and many recent feminist critics have argued that Female Gothic may be seen as a complex genre which simultaneously represents women's fears and offers fantasies of escape from them. Female Gothic enacts fantasies of female power in the heroine's courage and enterprise, while simultaneously, or by turns, representing the female condition as both confinement and refuge. Many of the Gothic elements of *Wuthering Heights* may be seen as examples of Female Gothic's representation and investigation of women's fears about the private domestic space which is at once refuge and prison. Indeed, Catherine Earnshaw's story might almost be read as an archetypal example of the genre. After a childhood which alternates between domestic confinement and freely roaming the unconfined spaces of the moors, Catherine's puberty is marked by her confinement to the couch of Thrushcross Grange. Womanhood and marriage to Edgar further confine her within the genteel household, and the denouement of her particular Gothic plot involves her imprisonment in increasingly confined spaces: the house, her room, and finally 'this shattered prison' (Penguin p. 196), her body, from which she longs to escape as she does from womanhood itself. □

(pp. 76–7)

■ Female Gothic explores women's power and powerlessness, their confinement within the domestic space, their role in the family, and their regulation by marriage and property laws not of their own making and, at this point in history, beyond their power to alter. Many of these concerns are represented, from a different perspective, in the increasingly dominant female genre of Domestic fiction. In a fascinating study of twentieth-century Gothics Tania Modleski has suggested that these similarities make for a continuity between Gothic and Domestic, since both are 'concerned with the (often displaced) relationships among family members and with driving home to women the importance of coping with enforced confinement and the paranoid fears it generates'.[13]

Certainly, in *Wuthering Heights* Gothic and Domestic are continuous, not simply because of this shared project, but also because the genres are mixed so as to produce a structural continuity. For example, although the Gothic is usually associated with the first generation plot and the Domestic with the second (or even with the last phase of the second generation plot), the novel's narrative structure, and particularly its dislocated chronology, tends to blur the boundaries between generations and genres. Emily Brontë's adaptation of the conventions of the Gothic frame tale is a particularly important element in this process. In earlier Gothic novels the central narrative is approached by way of diaries, letters and other documents which are transcribed or edited by the narrator(s) of the story. Similarly, the reader approaches the central narrative of *Wuthering Heights* via an outsider, Lockwood, who transmits or mediates Nelly's inner (and insider) narrative. To gain access to the extraordinary stories of the families of Wuthering Heights and Thrushcross Grange the reader must thus pass through, and ultimately pass beyond, the perceptual structures of a bemused genteel male narrator who mediates between the public world he shares with his readers and the inner, private, domestic world conveyed to him by Nelly's stories. □

(pp. 78–9)

■ The closing stages of the narrative seem to move towards the conventional closure of the Victorian Domestic novel: the restitution of family fortunes, the restoration of disrupted stability, and intimations of protracted domestic bliss in the protected space of the ideal nuclear family. However, as with so many aspects of this novel, appearances are deceptive. Although the second generation story revises the Gothic plot of the first generation in the direction of Domestic fiction, the Gothic is not simply written out or obliterated in the process. The Gothic persists in the person of Heathcliff who spans both generations. Indeed, his necrophilia and otherworldliness become more pronounced as the Domestic plot reaches its resolution. The Gothic persists too in the power of Catherine and Heathcliff which remains in the outer narrative, beyond the closure of the Catherine-Hareton plot.

Moreover the 'conventional' Domestic romance with which the novel ends not only revises the initial Gothic plot but is also a revisionary form of the genre in which it purports to be written. □

Pykett then instances the younger Catherine's devotion to books and her power with words, which she uses against Heathcliff.

■ Catherine's civilising of Hareton is an interesting variant of a common scene in eighteenth- and nineteenth-century fiction in which a male character offers improving reading to an 'ignorant' (but improvable) female . . . As the novel ends Catherine is about to regain control of her inheritance, and although at this period she would have been legally required to hand all her property back to Hareton when he became her husband, it is nevertheless at least of symbolic importance that Hareton's patrimony is returned to him via the female line. Like Jane Eyre's legacy, the restoration of Catherine's property equalises the balance of power between marriage partners. A degree of financial independence for the female partner seems to be a prerequisite for the companionate marriages with which both these novels end.

In its transition from patriarchal tyranny, masculine competition, domestic imprisonment and the Gothic to the revised Domestic romance of the courtship and companionate marriage of Catherine and Hareton, *Wuthering Heights* both participates in, and engages with, the feminisation of literature and the wider culture noted by Armstrong and Spencer. However, I would suggest that Emily Brontë's novel does not simply reflect or represent this process, but that it also investigates and explores . . . both changing patterns of fiction and the emergence of new forms of the family.

. . . It traces the process, minutely documented by Leonore Davidoff and Catherine Hall in *Family Fortunes* (1987), by which the modern family (represented by Catherine and Hareton) replaced the larger and more loosely related household (as exemplified by various stages of domestic life at the Heights), withdrawing to a private domestic space removed from the workplace. Catherine and Hareton are shown as inhabiting this newly privatised domestic realm even before their marriage and removal to the Grange. Their cultivation of the flower garden and Hareton's primrose-strewn porridge (Penguin p. 348) are emblematic of their transformation of the Heights into a domain of feminine values, a haven of tranquillity to which men retire from a workaday world of business and competition, in order to cultivate their gardens, their hobbies and the domestic ideal.

However, at the same time as *Wuthering Heights* traces the emergence of the modern family and its hegemonic fictional form of Domestic realism, other elements of the novel – its disrupted chronology, its dislocated narrative structure, and the persistence of the disturbing power of Catherine and Heathcliff – work together to keep other versions of domestic life before the reader: the domestic space as prison, the family as site of primitive passions, violence, struggle and control. □

(pp. 82–5)

Jacobs, Senf and Pykett, while allowing more freedom of action for the woman writer than Homans, still assume that her stance is reactive, giving at best a woman-centred view of an intransigent external 'history'. Anita Levy's 1986 article on *Wuthering Heights* draws on the theories of Michel Foucault to argue that *Wuthering Heights* shows four stages of transformation in the 'history of desire'. Nancy Armstrong's 1987 book, however, uses Foucauldian theory in a way which makes Levy look quite conventional; her thesis is nothing less than Oscar Wilde's, that 'Art does not imitate life, life imitates art'. Briefly, she argues that the ideological construction of 'separate spheres' for men and women in the nineteenth century, which is usually thought to follow the industrial separation of workplace and home, actually preceded and facilitated those changes, so that 'the formation of the modern political state . . . was accomplished largely through cultural hegemony' (p. 9). Because the domestic novel was one of the main ways in which men and women learned their separate roles, Armstrong argues that such novels became temporarily the site of social change, and women novelists thus the wielders of real power.

Like Musselwhite, Armstrong believes that *Wuthering Heights* disguises its own historicity, using tropes (figures of speech) which 'translated all kinds of political information into psychological terms' (p. 187).

■ As if to testify to the success of the Brontës' fables of desire, literary criticism has compulsively read these novels according to the same psychologizing tropes they formulated. Indeed, contemporary criticism has turned the Brontës' novels into sublimating strategies that conceal forbidden desires, including incest, which is generally considered the most plausible key to the novels. Critics still seem to be asking what else, if not such desire, could have motivated the elaborate sequences of substitutions that finally allow both *Wuthering Heights* and *Jane Eyre* to end with satisfactory marriages. The Brontës still entice us to extend their own aesthetic process to inscribe, finally, all their historical material within figures of desire. So powerful is the hermeneutic circle that makes their language of the self into its own basis for meaning that the noblest efforts to evade this trap are ensnared themselves as critics inevitably adopt a modern psychological vocabulary to interpret the Brontës' fiction. □

(p. 187)

Instead of seeing this psychologising as a dehistoricising process, however, Armstrong turns the priorities around. Because the regime of self-regulation which Foucault saw as characteristic of the nineteenth century required the self to be perceived as an object of knowledge, Armstrong contends that 'writing that constituted the self as such an object of knowledge was a primary agent of history'.

■ It is because the Brontës have encouraged readers to seek out the meaning of fiction in a recognizably modern form of consciousness that their novels have played an important part in British history. If one gives any credence to the notion of a history of subjectivity and to the priority of writing in constituting subjectivity as an object of knowledge, then it is a relatively simple step to see the Brontës as agents of history. We can assume their fiction produced – and continues with each act of interpretation to produce – figures of modern desire. These techniques have suppressed the political identity along with the knowledge of oneself as such. The production of the political unconscious has accompanied the production of the sexual subject, I believe, and in this way has constituted the repressive power actually exercised by a polite tradition of writing. ☐

(p. 191)

The Brontës' writing, then, can in this way be read as hegemonic rather than subversive. Nevertheless a comparison with Jane Austen demonstrates the newness of the Brontës' 'objects of desire':

■ Austen's heroines marry as soon as their desire has been correctly aimed and accurately communicated. But the Brontës broke up this congruity of personal and social experience by endowing their heroines with desire for the one object they could not possess, namely, Heathcliff and Rochester as first encountered in the novels . . . giving rise to the notion that social conventions are, in an essential way, opposed to individual desire . . . such a rhetorical opposition provides the necessary precondition for a modern theory of repression. ☐

(pp. 192–3)

Armstrong follows Jameson and Kavanagh in seeing in *Wuthering Heights* an exchange or displacement between the 'restless momentum' of capital and of sexual desire; unlike them, however, she sees this social unsettling as created by female desire for an impossible object.

■ Under these circumstances, marriage quite literally ceases to embody desire, or rather, it embodies desire only to the degree that desire has brutally misshapen the social conventions that seek to suppress and contain it. In this way, the novel locates desire elsewhere, in an extrasocial dimension of human experience . . .

In righting the order of social relations, then, the Brontës reconstitute the individual as a particular field of knowledge whose identity is neither socially nor genealogically determined because its fate or 'development' is propelled by female desires. Under such circumstances, the possibilities and prerogatives of female subjectivity seem to expand immensely . . . It is important to note that in the process of handing over such powers of motivation to the female, fiction does something to history. Understanding the configuration of social relationships which concludes both *Wuthering Heights* and *Jane Eyre* requires another order of history that is no longer considered history at all. It is a tale told by a woman. It is a history of sexuality. ☐

(pp. 196–7)

■ When the Brontës infuse their heroines with desire for the one male who cannot possess them, everyone within the field of social possibilities becomes a mere substitute for the original, and socially mediated forms of desire never again provide anything approximating *complete* gratification – to wit, Rochester's missing parts. This eternal deferral of gratification might appear to set desire forever in the realm of romance and therefore forever at odds with reality, but such is not the case. As the Brontës represent it, desire acquires a reality in its own right, a reality equivalent to, though often in conflict with, the reality principle. If anything, desire wins out over the reality principle, as these novels progressively reorganize disparate elements of the socioeconomic field into an artificial unity – that of the narrative consciousness. Not only social signs, but anatomical elements, biological functions, behaviors, sensations, and pleasures all become signs of male or female desire. And as they do so, the principle reorganizing the object world into this gender formation takes on the proportions of a causal principle and a universal meaning to be discovered. ☐

(p. 198)

Where Armstrong's main theoretical force comes from Michel Foucault, Patricia Yaeger draws on Bakhtinian theory in her 1988 article, 'Violence in the Sitting Room' (which is repeated with only minor changes in her book of the same date). Like Davies, Yaeger takes up Ellen Moers's hint about the 'joyous' aspects of *Wuthering Heights*; but Yaeger uses Bakhtin's theories to focus on the subversive power of laughter, reading his work in combination with the French feminist Julia Kristeva's *Revolution in Poetic Language* and Hélène Cixous's 'The Laugh of the Medusa'. In this context Yaeger is able to oppose readings by a number of other feminists (including Myra Jehlen and Rachel Brownstein)[14] who see the novel as a dangerous trap for women, arguing that

■ As a multi-voiced, multi-languaged form – a form inviting the novelist to parody other discourses and portray a dialogic 'struggle among socio-linguistic points of view', the novel is a genre which encourages its writers to assault the language systems of others and to admit into these language systems the disruptive ebullience of other speech and of laughter. ☐

(p. 207)

In place of Gilbert and Gubar's reading of Heathcliff as the symbol of the woman writer's anxiety, and of Jameson's reading of Heathcliff as 'the locus of *history*, Yaeger argues instead for a reading which

■ would locate the trauma and reenactment of the woman writer's anxiety of authorship in the beginning of the book – explicitly in the scene . . . in which Lockwood cuts Cathy's hand. If we read this scene as gothic and parodic, as a tragic exegesis of masculine power which is, at the same time, a weirdly comic expulsion of this power, we have begun to account for several items most critics of the novel ignore: (1) the novel's opening humour, (2) the novel's preoccupation with class, and (3) the novel's shift from a masculine to a feminine narrator. □

(p. 226)

The feminine narrator, Nelly Dean, now becomes the focus for some conflicting feminist interpretations. Yaeger argues that through Nelly's narrative, we are reminded of the tangle of economic and social factors which determine family membership, while being discouraged from identifying too closely with any single person. In the same year as Yaeger's article and book (1988), Bette London argues that Nelly's own story is repressed by, but affects her judgement of, the Earnshaw-Linton history, so that her fierce adherence to the 'law' (which dispossessed her of her love for Hindley) is undercut by her involuntary expressions of sympathy with other dispossessed characters. London thus offers a feminist revision of Matthews's argument about the literally interminable process by which the reader 'succumb[s] to the constant oscillation between figure and ground'.

In the following year (1989), Karen Chase makes a positive case for Nelly's role through the medium of gossip.

■ It is not Joseph with his scripture but Nelly with her gossip who works her way into the center of events and who is chiefly responsible for one of the most startling aspects of *Wuthering Heights*: its reliance on the methods and motives of voyeurism.

Observing, overhearing, snooping, skulking, eavesdropping – these are not incidental lapses, they are central activities in a book where being is never clearly distinguished from seeing. □

(pp. 25–6)

With an inflection reminiscent of Bakhtinian dialogism, Chase notes that

■ In every act of gossip there lives a tacit acknowledgement of a rival subjectivity, there lives the recognition that I who speak may soon be spoken of. Nelly Dean . . . is repeatedly caught in the act, repeatedly seen seeing; and yet just this failure of concealment ensures her importance – because to be seen seeing is to become at once subject and object, a constituting eye and a constituted body, a critic and a thing criticized. This is the deepest implication of that reversal of gaze which informs *Wuthering Heights* at every level and which allows it to become an exemplary text for heroines and also for historians.[15] □

(p. 28)

In the following year (1990), two feminist critics take up the two branches of Chase's argument: Beth Newman develops Chase's argument about the 'reversal of the gaze', and Regina Barreca discusses ways in which women 'appropriate the power of inscription' in *Wuthering Heights* (p. 227). Beth Newman (1990) draws on Lacan's theory of 'scopophilia' (love of looking) to discuss the question of 'the gaze'. Lacan explains that boys have their contact with the mother's body abruptly prohibited by their (prematurely complete) entry into the Symbolic order, so that adult men cultivate the gaze (at female objects) as a permitted mode of regress to that lost, 'imaginary' sense of wholeness (discussed in relation to Bersani and others in chapter three).[16] Because of its context within prohibition, however, the gaze is pleasurable only so long as it is not returned. Newman analyses the opening scenes of *Wuthering Heights* in which Lockwood provokes the dogs by a stare and has to fend off 'the canine mother' with a poker. Newman comments that 'to be the object of the gaze . . . is to lose one's position of mastery and control' (p. 1032). The younger Catherine also discomposes Lockwood by staring back, which earns her the epithet of 'witch':

■ Even Heathcliff finds the power of her gaze preternaturally disconcerting: 'What fiend possesses you to stare back at me, continually, with those infernal eyes? Down with them! and don't remind me of your existence again' (*WH* p. 318) . . . Through Catherine, the text parodically inscribes the dynamics involved in the gaze and articulates the psychological fact that when a woman looks back she asserts her 'existence' as a subject, her place outside the position of object to which the male gaze relegates her and by which it defines her as 'woman'. The novel even confronts these dynamics straightforwardly, having Catherine explicitly deny to Heathcliff that he has anything to fear from her gaze: 'I'll not take my eyes from your face, till you look back at me! No, don't turn away! *do* look! You'll see nothing to provoke you'. □

(*WH* p. 275).

Maja-Lisa Von Sneidern and Susan Meyer both use the reverse gaze in their postcolonial arguments (discussed above); unlike them, however, Newman does not overestimate the power of reversal:

■ By parodying and challenging what Mary Ann Doane calls 'the sexual politics of looking', the text even raises a question that feminist theory has been asking: Is the gaze male? That is, is it possible to elude the patriarchal 'regime of the specular'?[17] . . . Catherine's situation underscores the difficulty of doing that. In assuming the role of spectator, she seeks a 'masculine' position that because she is a woman, redefines her as a 'monster' or 'witch'. Even as a spectator, then, Catherine is locked into exaggerating the role of the woman whose gaze is dangerous to men, engaging in a kind of female impersonation or masquerade, an imitation of femininity as a construct. Such a masquerade can register a protest against the gender conventions it mimics, but there is no clear evidence that it can dismantle them. □

(pp. 1032–3)

As a further development, beyond evasion or reversal, 'the courtship of Catherine and Hareton at the end, read in the light of the gaze, tells the utopian story of a subtle but essential transformation of the structures the novel faults' (p.1036). In Vol. II Chapter 18, we hear how Catherine, by persevering, gets Hareton to return her look. At breakfast the following day, Hareton's knowledge of this shared look enables him to *laugh* (*WH* p. 318). Newman comments:

■ Hélène Cixous has written that the Medusa who has terrorized the male subject, looked at 'straight on', is actually 'beautiful . . . and . . . laughing' (p. 255). Brontë has uncannily anticipated Cixous's analysis of the masculine fear of the woman's gaze in suggesting that Hareton, alone among the male characters in the novel, is able to laugh back.[18] □

This book perhaps fittingly ends with an extract from Regina Barreca's chapter, 'The Power of Excommunication: Sex and the Feminine Text in *Wuthering Heights*'. She takes her argument from the same scene, in Vol. II Chapter 18, which begins with Nelly singing 'Fairy Annie's Wedding', and Joseph complaining that 'them glories tuh Sattan' prevent him from reading 't'Blessed Book' (*WH* p. 308). Barreca comments that 'the prevailing language of *Wuthering Heights* is . . . not the language of the law but . . . the song and the story . . . Nelly has in her possession the unwritten, contraband history of folk-lore, songs and ballads' (pp. 229–30). Women thus

■ create and shape all the language play of the text . . . They claim the authority of the 'author' – the initiator and the inscriber . . . They create a system of feminine 'excommunication', whereby they appropriate discourse and desire, surrounding the patriarchal text . . . and render it ineffective, if not obsolete . . . The system of feminine discourse in this book is expelled from, existing outside of, but more powerful than the traditional script. □

(p. 228)

NOTES

CHAPTER ONE

1 Charlotte Brontë to William Smith Williams, 22 November 1848; quoted in Juliet Barker, p.575.

2 See the unidentified review quoted by Simpson, pp.177–9; *CH*, p.243 and the *Spectator* (18 Dec 1847), p.1217; *CH*, p.217.

3 *The Economist* (1848) agrees that the novel lacks moral direction and *Tait's Magazine* repeats Whipple's point that 'its powerful writing was thrown away' (p.138); quoted in Melvin Watson, 'Critics', p.245).

4 Genesis 15:12.

5 An Afreet is 'an evil demon or monster of Mohammedan mythology' (*OED*). Cf. Byron, *The Giaour*, l.784.

6 Lewes joins Sydney Dobell in approving of Emily's handling of Catherine's simultaneous loves (*CH*, p.293); 1850 was the year in which he most amicably 'shared' his wife with Thornton Hunt (see Gordon S. Haight. *George Eliot: A Biography*. Oxford: Oxford University Press, 1968, p.131).

7 *North American Review* (1857), p.327.

CHAPTER TWO

1 'Canonised' is a metaphor deriving from ecclesiastical usage, where it would mean 'accepted as an authorised part of holy scripture, otherwise called the "canon"'. In literary terms, it means that a text has achieved 'classic' status.

2 John Milton, *L'Allegro*, line 134.

3 Willis's immediate purpose was to prove that *Wuthering Heights* had been written by Emily Brontë and not by Branwell. The question of disputed authorship will be dealt with in chapter four.

4 Discussed briefly in chapter one.

5 The word 'discursive' has a variety of meanings; here it appears to mean 'argumentative' [Ed.].

6 W.K. Wimsatt and Monroe C. Beardsley, 'The Intentional Fallacy', 1946. W.K. Wimsatt. *The Verbal Icon*, 1954.

7 This more scientific attitude to language can be seen in a more extravagant form in R.B. Pearsall's 1966 essay, 'The Presiding Tropes of Emily Brontë'.

8 Here there is a reference to Mark Schorer's 1949 essay.

9 See Gleckner (1959), McKibben (1960), Van de Laar (1969), Blondel (1975) and Melchiori (1975–6).

10 William Dean Howells (1901) and Arthur Symons (1918) also find the book ill-constructed, and Melvin Watson (1948–9) cites a number of others (p.255–7).

11 Sanger's chronology has been refined by later critics. See Charles Travis Clay, S.A. Power and A. Stuart Daley.

12 Quoted by J.A. Cuddon, p.33.

13 See C.P. Sanger.

14 Melvin R. Watson, 'Tempest', p.88; see also Allott 1958.

15 See James Hafley [Ed.].

16 Emily Jane Brontë, 'No Coward Soul Is Mine', in *Complete Poems*, ed. C.W. Hatfield, p.243.

17 This parallel is taken up by Mary Visick in 1967, and in 1998 Edward Chitham demonstrates that the poem and the speech were probably written within weeks of each other.

18 A 'rebus' is 'an enigmatical representation of a name, word or phrase by figures, pictures, arrangement of letters etc.' (*Shorter Oxford English Dictionary*) [Ed.].

19 'Endogamy' and 'exogamy' are anthropological terms indicating cultures which characteristically marry inside or outside the family grouping [Ed.].

20 'Pneumatology' is 'the science . . . of spirits or spiritual beings . . . God . . . angels and demons, and of the human soul' [Ed.].

21 'Hermeneutic' means 'interpretative' (*Shorter Oxford English Dictionary*) [Ed.].

22 Wolfgang Iser, 'Indeterminacy and the Reader's Response' in *Aspects of Narrative*, ed. J. Hillis Miller (1971), p.42.

23 An 'episteme' is a system of knowledge [Ed.].

24 Leo Bersani will be discussed in chapter three; Margaret Homans and Terry Eagleton in chapter five.

25 Jacques Derrida, 'Living On: *Border Lines*' in *Deconstruction and Criticism*, ed. Geoffrey Hartman (New York: Seabury, 1979).

26 A 'synecdoche' is a figure of speech in which the part stands for the whole [Ed.].

27 Bersani's article will be discussed in chapter three, below.

28 A 'palimpsest' is a manuscript written over an earlier text [Ed.].

29 Parker's references are to the Penguin *WH*.

30 'Apotropaic' means 'turning away from a place'; 'proleptically' means 'anticipating future events' [Ed.].

31 'Parataxis' is the placing of items of speech together without conjunctions [Ed.].

CHAPTER THREE

1 Claude Lévi-Strauss's books, *The Raw and the Cooked* and *The Elementary Structures of Kinship*, both appeared in 1969.

2 Norman O. Brown, *Life Against Death* (New York, 1959), p. 40.

3 Freud's 'fort-da game' is described in relation to Leo Bersani, below.

4 See James Hafley (1958), who argues that Nelly Dean is 'The Villain in *Wuthering Heights*'.

5 Jacques Lacan, *Les Ecrits techniques de Freud. Le Séminaire*. Vol. I (Paris: Seuil, 1975), p. 178.

6 Julia Kristeva, 'Psychoanalysis and the Polis' in *The Politics of Interpretation*, trans. Margaret Waller, ed. W. J. T. Mitchell (Chicago: University of Chicago Press, 1982), pp. 87–8.

7 Emily Brontë, *Complete Poems*, ed. C. W. Hatfield, p. 242.

CHAPTER FOUR

1 Other critics who believe that Branwell wrote or significantly influenced the writing of *Wuthering Heights* include the Hon. Mr Justice Vaisey (1946) and Peter Quennell (1947).

2 For many years, the 'definitive' edition of Emily's poems has been C. W. Hatfield's (1941). There are more recent editions by Janet Gezari (1992) and Derek Roper (with Edward Chitham, 1995).

3 'Gnostic' means 'having esoteric spiritual knowledge' (*Shorter Oxford English Dictionary*) [Ed.].

4 Goetz (1982) also makes this point.

5 'Heteroglossia' is a Bakhtinian term meaning 'the speech of the other'. Farrell here refers to Mikhail Bakhtin, *Problems of Dostoevsky's Poetics*, ed. and trans. Caryl Emerson, *Theory and History of Literature* 8 (Minneapolis: University of Minnesota Press, 1984), p. 284.

6 Bakhtin, *Problems*, p. 289.

7 Cited in Katrina Clark and Michael Holquist, *Mikhail Bakhtin* (Cambridge, Mass: Harvard University Press, 1984), p. 207.

8 Quotations from Terry Eagleton, *Literary Theory* (Oxford: Basil Blackwell, 1983), p. 210.

CHAPTER FIVE

1 *Complete Poems*, ed. Hatfield, p. 252.

2 Heathcliff is actually absent for more than three years (*WH*, p. 89) [Ed.].

3 See Frankenberg (1978) for a useful evaluative survey of Marxist criticism to date.

4 Virginia Woolf, *A Room of One's Own* (1928) (Harmondsworth: Penguin, 1945), p. 106.

5 Marxist-Feminist Literature Collective, 'Women's Writing' in *The Sociology of Literature: 1848*, ed. Francis Barker *et al.* (Colchester: University of Essex, 1978); Jenni Calder, *Women and Marriage in the Victorian Novel* (London, 1976); Elaine Showalter, *A Literature of Their Own* (London: Virago, 1978), p. 8.

6 'Etiological' (or 'aetiological') means 'having to do with causes or origins' [Ed.].

7 See Carolyn Heilbrun, pp. 80–2.

8 In Blake's mythic system, Urizen is the

representative of reason and constraint as opposed to joyful energy [Ed.].

9 See William Blake, *The Marriage of Heaven and Hell*, Plate 15.

10 The quotation is from the disinherited bastard son, Edmund, in William Shakespeare, *King Lear*: I ii lines 1–2 [Ed.].

11 See Lucille Fletcher, *Wuthering Heights: Libretto of the Opera by Bernard Herrmann* (Portland, Oregon: Portland Opera Society, 1982).

12 Q. D. Leavis (1969), p. 87.

13 Tania Modleski, *Loving With a Vengeance: Mass-produced Fantasy for Women* (London: Routledge, 1982), p. 20.

14 Yaeger's references are to Myra Jehlen, 'Archimedes and the Paradox of Feminist Criticism', in *The Signs Reader*, ed. Elizabeth Abel and Emily K. Abel (Chicago: University of Chicago Press, 1983); and Rachel Brownstein, *Becoming a Heroine: Reading About Women in Novels* (Harmondsworth: Penguin, 1984).

15 James Hill (1994) also argues that the novel invites two incompatible reading strategies, analogous to Biblical exegesis based on the belief that the text is the word of God, and a newer historical and scientific cause-and-effect linearity. Hill, however, implies that this is a flaw in the novel's discursive structure.

16 Jacques Lacan, 'Of the Gaze as *Objet Petit a*' (1973) in *The Four Fundamental Concepts of Psychoanalysis*, ed. Jacques-Alain Miller, trans. Alan Sheridan (New York: Norton, 1981), pp. 57–119.

17 Mary Ann Doane, 'Film and the Masquerade: Theorising the Female Spectator', *Screen* 23:3 (1982), pp. 74–87, p. 86. Nancy K. Miller, *Subject to Change: Reading Feminist Writing* (New York: Columbia University Press, 1988), p. 175.

18 Newman refers the reader to Patricia Yaeger (1988) for the emancipatory energies of laughter.

A BRIEF GUIDE TO FURTHER READING

The complete Bibliography of *Wuthering Heights* criticism is somewhat overwhelming. This brief guide is intended, therefore, to indicate the most important critical works in a number of different areas. It uses short titles only; full bibliographical details will be found in the Bibliography. Further information about the texts mentioned here will, of course, be found in the main body of the book, and can be traced *via* the Index.

Editions of *Wuthering Heights*

The (Oxford) Clarendon edition (1976), edited by Hilda Marsden and Ian Jack, is the most accurate and detailed edition.
The (Oxford) World's Classics edition (1995) has this same authoritative text, with Ian Jack's notes and a new Introduction by Patsy Stoneman, in a cheap paperback form.

Emily Brontë's Poetry

For many years the 'definitive' edition of the poetry has been C. W. Hatfield's (1941); there are two more recent complete editions by Janet Gezari (1992) and Derek Roper (with Edward Chitham, 1995).

Biographies of Emily Brontë

Juliet Barker's (1994) biography, *The Brontës*, is the most complete and accurate source of information about the Brontë family, but pays relatively little attention to Emily because of the lack of primary sources about her life. Other recent biographies include Winifred Gérin's (1978) and Edward Chitham's (1987).

Anthologies of Criticism

There are thirteen anthologies of *Wuthering Heights* criticism listed in the 'Note on Sources and References' at the beginning of this book. The essential source for nineteenth-century criticism is Miriam Allott's *The Brontës: The Critical Heritage* (1974); Allott's 'Casebook' (new edition 1992) covers criticism from 1900 to 1970, and Patsy Stoneman's 'New Casebook' (1993) covers criticism from 1969–92.

Humanist Readings

The most influential of the studies which attribute *Wuthering Heights* to Emily Brontë's timeless and universal genius is from Lord David Cecil's 1934 book, *Early Victorian Novelists*.

Formalist Readings

The most important essay dealing with imagery and structure is Dorothy Van Ghent's 'The Window Figure and the Two Children Figure in *Wuthering Heights*' (1952).

Deconstructive Readings

The best-known essay in this category is from J. Hillis Miller's 1982 book, *Fiction and Repetition*; John T. Matthews's 1985 essay on 'Framing in *Wuthering Heights*' is rich and suggestive.

Psychoanalytic Readings

Leo Bersani's 1976 essay from *A Future for Astyanax* is widely cited but difficult. Jay Clayton's 1987 book, *Romantic Vision and the Novel*, includes a humane and approachable psychoanalytic study.

Source Studies

Jacques Blondel summarised 'Literary Influences on *Wuthering Heights*' in 1970; Edward Chitham also gives some attention to sources in his 1987 biography.

Readings using Discourse Theory

Heather Glen, in the 1988 'Introduction' to the Routledge edition of *Wuthering Heights*, talks about discourses without using theoretical terminology. Michael Macovski (1987) reads the Catherine–Heathcliff relationship in terms of Bakhtinian dialogism, and Nancy Armstrong (1987) claims importance for the text in terms of Foucauldian discourse theory.

Cultural Studies or Dissemination Studies

The most comprehensive book in this area is Patsy Stoneman's 1996 book, *Brontë Transformations*.

Marxist Readings

The two most influential readings in this category are Arnold Kettle's 1951 essay in his *Introduction to the English Novel* and Terry Eagleton's book, *Myths of Power: A Marxist Study of the Brontës* (1975, new edition 1988).

Postcolonial Readings

The only extended study in this area so far is Susan Meyer's book, *Imperialism at Home* (1996).

Feminist Readings

There is a great deal of material here; outstanding examples are Gilbert and Gubar in *The Madwoman in the Attic* (1979), and Stevie Davies's four books (1987, 1988, 1994 and 1998). *Wuthering Heights* is used as an exemplary text in three chapters of *Feminist Readings: Feminists Reading* (1996), edited by Sara Mills *et al.*, which forms a useful introduction to feminist criticism.

BIBLIOGRAPHY

Code letters after entries refer to sources in anthologies; the key will be found in the 'Note on Sources and References' at the beginning of the book.

Abercrombie, Lascelles. 'The Brontës Today'. *Brontë Society Transactions* 6 (1924): pp. 179–200; A pp. 106–8. (A)

Adams, Ruth M. 'The Land East of Eden'. *Nineteenth-Century Fiction* 13 (June 1958): pp. 56–62. (L&M)

Allott, Miriam. 'The Rejection of Heathcliff?' *Essays in Criticism* 8 (1958): pp. 27–47; A pp. 166–80. (A, O, PJ)

Allott, Miriam (ed.). *The Brontës: The Critical Heritage*. London: Routledge and Kegan Paul, 1974.

Allott, Miriam (ed.). A Casebook. *Emily Brontë: Wuthering Heights: A Selection of Critical Essays*. Basingstoke: Macmillan, 1992.

Ankenbrandt, Katherine. 'Songs in *Wuthering Heights*'. *Southern Folklore Quarterly* 33 (1969): pp. 92–115.

Apter, T. E. 'Romanticism and Romantic Love in *Wuthering Heights*'. Ed. Anne Smith. *The Art of Emily Brontë*. London: Vision Books, 1976: pp. 205–22. (SA)

Armstrong, Nancy. 'Emily Brontë in and out of her Time'. *Genre* 15 (1982): pp. 243–64. (S&D)

Armstrong, Nancy. *Desire and Domestic Fiction: A Political History of the Novel*. Oxford: Oxford University Press, 1987.

Armstrong, Nancy. 'Imperialist Nostalgia and *Wuthering Heights*'. Ed. Linda H. Peterson. *Wuthering Heights*. Case Studies in Contemporary Criticism. Boston: Bedford-St Martin's, 1992: pp. 428–49.

Arnold, Matthew. 'Haworth Churchyard'. *Fraser's Magazine* (May 1855). (A, CH, PJ)

Atlas (22 January 1848): p. 59; *CH* pp. 230–3. (PJ, S&D)

Azim, Firdous. *The Colonial Rise of the Novel*. London: Routledge, 1993.

Barker, Juliet. *The Brontës*. London: Weidenfeld and Nicolson, 1994.

Barreca, Regina. 'The Power of Excommunication: Sex and the Feminine Text in *Wuthering Heights*'. *Sex and Death in Victorian Literature*. Bloomington, Indiana: Indiana University Press and Basingstoke: Macmillan, 1990: pp. 227–40.

Bataille, Georges. *La Littérature et le mal*. 1957. Trans. as *The Literature of Evil*. London: Calder and Boyars, 1973. (PJ)

Bayne, Peter. 'Ellis, Acton and Currer Bell'. *Essays in Biography and Criticism* first series, 1857: pp. 393–424; *CH* pp. 321–8. (A, PJ)

Bayne, Peter. *Two Great Englishwomen: Mrs Browning and Charlotte Brontë*. 1881; *CH* pp. 423–30.

Bentley, Phyllis. *The Brontës*. 1947. London: Arthur Baker, 1957.

Bentley's Miscellany 29 (1851): pp. 448–9.

Bersani, Leo. *A Future for Astyanax: Character and Desire in Literature*. Boston: Little Brown, 1976.

B[ickley], F[rances]. 'Christmas Dinner at Haworth Parsonage'. *Punch* (25 December 1935): p. 708.

Blondel, Jacques. 'Literary Influences on *Wuthering Heights*'. 1955. A pp. 229–41. (PJ)

Blondel, Jacques. 'Imagery in *Wuthering Heights*'. *Durham University Journal* n.s. 37 (December 1975): pp.1–7.

Bloom, Harold (ed.). *Emily Brontë's 'Wuthering Heights'*. Modern Critical Interpretations. New York: Chelsea, 1987.

Bluestone, George. *Novels into Film*. Baltimore: Johns Hopkins Press, 1957.

Booth, Wayne C. *The Rhetoric of Fiction*. Chicago: University of Chicago Press, 1961.

Bradbury, Malcolm and James McFarlane. 'The Name and Nature of Modernism'. Ed. Malcolm Bradbury and James McFarlane. *Modernism 1890–1930*. Harmondsworth: Penguin, 1976.

Bradby, Godfrey Fox. 'Emily Brontë'. *Nineteenth-Century Fiction* 108 (October 1930): pp.533–40.

Bradner, Leicester. 'The Growth of *Wuthering Heights*'. *PMLA* 48 (March 1933): pp.129–46. (E)

Brick, Allan R. '*Wuthering Heights*: Narrators, Audience, and Message'. *College English* 21 (November 1959): pp.80–86. (L&M, PJ)

Bronfen, Elisabeth. *Over Her Dead Body: Death, Femininity and the Aesthetic*. Manchester: Manchester University Press, 1992: pp.305–13.

Brontë, Charlotte. 'Biographical Notice' and 'Editor's Preface' appended to 2nd edn of Emily Brontë, *Wuthering Heights*. London: Smith Elder, 1850. Ed. Ian Jack. Intro. Patsy Stoneman. The World's Classics. Oxford: Oxford University Press, 1995: pp.361–71. (A, CH, O, PJ, S&D)

Brontë, Emily. Ed. Janet Gezari. *Emily Jane Brontë: The Complete Poems*. Harmondsworth: Penguin, 1992.

Brontë, Emily Jane. Ed. C.W. Hatfield. *The Complete Poems of Emily Jane Brontë*. New York: Columbia University Press, 1941.

Brontë, Emily. Ed. Derek Roper with Edward Chitham. *The Complete Poems*. Oxford: The Clarendon Press, 1995.

Burgan, Mary. 'Some Fit Parentage: Identity and the Cycle of Generations in *Wuthering Heights*'. *Philological Quarterly* 61:4 (Fall 1982): pp.395–413.

Cecil, Lord David. 'Emily Brontë and *Wuthering Heights*'. *Early Victorian Novelists: Essays in Revaluation*. London: Constable, 1934. (A, L&M, PJ, V)

Chase, Karen. '"'Bad' was my commentary" – Propriety, Madness, Independence in Feminist Literary History'. Ed. Jerome J. McGann. *Victorian Connections*. Charlottesville: University of Virginia Press, 1989: pp.11–30.

Chitham, Edward. 'Emily Brontë and Shelley'. *Brontë Society Transactions* 17 (1978): pp.189–96.

Chitham, Edward. *The Brontës' Irish Background*. London: Macmillan, 1986.

Chitham, Edward. *A Life of Emily Brontë*. Oxford: Blackwell, 1987.

Chitham, Edward. *The Birth of Wuthering Heights: Emily Brontë at Work*. Basingstoke: Macmillan; New York: St Martin's Press, 1998.

Chodorow, Nancy. *The Reproduction of Mothering: Psychoanalysis and the Sociology of Gender*. Berkeley, Los Angeles and London: University of California Press, 1978.

[Chorley, H.F.] *Athenaeum* (25 December 1847): pp.1324–5; *CH* pp.218–19.

Christian Remembrancer n.s. 97 (July 1857): pp.87–145; *CH* pp.364–71.

Cixous, Hélène. 'The Laugh of the Medusa'. 1976. Ed. Elaine Marks and Isabelle de Courtivron. *New French Feminisms*. Amherst: University of Massachusetts Press, 1980: pp.245–64.

Clay, Charles Travis. '*Wuthering Heights* Chronology'. *Brontë Society Transactions* 12:62 (1952): pp. 100–105.

Clayton, Jay. *Romantic Vision and the Novel*. Cambridge: Cambridge University Press, 1987: pp. 81–102.

Collister, Peter. 'After "Half a Century": Mrs Humphry Ward on Charlotte and Emily Brontë'. *English Studies* 66:5 (October 1985): pp. 410–31.

Conger, Syndy McMillen. 'The Reconstruction of the Gothic Feminine Ideal in Emily Brontë's *Wuthering Heights*'. Ed. Juliann E. Fleenor. *The Female Gothic*. Montreal: Eden Press, 1983: pp. 91–106.

Cooper, Dorothy. 'The Romantics and Emily Brontë'. *Brontë Society Transactions* 12 (1952): pp. 106–12.

Cox, Philip. '*Wuthering Heights* in 1939: Novel, Film and Propaganda'. *Brontë Society Transactions* 20:5 (1992): pp. 283–8.

Crompton, D. 'The New Criticism: A Caveat'. *Essays in Criticism* 10 (1960): pp. 359–64.

Cross, Gilbert B. and Peggy L. Cross. 'Farewell to Hoffmann?' *Brontë Society Transactions* 15 (1970): pp. 412–16.

Cross, Wilbur L. *The Development of the English Novel*. New York, 1899.

Cuddon, J. A. *A Dictionary of Literary Terms*. 1977. Harmondsworth: Penguin, 1982.

Cunliffe, Walter R. 'The Brontës in Other People's Books'. *Brontë Society Transactions* 11:60 (1950): pp. 332–6.

Daiches, David. 'Introduction'. Emily Brontë. *Wuthering Heights*. Harmondsworth: Penguin, 1965; V pp. 109–10.

Daley, A. Stuart. 'The Moons and Almanacs of *Wuthering Heights*'. *Huntingdon Library Quarterly* 37 (1974): pp. 337–53. (S&D)

Daley, A. Stuart. 'A Revised Chronology of *Wuthering Heights*'. *Brontë Society Transactions* 21:5 (1995): pp. 169–73.

[Dallas, E. S.] *Blackwood's Magazine* 82 (July 1857): pp. 77–94; CH pp. 358–63. (A)

Davies, Stevie. *Emily Brontë: the Artist as a Free Woman*. Manchester: Carcanet, 1983. (B, PJ)

Davies, Stevie. *Emily Brontë*. Key Women Writers. Hemel Hempstead: Harvester Wheatsheaf/Prentice-Hall, 1988. (SP)

Davies, Stevie. *Emily Brontë: Heretic*. London: The Women's Press, 1994.

Davies, Stevie. *Emily Brontë*. Writers and their Work. Plymouth: Northcote House, 1998.

[Deardon, William] Pseud. 'William Oakendale'. 'Who wrote "Wuthering Heights"?' *Halifax Guardian* (15 June 1867). Reprinted in 'Patrick Branwell Brontë and *Wuthering Heights*'. *Brontë Society Transactions* 7 (1927): pp. 97–102.

[Dobell, Sydney]. '"Currer Bell" and *Wuthering Heights*'. *Palladium* (September 1850): pp. 161–75; CH pp. 277–83. (A, O)

Dodds, Madeleine Hope. 'Gondoliand'. *Modern Language Review* (January 1923).

Dodds, Madeleine Hope. 'A Second Visit to Gondoliand'. *Modern Language Review* (October 1926).

Dodds, Madeleine Hope. 'Heathcliff's Country'. *Modern Language Review* 39 (April 1944): pp. 116–29.

Douglas Jerrold's Weekly Newspaper 15 (January 1848): p. 77; CH pp. 227–8.

Downing, Crystal. 'Hieroglyphics (De)Constructed: Interpreting Brontë Fictions'. *Literature Interpretation Theory* 2:4 (1991): pp. 261–73.

Drew, Philip. 'Charlotte Brontë as a Critic of *Wuthering Heights*'. *Nineteenth-Century Fiction* 18:4 (March 1964): pp. 365–8; A pp. 197–208. (E, G)

Dworkin, Andrea. 1987. 'A Chauvinist Monster'. *Observer* (29 May 1988): pp. 35–6.

Eagleton, Terry. *Myths of Power: A Marxist Study of the Brontës*. 1975. Basingstoke: Macmillan, 2nd edn 1988. (A, PL, SP)

Eagleton, Terry. *Heathcliff and the Great Hunger*. London: Verso, 1995.

Eastlake: see Rigby

Eclectic Review (February 1851): pp. 222–7; *CH* pp. 296–8.

Economist 6 (1848): p. 126.

Economist 9 (1851): p. 15.

Empson, William. *Seven Types of Ambiguity*. London: Chatto and Windus, 1930.

Evans, Margiad. 'Byron and Emily Brontë: An Essay'. *Life and Letters* 47 (June 1948): pp. 193–216.

Ewbank, Inga-Stina. *Their Proper Sphere: The Brontë Sisters as Early Victorian Female Novelists*. London: Edward Arnold, 1966. (PJ)

Examiner (January 1848): pp. 21–2; *CH* pp. 220–2. (PJ, S&D)

Farrell, John P. 'Reading the Text of Community in *Wuthering Heights*'. *ELH* 56:1 (Spring 1989): pp. 173–208.

Fenton, Edith Maud. 'The Spirit of Emily Brontë's *Wuthering Heights* as Distinguished from That of Gothic Romances'. *Washington University Studies, Humanities Series* 8 (1920): pp. 103–22.

Fine, Ronald E. 'Lockwood's Dreams and the Key to *Wuthering Heights*'. *Nineteenth-Century Fiction* 24:1 (June 1969): pp. 16–30.

Forster, E. M. *Aspects of the Novel*. London: Edward Arnold, 1927: pp. 134–5.

Frankenberg, Ronald. 'Styles of Marxism, Styles of Criticism: *Wuthering Heights*: A Case Study'. *The Sociology of Literature: Applied Studies*. Monograph 26. Keele, Staffs: University of Keele Press, 1978: pp. 109–44.

Fraser, John. 'The Name of the Action: Nelly Dean and *Wuthering Heights*'. *Nineteenth-Century Fiction* 20 (December 1965): pp. 223–36.

Galaxy (February 1873): pp. 226–38; *CH* pp. 392–6.

Garrett, Peter K. *The Victorian Multi-Plot Novel: Studies in Dialogical Form*. New Haven, Conn: Yale University Press, 1980.

Garrod, H.W. 'Introduction'. Emily Brontë. *Wuthering Heights*. World's Classics. Oxford: Oxford University Press, 1930; A pp. 118–19.

Gaskell, Elizabeth. 1857. *The Life of Charlotte Brontë*. Ed. Alan Shelston. Harmondsworth: Penguin, 1975. (PJ)

Gérin, Winifred. *Emily Brontë: A Biography*. Oxford: Oxford University Press, 1971.

Gérin, Winifred. 'Byron's Influence on the Brontës'. Ed. Robert Speight. *Essays by Divers Hands, Being the Transactions of the Royal Society of Literature of the UK* n.s. 37. London: Oxford University Press, 1972: pp. 47–62.

Gilbert, Sandra and Susan Gubar. *The Madwoman in the Attic: The Woman Writer and the Nineteenth-Century Literary Imagination*. New Haven and London: Yale University Press, 1979. (B, SP)

Gilmour, Robin. 'Scott and the Victorian Novel: the Case of "*Wuthering Heights*"'. Ed. J.H. Alexander and David Hensitt. *Scott and His Influence*. Aberdeen: Association for Scottish Literary Studies, 1983.

Girdler, Lew. '*Wuthering Heights* and Shakespeare'. *Huntingdon Library Quarterly* 19 (August 1956): pp. 385–92.

Gleckner, Robert. 'Time in *Wuthering Heights*'. *Criticism* 1 (Fall 1959): pp. 328–38.

Glen, Heather. 'Introduction'. Emily Brontë. *Wuthering Heights*. 1847. London & New York: Routledge, 1988: pp. 1–33.

Goetz, William R. 'Genealogy and Incest in *Wuthering Heights*'. *SNNTS (Studies in the Novel)* 14:4 (Winter 1982): pp. 359–76.

Goodman, Charlotte. 'The Lost Brother, the Twin: Women Novelists and the Male-Female Double *Bildungsroman*'. *Novel* 17:1 (Fall 1983): pp. 28–43.

Gordon, Marci M. 'Kristeva's Abject and Sublime in Brontë's *Wuthering Heights*'. *Literature and Psychology* 34:3 (1988): pp. 44–58.

Gose, Elliott B., Jr. '*Wuthering Heights*: The Heath and the Hearth'. *Nineteenth-Century Fiction* 21 (June 1966): pp. 1–19.

Graham's Magazine (July 1848): p. 60; *CH* pp. 242–3.

Guerard, Albert J. 'Preface'. Emily Brontë. *Wuthering Heights*. New York: Washington Square Press, 1960; V pp. 63–8.

Hafley, James. 'The Villain in *Wuthering Heights*'. *Nineteenth-Century Fiction* 13 (December 1958): pp. 199–215. (L&M)

Hagan, John. 'Control of Sympathy in *Wuthering Heights*'. *Nineteenth-Century Fiction* 21:4 (1967): pp. 305–23. (G)

Hanson, T. W. 'The Local Colour of *Wuthering Heights*'. *Brontë Society Transactions* 6:34 (1924): p. 201.

Harrington, John. 'Wyler as *Auteur*'. Ed. Michael Klein and Gillian Parker. *The English Novel and the Movies*. New York: Frederick Ungar, 1981: pp. 67–82.

Harris, Anne Leslie. 'Psychological Time in *Wuthering Heights*'. *International Fiction Review* 7:2 (Summer 1980): pp. 112–17.

Harrison, Grace Elsie. *The Clue to the Brontës*. London: Methuen, 1948.

Harvey, W. J. *Character and the Novel*. Ithaca, New York: Cornell University Press, 1965.

Hatfield: see Brontë, Emily Jane.

Heilbrun, Carolyn. *Towards Androgyny: Aspects of Male and Female in Literature*. London: Gollancz, 1973: pp. 79–82.

Hewish, John. *Emily Brontë: A Critical and Biographical Study*. London: Macmillan, 1969. (PJ)

Heywood, Christopher. 'Yorkshire Slavery in *Wuthering Heights*'. *Review of English Studies* 38:150 (May 1987): pp. 184–98.

Heywood, Christopher. 'Africa and Slavery in the Brontë Children's Novels'. *Hitotsuhashi Journal of Arts and Sciences* 30:1 (December 1989): pp. 75–87.

Heywood, Christopher. '"The Helks Lady" and Other Legends Surrounding *Wuthering Heights*'. *Lore and Language* 11:2 (1992–3): pp. 127–42.

Heywood, Christopher. 'A Yorkshire Background for *Wuthering Heights*'. *Modern Language Review* 88:4 (October 1993): pp. 817–30.

Hill, James. 'Joseph's Currants: The Hermeneutic Challenge of *Wuthering Heights*'. *Victorian Literature and Culture* 22 (1994): pp. 267–85.

Hinkley, Laura. *Ladies of Literature*. New York: Hastings House, 1946.

Homans, Margaret. 'Repression and Sublimation of Nature in *Wuthering Heights*'. *PMLA* 93 (January 1978): pp. 9–19. (B)

Homans, Margaret. 'Dreaming of Children: Literalization in *Jane Eyre* and *Wuthering Heights*'. Ed. Juliann E. Fleenor. *The Female Gothic*. Montreal & London: Eden Press, 1983: pp. 257–79, 308–11.

Homans, Margaret. 'The Name of the Mother in *Wuthering Heights*'. *Bearing the Word: Language and Female Experience in Nineteenth-Century Women's Writing*. Chicago: University of Chicago Press, 1986. (PL)

Howells, William Dean. 'The Two Catherines of Emily Brontë'. *Heroines of Fiction*. New York: Harper, 1901.

Jacobs, Carol. '*Wuthering Heights*: At the Threshold of Interpretation'. *boundary 2* 7:3 (Spring 1979): pp.49–71; B pp.99–118. (S&D)

Jacobs, Naomi. 'Gender and Layered Narrative in *Wuthering Heights* and *The Tenant of Wildfell Hall*'. *Journal of Narrative Technique* 16:3 (Fall 1986): pp.204–19. (SP)

James, Henry. 'The Lesson of Balzac'. 1905. Ed. Leon Edel. *Henry James. The House of Fiction*. Westport, CT: Greenwood, 1957: pp.60–85. (PJ)

Jameson, Fredric. *The Political Unconscious*. Ithaca: Cornell University Press, 1981.

Kavanagh, Coleman. *The Symbolism of Wuthering Heights*. London: John Long, 1920.

Kavanagh, James. *Emily Brontë*. Oxford: Blackwell, 1985.

Kermode, Frank. *The Sense of an Ending: Studies in the Theory of Fiction*. New York: Oxford University Press, 1967.

Kermode, Frank. *The Classic*. London: Faber and Faber, 1975: pp.115–41. (B, SP)

Kettle, Arnold. *An Introduction to the English Novel*. 2 vols. London: Hutchinson, 1951. Vol. I: pp.139–55. (L&M, V)

Kiely, Robert. *The Romantic Novel in England*. Cambridge, Mass.: Harvard University Press, 1972: pp.233–51.

Kinkead-Weekes, Mark. 'The Place of Love in *Jane Eyre* and *Wuthering Heights*'. Ed. Ian Gregor. *The Brontës: A Collection of Critical Essays*. Englewood Cliffs, NJ: Prentice-Hall, 1970: pp.76–95.

Klingopulos, G.D. 'The Novel as Dramatic Poem (II): *Wuthering Heights*'. *Scrutiny* 14 (1946–7): pp.269–86. (A)

Knoepflmacher, U.C. '*Wuthering Heights*'. Basingstoke: Macmillan, 1989.

Kristeva, Julia. *Revolution in Poetic Language*. Trans. Margaret Waller. New York: Columbia University Press, 1984.

Lane, Margaret. 'Emily Brontë in a Cold Climate'. *Brontë Society Transactions* 15 (1968): pp.187–200.

Law, Alice. *Patrick Branwell Brontë*. London: A.M. Philpot, 1923.

Lawson-Peebles, Robert. 'European Conflict and Hollywood's Reconstruction of English Fiction'. *Yearbook of English Studies* 26 (1996): pp.1–13.

Leavis, F.R. *The Great Tradition: George Eliot, Henry James, Joseph Conrad*. 1948. Harmondsworth: Penguin, 1962.

Leavis, Q.D. *Fiction and the Reading Public*. London: Chatto and Windus, 1932.

Leavis, Q.D. 'A Fresh Approach to *Wuthering Heights*.' 1969. Ed. G. Singh. *Collected Essays*. 3 vols. Cambridge: Cambridge University Press, 1983–9: Vol. 1, pp.228–74. (A, PJ, SP)

Lee, Vernon [Violet Paget]. *The Handling of Words*. London: Bodley Head, 1922. (A)

Levy, Anita. 'The History of Desire in *Wuthering Heights*'. *Genre* 19:4 (Winter 1986): pp.409–30.

[Lewes, G.H.] Review of *Wuthering Heights*. *The Leader* (28 December 1850): p.953; *CH* pp.291–3. (O, PJ)

Literary Images. *Wuthering Heights by Emily Brontë: A Critical Guide to the Novel*. Braceborough, Lincs: Literary Images Limited, 1992: jacket blurb.

Literary World 3, 65 (April 1848): p.243; *CH* pp.233–4.

Livermore, Ann Lapraik. 'Byron and Emily Brontë'. *Quarterly Review* 300 (July 1962): pp.337–44.

London, Bette. '*Wuthering Heights* and the Text Between the Lines'. *Papers on Language and Literature* 24:1 (Winter 1988): pp.34–52.

Lonoff, Sue (ed. & trans.). *The Belgian Essays: Charlotte Brontë and Emily Brontë*. New Haven, CT: Yale University Press, 1996.

[Lorimer, James]. Review of *Wuthering Heights*. *North British Review* 11 (August 1849): pp.475–93; *CH* pp.113–16.

Lovell-Smith, Rose. 'Qu'a donc pu lire Emily Brontë? Arrivals in the Waverley Novels and *Wuthering Heights*'. *Brontë Society Transactions* 21:3 (1994): pp.79–87.

Lovell-Smith, Rose. 'Walter Scott and Emily Brontë: The Rhetoric of Love'. *Brontë Society Transactions* 21:4 (1994): pp.117–24.

McCarthy, Terence. 'A Late Eighteenth Century Ballad Community: *Wuthering Heights*'. *Southern Folklore Quarterly* 43 (1979): pp.241–52.

MacFarlane, Kathryn Jean. *Divide the Desolation: based on the life of Emily Jane Brontë*. New York: Simon and Schuster, 1936.

Mackay, Angus. 'On the Interpretation of Emily Brontë'. *Westminster Review* 150 (August 1898): pp.203–18; *CH* pp.446–7. (A, PJ)

MacKereth, J. A. *Storm-Wrack. A Night with the Brontës and Other Poems*. London: Lane, 1927.

MacKereth, James A. 'The Greatness of Emily Brontë'. *Brontë Society Transactions* 7 (1929): pp.175–200.

McKibben, Robert C. 'The Image of the Book in *Wuthering Heights*'. *Nineteenth-Century Fiction* 15:2 (September 1960): pp.159–69. (G, L&M)

Macherey, Pierre. *A Theory of Literary Production*. 1966. Trans. G. Wall. London: Routledge and Kegan Paul, 1978.

Macovski, Michael. '*Wuthering Heights* and the Rhetoric of Interpretation'. *ELH* 54:2 (Summer 1987): pp.363–84. (SP)

Madden, William A. '*Wuthering Heights*: The Binding of Passion'. *Nineteenth-Century Fiction* 27 (1972): pp.127–54.

Malham-Dembleby, J. *The Key to the Brontë Works*. London: Walter Scott, 1911.

Marsden, Hilda. 'The Scenic Background of *Wuthering Heights*'. *Brontë Society Transactions* 13:67 (1957): p.111.

Marsden, Hilda. 'The Moorlands: The Timeless Contemporary'. *Brontë Society Transactions* 20:4 (1991): pp.205–12.

Masson, Flora. *The Brontës*. The People's Books. London: T.C. & E.C. Jack; New York: Dodge Publishing, 1912.

Mathison, John K. 'Nelly Dean and the Power of *Wuthering Heights*'. *Nineteenth-Century Fiction* 11 (1956): pp.102–29. (L&M)

Matthews, John T. 'Framing in *Wuthering Heights*'. *Texas Studies in Literature and Language* 27:1 (Spring 1985): pp.25–61. (SP)

Maugham, W. Somerset. 'The Ten Best Novels: *Wuthering Heights*'. *Atlantic Monthly* 181 (February 1948): pp.89–94.

Melchiori, Barbara. 'The Windows of the Victorians'. *English Miscellany* 25 (1975–6): pp.335–54.

Mellor, Anne K. *Romanticism and Gender*. New York: Routledge, 1993: pp.186–208.

Meyer, Susan. *Imperialism at Home: Race and Victorian Women's Fiction.* Ithaca, New York: Cornell University Press, 1996: pp.96–125.

Meynell, Alice. 'Unparalleled Power of Imagery'. 1911; A pp.104–5.

Michie, Elsie. 'From Simianized Irish to Oriental Despots: Heathcliff, Rochester, and Racial Difference'. *Novel* 25 (1992): pp.125–40.

Miller, J. Hillis. *The Disappearance of God: Five Nineteenth-Century Writers.* Cambridge, Mass: Harvard University Press, 1963: pp.157–211. (O, PJ, V)

Miller, J. Hillis. *Fiction and Repetition: Seven English Novels.* Cambridge, Mass.: Harvard University Press, 1982. (A, PL, S&D)

Mitchell, Juliet. *Women, the Longest Revolution: Essays on Feminism, Literature and Psychoanalysis.* London: Virago, 1984.

Moers, Ellen. *Literary Women.* 1976. London: The Women's Press, 1978.

Moglen, Helen. 'The Double Vision of *Wuthering Heights*: A Clarifying View of Female Development'. *Centennial Review* 15 (Fall 1971): pp.391–405.

Montégut, Emile. *Revue des deux mondes* 4 (1 July 1857): pp.139–84; *CH* pp.372–8. (A)

Moore, Virginia. *The Life and Eager Death of Emily Brontë.* London: Rich and Cowen, 1936.

Moser, Thomas. 'What Is the Matter with Emily Jane? Conflicting Impulses in *Wuthering Heights*'. *Nineteenth-Century Fiction* 17 (June 1962): pp.1–19.

Musselwhite, David. '*Wuthering Heights*: The Unacceptable Text'. 1976. Ed. Francis Barker *et al. Literature, Society and the Sociology of Literature.* Colchester: University of Essex, 1977: pp.154–60.

Musselwhite, David. '*Wuthering Heights*: The Unacceptable Texts'. *Partings Welded Together: Politics and Desire in the Nineteenth-Century English Novel.* London and New York: Methuen, 1987: pp.75–108.

Myer, Michael Grosvenor. '"Traditional" Lullabies in Victorian Fiction: *Wuthering Heights* and *Tess of the d'Urbervilles*'. *Notes and Queries* 35 (233):3 (September 1988): pp.319–20.

Nemesvari, Richard. 'Strange Attractors on the Yorkshire Moors: Chaos Theory and *Wuthering Heights*'. *The Victorian Newsletter* 92 (1997): pp.15–21.

New Monthly Magazine 82 (January 1848): p.140; *CH* p.229.

Newman, Beth. 'The Situation of the Looker-On: Gender, Narration and Gaze in *Wuthering Heights*'. *PMLA* 105:5 (October 1990): pp.1029–41.

North American Review 85:2 (October 1857): pp.293–392.

Ohmann, Carol. 'Emily Brontë in the Hands of Male Critics'. *College English* 32 (1971): pp.906–13.

Osborn, Judi. 'The Byronic Heroine: Is She Different?' *Pleiades* 10:1 (Winter 1990): pp.45–51.

Paris, Bernard. '"Hush, hush! He's a human being": A Psychological Approach to Heathcliff'. *Women and Literature* 2 (1982): pp.101–17.

Parker, Patricia. 'The (Self-)Identity of the Literary Text: Property, Proper Place, and Proper Name in *Wuthering Heights*'. *Literary Fat Ladies: Rhetoric, Gender, Property.* London: Methuen, 1987: pp.155–64. (SP)

Pater, Walter. 1889. *Appreciations.* London: Macmillan, 1910: p.242; *CH* p.445. (A)

Patterson, Charles I. 'Empathy and the Daemonic in *Wuthering Heights*'. Ed. George Goodin. *The English Novel in the Nineteenth Century: Essays on the Literary Mediation of Human Values.* Illinois Studies in Language and Literature 63. Urbana, Illinois: University of Illinois Press, 1972: pp.81–96.

Pearsall, R.B. 'The Presiding Tropes of Emily Brontë'. *College English* 27 (1966): pp.267–73.

[Peck, George Washington]. Review of *Wuthering Heights*. *American Review* 7 (June 1848): pp.572–85; *CH* pp.235–42.

Pinion, F.B. *A Brontë Companion: Literary Assessment, Background, and Reference*. London and Basingstoke: Macmillan, 1975.

Pinion, F.B. 'Byron and *Wuthering Heights*'. *Brontë Society Transactions* 21:5 (1995) pp.195–201.

Pinion, F.B. 'Scott and *Wuthering Heights*'. *Brontë Society Transactions* 21:7 (1996): pp.313–22.

Power, S.A. 'The Chronology of *Wuthering Heights*'. *Brontë Society Transactions* 16 (1972): pp.139–43.

Pritchett, V.S. 'Implacable, Belligerent People of Emily Brontë's Novel, *Wuthering Heights*'. *New Statesman and Nation* 31 (22 June 1946): p.453. (E, L&M, V)

Pykett, Lyn. *Emily Brontë*. Basingstoke: Macmillan, 1989. (SP)

Quennell, Peter. 'Foreword'. *Novels by the Brontë Sisters*. London: Pilot Press, 1947.

Ratchford, Fannie E. *The Brontës' Web of Childhood*. New York: Columbia University Press, 1941.

Ratchford, Fannie E. (ed.). *Gondal's Queen: A Novel in Verse by Emily Jane Brontë*. Austin: University of Texas Press, 1955.

Reed, Walter L. *Meditations on the Hero: A Study of the Romantic Hero in Nineteenth-Century Fiction*. New Haven and London: Yale University Press, 1974.

Reid, T. Wemyss. *Charlotte Brontë: A Monograph*. 1877. *CH* pp.397–403. (A)

Rigby, Elizabeth. 'A Review of *Jane Eyre* with Comments on *Wuthering Heights*'. *Quarterly Review* 84 (1848): pp.153–85; *CH* p.111.

Robinson, A. Mary F. *Emily Brontë*. Eminent Women Series. London: WH Allen, 1883. 3rd edn 1890. (A, *CH*, E, PJ)

Romberg, Bertil. *Studies in the Narrative Technique of the First-Person Novel*. [No place]: Almquist and Wiksell, 1962: pp.65–6. (PJ)

Romieu, Emilie and Georges. *The Brontë Sisters*. Trans. Roberts Tapley. London: Skeffington, 1931.

Roper, Derek. 'Emily Brontë's Lover'. *Brontë Society Transactions* 21:1&2 (1993): pp.25–31.

[Roscoe, W.C.]. *National Review* 5 (June 1857): pp.127–64; *CH* pp.346–57. (A)

Rossetti, Dante Gabriel. Letter to William Allingham, 19 September 1854. Ed. O. Doughty and R.J. Wahl. *Letters of Dante Gabriel Rossetti*. London: Oxford University Press, 1965: i 224; *CH* p.300. (A, PJ)

Sagar, Keith. 'The Originality of *Wuthering Heights*'. Ed. Anne Smith. *The Art of Emily Brontë*. London: Vision Books, 1976: pp.121–59.

Sanger, C.P. *The Structure of 'Wuthering Heights'*. London: Hogarth Press, 1926. (A, E, L&M, G, O, PJ, S&D, V)

Schapiro, Barbara. 'The Rebirth of Catherine Earnshaw: Splitting and Regeneration of Self in *Wuthering Heights*'. *Nineteenth Century Studies* 3 (1989): pp.37–51.

Schorer, Mark. 'Fiction and the "Matrix of Analogy"'. *The Kenyon Review* 11:4 (Autumn 1949): pp.539–60. (A, L&M, O, PJ, V)

Scheuerle, William H. 'Emily Brontë's *Wuthering Heights*'. *Explicator* 33:9 (May 1975): item 69.

Selby, Sara E. 'The Influence of the Yorkshire Moors and Folk Balladry on Emily Brontë's Literary Imagination'. *Mississippi Folklore Register* 22:1–2 (Spring–Fall 1988): pp. 71–8.

Senf, Carol. 'Emily Brontë's Version of Feminist History – *Wuthering Heights*'. *Essays in Literature* 12 (1985): pp. 204–14.

Shannon, Edgar F., Jr. 'Lockwood's Dreams and the Exegesis of *Wuthering Heights*'. *Nineteenth-Century Fiction* 14 (September 1959): pp. 95–110. L&M, V)

Shunami, Gideon. 'The Unreliable Narrator in *Wuthering Heights*'. *Nineteenth-Century Fiction* 27 (March 1973): pp. 449–68.

Simpson, Charles. *Emily Brontë*. London: Country Life, 1929.

Simpson-Housley, Paul, Andrea O'Reilly and Deborah Carter Park. 'Geographic Reality: Symbolic Landscapes of *Wuthering Heights*'. *Brontë Society Transactions* 19:8 (1989): pp. 369–75.

Sinclair, May. *The Three Brontës*. London: Hutchinson, 1912. (PJ)

Sitwell, Edith. 'Emily Brontë: 1818–1848'. *English Women*. London: William Collins, 1942: pp. 35–6.

[Skelton, Sir John]. *Fraser's Magazine* 55 (May 1857): pp. 569–82; *CH* pp. 331–42. (A)

Smith, George Barnet. 'The Brontës'. *Cornhill Magazine* 28 (July 1873): pp. 54–71.

Smith, Sheila. '"At once strong and eerie". The Supernatural in *Wuthering Heights* and its debt to the traditional ballad'. *Review of English Studies* 43:172 (November 1992): pp. 498–517.

Snowden, Keighley. 'The Enigma of Emily Brontë'. *Fortnightly Review* 130 (1928): pp. 200, 202.

Solomon, Eric. 'The Incest Theme in *Wuthering Heights*'. *Nineteenth-Century Fiction* 14 (June 1959): pp. 80–3. (L&M, V)

Sonstroem, David. '*Wuthering Heights* and the Limits of Vision'. *PMLA* 86:1 (January 1971): pp. 51–62. (B)

Spacks, Patricia. *The Female Imagination*. London: Allen and Unwin, 1976: pp. 134–44.

Spectator 20 (18 December 1847): p. 1217. (*CH*)

Stephen, Leslie. 'Charlotte Brontë'. *Cornhill Magazine* (December 1877): pp. 723–9; *CH* pp. 413–23. (A)

Stoneman, Patsy. 'The Brontës and Death: Alternatives to Revolution?' Ed. Francis Barker *et al. The Sociology of Literature: 1848*. Colchester: University of Essex, 1978.

Stoneman, Patsy. 'Feminist Criticism of *Wuthering Heights*'. *Critical Survey* 4:2 (1992): pp. 147–53.

Stoneman, Patsy. 'Reading Across Media: the Case of *Wuthering Heights*'. Ed. Richard Andrews. *Rebirth of Rhetoric: Essays in language, culture and education*. London: Routledge, 1992, pp. 172–96.

Stoneman, Patsy (ed.). *Wuthering Heights*. A New Casebook. Basingstoke: Macmillan, 1993.

Stoneman, Patsy. *Brontë Transformations: The Cultural Dissemination of 'Jane Eyre' and 'Wuthering Heights'*. Hemel Hempstead: Harvester Wheatsheaf/Prentice Hall, 1996.

Stoneman, Patsy. 'Catherine Earnshaw's Journey to her Home Among the Dead: Fresh Thoughts on *Wuthering Heights* and "Epipsychidion"'. *Review of English Studies* n.s. 47:188 (1996): pp. 521–33.

Sutcliffe, Halliwell. 'The Spirit of the Moors'. *Brontë Society Transactions* 2 (January 1903): pp. 174–90.

Sutton-Ramspeck, Beth. 'The Personal is Poetical: Feminist Criticism and Mary Ward's Readings of the Brontës'. *Victorian Studies* 34:1 (Autumn 1990): pp. 55–75.

Swinburne, Algernon. 'Emily Brontë'. *Athenaeum* (16 June 1883): pp. 762–3; *CH* pp. 438–44. (A, PJ)

Symons, Arthur. 'Emily Brontë'. *The Nation* 23 (24 August 1918): pp. 546–7. *The Living Age* (October 1918): pp. 119–21.

Tait's Magazine 15 (1848): p. 138. Melvin Watson. '*Wuthering Heights* and the Critics': pp. 243–6.

Taylor, Irene. *Holy Ghosts: The Male Muses of Emily and Charlotte Brontë*. New York: Columbia University Press, 1990.

Thompson, Nicola Diane. *Reviewing Sex: Gender and the Reception of Victorian Novels*. Basingstoke: Macmillan, 1996.

Thompson, Wade. 'Infanticide and Sadism in *Wuthering Heights*'. *PMLA* 78:1 (March 1963): pp. 69–73. (E, O, PJ)

Tobin, Patricia Dreschel. '*Wuthering Heights*: Myth and History, Repetition and Alliance'. *Time and the Novel: the Genealogical Imperative*. Princeton: Princeton University Press, 1978: pp. 38–42.

Totheroh, Dan. *Moor Born: A Play*. New York, Los Angeles, London: Samuel French, 1934.

Traversi, Derek. '*Wuthering Heights* after a Hundred Years'. *Dublin Review* 202 (Spring 1949): pp. 154–68. (A, O, V) As 'The Brontë Sisters and *Wuthering Heights*'. Ed. Boris Ford. Pelican Guide to English Literature. Vol. 6. *From Dickens to Hardy*. Harmondsworth: Penguin, 1958: pp. 256–73.

Twitchell, James. 'Heathcliff as Vampire'. *Southern Humanities Review* 11 (1977): pp. 355–62.

Urquhart, Jane. *Changing Heaven*. Sevenoaks: Hodder & Stoughton, 1990.

Vaisey, Hon Mr Justice. '*Wuthering Heights*: A Note on Its Authorship'. *Brontë Society Transactions* 11 (1946): pp. 14–15.

van de Laar, Elisabeth. T*he Inner Structure of 'Wuthering Heights'*. The Hague, Paris: Mouton, 1969.

Van Ghent, Dorothy. 'The Window Figure and the Two Children Figure in *Wuthering Heights*'. *Nineteenth-Century Fiction* 7 (December 1952): pp. 189–97. *The English Novel, Form and Function*. New York: Rinehart, 1953: pp. 153–70. (A, B, E, L&M, O, PJ, V)

Vine, Steven. 'The Wuther of the Other in *Wuthering Heights*'. *Nineteenth-Century Literature* 49:3 (December 1994): pp. 339–59.

Visick, Mary. *The Genesis of 'Wuthering Heights'*. Hong Kong: Hong Kong University Press, 1958. (A, O, PJ)

Vogler, Thomas A. *Twentieth-Century Interpretations of Wuthering Heights: A Collection of Critical Essays*. Englewood Cliffs, NJ: Prentice-Hall, 1968.

Von Sneidern, Maja-Lisa. '*Wuthering Heights* and the Liverpool Slave Trade'. *ELH* 62:1 (Spring 1995): pp. 171–96.

Wagner, Geoffrey. *The Novel and the Cinema*. London: Associated University Presses, 1975.

Wallace, Robert K. 'Emily Brontë and Music: Haworth, Brussels and Beethoven'. *Brontë Society Transactions* 18:2 (1982): pp. 136–42.

Ward, Mary Augusta. 'Introduction' to *Wuthering Heights. The Lives and Works of the Sisters Brontë*. Haworth edition. New York: Harper, 1900; *CH* pp. 448–60. (A, PJ)

Watson, Melvin R. '*Wuthering Heights* and the Critics'. *Nineteenth-Century Fiction* 3:1–4 (1948–9): pp. 243–63. (E)

Watson, Melvin R. 'The Tempest in the Soul: The Theme and Structure of *Wuthering Heights*'. *Nineteenth-Century Fiction* 4:1–4 (September 1949): pp. 87–100. (L&M)

West, Rebecca. 'The Role of Fantasy in the Work of the Brontës.' *Brontë Society Transactions* 12 (1954): pp. 255–67.

Whipple, E. P. *North American Review* 141 (October 1848): pp. 354–69; *CH* pp. 247–8.

Widdowson, Peter. 'Emily Brontë: Romantic Novelist'. *Moderna Sprak* 66 (February–March 1972): pp. 1–19.

Williams, Anne. '"The Child is *Mother* of the Man": The "Female" Aesthetic of *Wuthering Heights*'. *Cahiers Victoriens et Edouardiens* 34 (October 1991): pp. 81–94.

Williams, Raymond. *The Country and the City*. London: Chatto and Windus, 1973.

Willis, Irene Cooper. *The Authorship of 'Wuthering Heights'*. London: Hogarth Press, 1936; A pp. 126–9. (E, O, PJ)

Wilson, David. 'Emily Brontë: First of the Moderns'. *Modern Quarterly Miscellany* 1 (1947): pp. 94–115. (SA)

Wilson, Romer. *All Alone: The Life and Private History of Emily Jane Brontë*. London: Chatto and Windus, 1928.

Wimsatt, W. K. 'The Intentional Fallacy'. 1946. Reprinted in *The Verbal Icon*, 1954.

Wion, Philip. 'The Absent Mother in Emily Brontë's *Wuthering Heights*'. *American Imago* 42 (1985): pp. 143–64. (PL)

Woodring, Carl R. 'The Narrators of *Wuthering Heights*'. *Nineteenth-Century Fiction* 11 (1957): pp. 298–305. (L&M)

Woolf, Virginia. 1916. '*Jane Eyre* and *Wuthering Heights*'. *The Common Reader*. New York: Harcourt, Brace & Co., 1925; A pp. 108–9. (L&M, O, PJ, V)

Woollcott, Alexander. '"Our Greatest Women", or Screen Credits for Emily'. *Lady's Home Journal*, 1939. *Long, Long Ago*. New York: Viking, 1943.

Yaeger, Patricia. 'Violence in the Sitting Room: *Wuthering Heights* and the Woman's Novel'. *Genre* 21:2 (1988): pp. 203–29.

ACKNOWLEDGEMENTS

The editor and publishers wish to thank the following for their permission to reprint copyright material: Cambridge University Press (for material from *Romantic Vision and the Novel*); Harvester Wheatsheaf/Prentice-Hall (for material from *Emily Brontë*); Macmillan (for material from *Myths of Power: A Marxist Study of the Brontës* and *Emily Brontë*); Sandra Gilbert (for material from *The Madwoman in the Attic: The Woman Writer and the Nineteenth-Century Literary Imagination*); Routledge (for material from *Wuthering Heights*, Introduction); Eden Press (for material from 'Dreaming of Children: Literalization in *Jane Eyre* and *Wuthering Heights*'); Faber and Faber (for material from *The Classic*); Hutchinson (for material from *An Introduction to the English Novel*); Chatto and Windus (for material from *Lectures in America*); Rinehart (for material from *The English Novel, Form and Function*); Methuen (for material from *Literary Fat Ladies: Rhetoric, Gender, Property*).

There are instances where we have been unable to trace or contact copyright holders before our printing deadline. If notified, the publisher will be pleased to acknowledge the use of copyright material.

Patsy Stoneman is a Senior Lecturer in English at the University of Hull, where she teaches in the fields of Victorian and Women's studies. Major publications include *Elizabeth Gaskell* (1987), the New Casebook on *Wuthering Heights* (1993) and *Brontë Transformations: the Cultural Dissemination of 'Jane Eyre' and 'Wuthering Heights'* (1996).

The editor wishes to thank Colin Stoneman for indefatigable help of all kinds and Richard Beynon for cheerful editorial support.

INDEX

Columbia Critical Guides Series

Toni Morrison: Beloved
Edited by Carl Plasa
0–231–11526–1 (cloth)
0–231–11527-X (paper)

William Shakespeare: King Lear
Edited by Susan Bruce
0–231–11528–8 (cloth)
0–231–11529–6 (paper)

James Joyce: Ulysses / A Portrait of the Artist As a Young Man
Edited by John Coyle
0–231–11530-X (cloth)
0–231–11531–8 (paper)

Virginia Woolf: To the Lighthouse / The Waves
Edited by Jane Goldman
0–231–11532–6 (cloth)
0–231–11533–4 (paper)

Mark Twain: Tom Sawyer and Huckleberry Finn
Edited by Stuart Hutchinson
0–231–11536–9 (cloth)
0–231–11537–7 (paper)

Shakespeare: Richard II
Edited by Martin Coyle
0–231–11536–9 (cloth)
0–231–11537–7 (paper)

Herman Melville: Moby-Dick
Edited by Nick Selby
0–231–11538–5 (cloth)
0–231–11539–3 (paper)

F. Scott Fitzgerald: The Great Gatsby
Edited by Nicolas Tredell
0–231–11534–2 (cloth)
0–231–11535–0 (paper)

The Poetry of Seamus Heaney
Edited by Elmer Andrews
0–231–11926–7 (cloth)
0–231–11927–5 (paper)

Charles Dickens: Great Expectations
Edited by Nicolas Tredell
0–231–11924–0 (cloth)
0–231–11925–9 (paper)

Emily Brontë: Wuthering Heights
Edited by Patsy Stoneman
0–231–11920–8 (cloth)
0–231–11921–6 (paper)

Joseph Conrad: Heart of Darkness
Edited by Nicolas Tredell
0–231–11922–4 (cloth)
0–231–11923–2 (paper)